December 2019

Chris,

Happy C...

Much love,

Debbie xx

William Flint

Leicester's Classical Architect

William Flint

Leicester's Classical Architect

Mark Mitchley

ISBN 978-1-9161147-0-8

Published by Fuzzy Flamingo
36 Charnwood Avenue
Thurmaston, Leicester
LE4 8FJ
www.fuzzyflamingo.co.uk
07588 966 425

Printed by CPI Group (UK) Ltd, Croydon CR0 4YY

For Mark, of course.

In memory of Viv Liptrot because she was the best of us.

And also to the younger members of my family in the hope that they will look kindly upon history and see its interest, use and value.

So, to my nieces and nephew Juliette and Joseph Mitchley and Lily and Amber Parker; my brother-in-law Alex Liptrot and my cousins Lewis and Connor Julian; Rebecca and Harry Mitchley; Eleanor and Emma Mitchley; Andreas and Emilie Mitchley; Bertrand Mitchley-Park; Leah and Aleksander Mitchley-Peterson and Daniel, Rebecca and Oliver Seymour. Also to my Godson Sam Rigby (and his sister Katie) and my Goddaughter Florence Dobney, who first lived in a Flint house.

Contents

Foreword

Leicester has lost much of its architectural heritage and, as a city, has in the past, at least, seemed slower than many to preserve its finest and most interesting buildings. Consequently, it is no surprise to learn that some of the best examples of the Georgian, William IV and early Victorian work of William Flint have been lost. That said, there is a lot that has survived and it is perhaps surprising that so much of his work is still in use whether as places of worship, homes or offices.

Flint has held the casual historian's interest from time to time but there has never been attempted a more detailed study of the man and his work. What follows is a consideration of his life and work and a survey of what remains of it in Leicestershire, the only county in which he transacted business. Several of the buildings are shrouded in mystery and where I have suspected that he may be the architect but have little or no evidence, I have included the building in chapter 12: Flint or Not Flint?

William Flint is a rather forgotten figure; facts about his life are not well known and concrete attribution of his buildings and designs has been (and to some extent remains) hazy. What follows is also an attempt to enlarge and clarify what we know about him and his buildings and many of the facts that have been included appear in print for the first time. As an architect, his work stands for itself, but as a teacher, his influence is even greater with his pupil Isaac Barradale and his pupil in turn, Ernest Gimson, prominent among them.

As well as a biography and an examination of his work, I have included chapters on his pupils, partners and his apprentice masters. There is also some more trivial information to add a little more colour to the life of the man which is still far too sketchy I have tried to capture some of the noise, commerce and sense of expansion in early Victorian Leicester and the footnotes proliferate with examples of good solid Victorian worthies, many of whom were related to each other and many of whom worked for and with each other to an almost exclusive degree.

Acknowledgements

I owe a great debt to the many people who helped me in the course of writing this book and feel that Leicester has rallied round to help me celebrate the life of one of its sons.

The staff at the Leicestershire and Rutland Record Office (LRO) (particularly Jenny Moran and Lynsey Swift) were very patient and helped me look through several hundred building plans, all of which were heavy and awkward to handle. Alison Clipsham of the Land Registry was generous with her time and knowledge about the Whitmore Ellis mill at West Bridge. Roger Beeby was similarly generous with his time about Charles Street Baptist Church and also with his warm and friendly encouragement.

Neil Crutchley has been a real guide through the process; encouraging and fulsome in his support and sharing his considerable knowledge of Leicester. He also put me in touch with Rowan Roenisch who was kind enough to read the manuscript and save me from various mistakes. J. D. Bennett, whose book on Leicestershire architects remains essential reading, was also helpful sharing his sources. I also owe thanks to Dr Helen Boynton for putting me in touch with him and I thank Michael Smith (a fellow ex-Castle Donington College man) for his friendly mentoring.

Colin Young of Golding, Young and Mawer Auctioneers was sporting with his help and Graham Barker pointed me in the right direction with the Corah warehouse, later Post Office. Thank yous are also due to the friendly staff at the R.I.B.A. Library in London and to Ian and Manny, for providing a place to write, and also to Caroline Wessel. Similar thanks to Thomas Barnes and Anna Stone of Aviva.

Colin Hyde liaised with Denis Calow to secure permission to use examples from his unique photograph collection. His generosity in freely allowing their use is an example to all historians. Alan and Sandy White have saved the portrait of William Flint for posterity and were good enough to let me use the image for the front cover.

Finally, without Jennifer Parker of Fuzzy Flamingo and her skill, judgement and wisdom, this book would never have been published.

Most of all, Mark Liptrot has shown saintly levels of patience being dragged round the various Flint or Flint-related buildings in the county.

To everyone above, my grateful thanks. Any errors in the text are mine and I would welcome any revisions via markmitchley@yahoo.com or through the publisher. I intend ultimately to donate the research for this book to the LRO.

Picture Acknowledgements

All photographs are by the author other than the following which are reproduced with the kind permission of:

Denis Calow: pages 24, 147, 153, 154, 158, 177, 192, 208, 262

Norwich Union: page 181

Record Office for Leicestershire, Leicester and Rutland: pages 8, 10, 17, 34, 35, 40, 49, 51, 53, 54, 57, 61, 62, 64, 68, 73, 75, 80, 88, 89, 90, 93, 98, 103, 104, 113, 117, 118, 122, 125, 132, 134, 139, 142, 145, 146, 150, 156, 164, 172, 178, 186, 189, 201, 216, 220, 223, 235, 237, 241, 246, 248, 250

Sandy and Alan White: Front cover and pages 14 and 15

CHAPTER 1

The Life of William Flint

William Flint was born in Leicester on 18th February 1801 and baptised eight days later at St Mary de Castro.

Family

He was the son of John Loyley Flint[1] and Ann Birchnell,[2] both of the Newarke, who had married at St Mary de Castro on 6th October 1796; John being the son of Robert Flint[3] and Elizabeth Loyley[4] who had married in 1766. Robert died '...*in the service of King and Country*' at Tobago in 1781.[5] It is not clear what he was doing in the West Indies during this turbulent time, but it is likely he was a victim of the French reconquest of the islands, which started in 1781. It is possible that the family lived at Castle View as there is a William Flint described as a schoolmaster residing there, as listed in the 1800 Poll Book, and Robert and Elizabeth Flint did indeed have a son called William.

John and Ann had at least five children: the eldest was John[6], born in 1798, who died at King Street in 1826.[7] Robert[8] was next in 1799, followed by William and then Elizabeth,[9] in 1803, who married Arthur Whitewood[10] in 1837 as his second wife. The last sibling was James,[11] born

1 John Loyley Flint (1768-1840). Schoolmaster.
2 Ann Flint (1770-1806).
3 Robert Flint (1735-1781).
4 Elizabeth Flint (1746-1803).
5 Gravestone, St Mary de Castro.
6 John Flint (1798-1826).
7 *Leicester Chronicle*, 18th February 1826.
8 Robert Flint (1799-1810).
9 Elizabeth Flint (1803-1885).
10 Arthur Whitewood (c.1788-1853). Cabinet maker and upholsterer of Charles Street.
11 James Flint (1805-1806).

Flint's birthplace? Castle View which has changed little since Flint's time.

in 1805 who died as an infant. Ann Flint died on 13th November 1806 and was buried at St Mary's, next to her parents-in-law, six days later.

William was only five years old when his mother died. John remarried by licence at St Mary's on 24th September 1807 to Mary Elson[12] who was a spinster of the parish.

John Flint was a schoolmaster and the family home was in King Street from at least 1814. He is listed in trade directories at King Street under *'Schools and academies'* from 1827 to 1831. He was also Secretary to the Board of the Leicester Infirmary for 14 years and was elected to the post on 16th February 1809 by 49 votes to 21 against Mr Martin,[13] being proposed and seconded by the Rev Mr Thomas Robinson[14] and Mr Robert Clarke.[15] The vacancy was caused by his predecessor, John Throsby,[16] who was forced to resign amidst allegations of defrauding asylum patients to

12 Mary Flint (1767-1854).
13 Isaac Martin (d.1851). Master of St Martin's House of Industry.
14 Thomas Robinson (1748-1813). Chaplain to the Infirmary and vicar of St Mary's, who presumably christened William Flint. For obituary see *Leicester Chronicle* 27th March 1813.
15 Robert Clarke (1749-1814). House visitor to the Infirmary (with William Firmadge).
16 John Throsby (1775-1847). Son of the historian of the same name.

the tune of £500.[17] John Flint was obliged to provide a bond of £200 to protect the Board from any losses.

Financial irregularity featured in John Flint's own resignation on 7th October 1823 after pressure from John Ellis[18] due to Flint's inability to account for subscription money! After an abortive attempt to justify his actions, Flint wrote to the Board to resign:

> 'I beg leave to resign the office of your secretary. In so doing I shall plead no mitigation of circumstances, I feel a strong support in the integrity of my motives and enjoy a solace in the remembrance of unrequited and unrewarded services.' [19]

He was a man of many talents as it would appear that, for some time during the second decade of the nineteenth century, he combined his Infirmary work with holding the office of Overseer for the Parish of St Mary as well as acting as agent for The Commercial Hall Wine Company for whom he put on tastings at his King Street home.

Flint family graves at St. Mary de Castro.

17 Minutes Leicester Infirmary Board, 16th February 1809.
18 John Ellis (1789-1862). Prominent businessman, railway builder, Quaker and later Liberal MP for Leicester.
19 Minutes, Leicester Infirmary Board 7th October 1823.

John Flint died of 'waters in the chest' (a pleural effusion) on 18th July 1840 at King Street and is buried at St Mary de Castro. His widow continued to live with William Flint first at King Street and then at Regent Street (now Road) until her death, aged 87, on 14th November 1854. Mary Flint is also buried at St Mary de Castro.

Early life

William was apprenticed to local builder, John Edwyn, on 10th July 1812 and afterwards was bound to a second master, William Parsons, from 10th October 1818 for three years. Parsons by this time had already made a name for himself as a local architect. Flint became a freemason at Leicester's St John's Lodge on 28th August 1823, and is already described as an architect. Parsons had joined two years previously and perhaps nominated him;[20] he rose quickly through its ranks to become Junior Warden in 1828; Senior Warden in 1830 and finally Worshipful Master in 1835. Unusually, he resigned his membership in 1836 and it is not known why, although a dispute which couldn't be settled with a fellow mason is the most likely answer. Did he fall out with William Parsons? They had both been in contention during the very acrimonious process to choose an architect for the new Work House.

In business

Three years after his masonic induction, he was ready to set up business on his own. His bold and proud statement of business is found in the *Leicester Journal* on 22nd September 1826:

'William Flint
(The Clerk of the Works at the New Church, Leicester)
Architect & Surveyor
BEGS to inform the Public, that he has COMMENCED THE
BUSINESS OF HIS PROFESSION, and respectfully solicits a portion
of its patronage.
King-street, Leicester, Sept. 12, 1826.'

---

20 Freemasons' Register, St John's Lodge, Halford Street, 1823.

St. George's Church; Flint's first serious work.

The 'New Church' was William Parsons's recently constructed St George's Church in Rutland Street. It is still standing but was internally largely rebuilt after a fire in 1911 and is now a Serbian Orthodox church.

The business gradually took off and Flint acquired offices at 18, Friar Lane, by 1832. Common with many architects at the time, he was engaged in building as well as surveying and also acted as an estate agent.

Business in the 1830s

This decade saw a confident Flint at the height of his powers. His commissions were large, grand and elegant: many still survive. The Baptist Church in Charles Street was finished in early 1830 in the reign of George IV before he went on to the new Hall in Wellington Street in 1831 and the Catholic Church at Loughborough in 1832, by now in the reign of William IV. This was followed by the General Newsroom in 1836 then the West Bridge and the eye-catching workhouse in 1837 before the decade came to an end with Leicestershire Banking House in Granby Street in 1838, a year after Victoria's ascent to the throne. In 1837,

Charles Street Baptist Church – a commission that really put Flint on the map.

the business was doing well enough for Flint to advertise for a pupil, but it is not known if he found one.[21]

Work for the Borough

The Borough of Leicester was reorganised in 1836 as a result of the 1835 Municipal Corporations Act. William Parsons was appointed Land Steward to the Corporation on 13th January 1836 with £100 salary. At the same meeting it was agreed to create an Estates Committee which was:

> '…authorised to appoint or employ an architect or surveyor whenever occasion they may require.' [22]

Thus opened a steady source of business and revenue for Flint for the next thirteen years. Various sources state that Flint was 'Borough architect and surveyor'. In fact, this post was not created until 1849 when Samuel Smith

---

21 *Leicester Mercury*, 20th May 1837.
22 Corporation meeting minutes, 13th January 1836.

St. Mary de Castro; the church of Flint's christening and a source of work for several years.

Harris[23] defeated William Flint in a vote, by 21 votes to 16, to appoint the first holder with its £150 salary.[24] Harris resigned in 1854 amidst allegations of corruption.[25] Although Flint was never formally architect and surveyor, he was certainly the Borough's 'go-to-man' for such work. Valuations and assessments are common and from his association fall several valuable commissions such as building the new West Bridge, restoring St Mary de Castro or repairing the Town Hall.

Work was at times grand and lengthy and at others pedestrian, not to say trivial. For example, Mr Willey[26] and his barn dispute take up the first few months of 1838 before the Corporation moved onto an examination of the West Bridge and then spent most of the next few months concerned with painting the Town Hall. In April 1839, he is measuring Cow Lane for paving, valuing land in Regent Street for house building and looking at paving Prince's (Princess) Street with the coming of the railway. The council obviously valued his expertise as this typical extract from an 1839 meeting illustrates:

---

23 Samuel Smith Harris (1796-1863), sometime town councillor and surveyor.
24 *Leicester Mercury*, 8th September 1849.
25 *Leicester Mercury*, 25th March 1854.
26 George Willey (1796-1885). Grocer and cheese and bacon factor with premises on Granby Street.

The Nag's Head in High Cross Street.

'RESOLVED – That Mr. Flint's opinion be taken as to the best mode if improving the appearance and convenience of the conduit, Market Place.'[27]

He often attends meetings and at times reads out his own reports, for example in December 1841 he reads two reports; the first about Watts Causeway and the second about a schoolhouse in Free School Lane. There are many valuations, often of properties and land owned by the Corporation, for example in High Cross Street in 1846 or about David Orange's[28] factory in Mill Lane the same year. He spends over a year from 1839 looking into drainage at the Fish Market and examines different ways of heating the Town Hall in 1842. Much work seems to have gone into assessing the Nag's Head in High Cross Street with councillors constantly quibbling with Flint's plans due to the cost, estimated at a paltry £73. They are still debating the repairs and costs after Flint's death in 1862!

---

27 Estates Committee minutes, 2nd September 1839.
28 David Orange (1801-1868). Worsted spinner who lived at New Walk then Crow Mills, Wigston. Isaac Barradale Sr was one of his executors.

In 1844 there is even a complaint:

'Mr Oldfield[29] attends to make his complaint respecting Mr Flint's treatment of him in reference to painting the Town Hall and Mr Flint enters into an explanation in vindication of the course he has adopted.

Resolved – that the committee having attentively listened to the statements of Mr Oldfield and Mr Flint are of the opinion that Mr Oldfield might misunderstand the specification from the term "completely removed" being used there – at the same time they are of opinion that he has failed to substantiate his charges against Mr Flint.'[30]

Flint certainly gains from his association with the Corporation, for instance he is asked to lay or repair the Town Hall floor in 1847 for £23 10s 0d and he gets the job of mapping the Corporation estate in 1849 at one shilling an acre.

Leicester is changing and growing rapidly and the town's infrastructure is struggling to cope, as can be seen by the Corporation's concern about Bow Bridge in 1845 (it had already spent a considerable sum on Flint's new West Bridge):

'I have examined Bow Bridge and I beg to report to you my opinion that it is in a ruinous state and unfit to sustain the passage of heavy weights over it. I may add that I surveyed the bridge at the commencement of the year 1842 and that the fractures and decay in it have much increased since that time.'[31]

He wrote again in May 1845 and there is a sense of frustration and determination: *'I do not think it can be made certainly secure.'* Flint underlines 'certainly' and this is strong stuff for him as his letters are unfailingly diplomatic and polite.[32] Nothing came of this either and Flint produced yet another inspection report in 1848.

The arrival of the railway (about which Flint made a report in 1848) acts as a further stimulus for growth. Whole streets are laid out and the Corporation is busy selling plots of land for building, particularly in the

---

29 Edward Oldfield (1798-1875), painter of Belgrave Gate.
30 Estates Committee minutes, 26th November 1844.
31 Estates Committee minutes, 30th January 1845.
32 Estates Committee minutes, 26th May 1845.

Old Bow Bridge, rebuilt in 1862. Note the Richard III stone, another Flint commission.

Southfields area. From time to time ad hoc committees would be formed to respond to large projects. There is one for the new West Bridge, the new Museum, the Borough Gaol, the Fish Market and the largest one, Town Improvement, which spent much of the 1840s trying to create an Act of Parliament to give the Corporation a host of executive powers.

Names of roads change to reflect a smarter outlook: in April 1850 Gaol Lane becomes Lancaster Street and (de) Montfort Street is named and laid out to link it to Victoria Road, the new name of Occupation Road. There is a very large auction in July the same year of land plots that Flint laid out in (de) Montfort Street and Square, Regent Road and Princess Street. There are plots for 67 houses in 33 lots; the quantity of ground 23,817 square yards or four acres three roods and four perches. Flint would build on this land, for his own residence and for a variety of clients, throughout the 1850s and future partner Henry Shenton would also buy land to build his house here. Later in 1851, Flint was greatly engaged in plans to re-site the race course which in those days was located near New Walk and the Corporation are still debating what to do in 1856 when Flint submits yet another plan.

Corporation work for Flint is thin on the ground from about the time of Harris's appointment as Borough Surveyor and this is not perhaps surprising; in 1858, Flint's only involvement with the Corporation is to present plans on behalf of the Leicester Freehold Land Society for the continuance of roads in Jarrom Street, Deacon Street and Laxton Street. The last entry mentioning him is at the 12th March meeting where payment of the firm's bill for £4 3s 0d is authorised for an unknown valuation. It is a small ending to a long association.

Business in the 1840s

This decade saw more large commissions, most of them still standing. 1842 saw the start of the Congregational Church at Market Harborough and circa 1845 the Richard Harris[33] warehouses on King Street. There is very little work other than the Market Harborough church during 1843. This may indicate that Flint was working elsewhere, or he was perhaps unwell. The surviving correspondence for the Harborough Church indicates

Market Harborough Congregational Chapel: in mature style with echoes of Charles Street.

---

33 Richard Harris (1777-1854). Mill owner and sometime Liberal MP for Leicester.

money worries in late 1843 and illness in 1844.[34] No work has been found out of the county and there are very few lettings. A notice to iron founders appeared for a Leicester warehouse in the Derby press in May,[35] but other than that, there is nothing to suggest he was busy elsewhere. In 1847, Flint took on his first identified pupil, William Millican and in the same year advertised for five to ten acres of freehold land eligible for building within the precincts of the Borough.[36] Was he trying property speculation? In 1848 he started the enormous and statesmanlike Italianate Whitmore Ellis spinning mill at West Bridge. He finished the decade in partnership with Charles Wickes from early 1849 and found a new role with a new and radical society.

The Leicester Freehold Land Society

In 1849 he secured the position of surveyor at the first meeting of the newly formed Leicester Freehold Land Society[37] and this must have been some consolation for his not securing the Borough's equivalent post. Newspaper adverts from this period show that Flint was energetic on the society's behalf. It was a political movement and, as John Biggs MP[38] said:

'The object of the society was to overthrow Tory domination in the county of Leicester'.[39]

The Society had its roots in the National Freehold Land Society, set up by quondam Leicester Whig MP Sir Joshua Walmsley[40] and Stockport MP Richard Cobden.[41] It used the 1835 Buildings Act to create what ultimately became building societies such as the Abbey National, which the society

---

34 LRO N/C/215/152/1-26.

35 *Derby Mercury*, 17th May 1843.

36 *Leicester Mercury*, 17th July 1847.

37 *Leicester Mercury*, 25th August 1849.

38 Sir John Biggs (1801-1871). Hosier and reforming Liberal MP for Leicester 1855-1862.

39 *Leicester Mercury*, 1st September 1849.

40 Sir Joshua Walmsley (1794-1871), reformer and campaigner several times elected Liberal MP for Leicester.

41 Richard Cobden (1804-1865), free trade and anti-Corn Law campaigner and liberal MP for Stockport.

became in 1874. It was concerned with the enfranchisement of a wider section of the British population, as in order to be a parliamentary voter, it was necessary to be a land owner. The Society organised itself to buy and sell plots of land at affordable prices so that a greater proportion of society could obtain suffrage. An offshoot, in the form of British Land Company, still exists in the twenty-first century. Contemporary newspaper reports are fascinating and the bile expended on the subject either from the Liberal *Mercury* or the Conservative *Journal* is eye-popping and reaches fever pitch with the *Journal's* horror at the fact that women were office holders in the Society.[42]

Home life

In 1841, Flint is unmarried and living with his stepmother, Mary, in King Street.

However, on 20th November 1845, Flint married Ann Hull by licence at Christ Church, Herne Bay. On the marriage certificate he is described as an architect from St Mary's parish in Leicester whose father is John Flint, Gentleman. Ann Hull was born in Leicester on 20th May 1810 and baptised at St Mary de Castro (like her husband) on 29th May the same year. She was the daughter of Samuel Hull[43] and his wife Sarah Bridget.[44] She and her family are from Leicester and in 1841 are living just a stone's throw from the Flints in Duke Street. She is a spinster without rank or profession, giving her residence as Herne Bay. Samuel Hull was a builder and carpenter and probably he and Flint had a professional connection. Despite an extensive search, no information has come to light as to why the couple married so far from home or what Ann Hull was doing there. Flint does not appear to have any professional engagements in Kent and seems confined to Leicestershire for his entire career. There is a Flint family in the area, but no connection has yet been established between them, although Flint's sister, Elizabeth Whitewood, was with him at the time and acted as a witness, adding to the idea that that there may be a family link.

---

42 *Leicester Journal*, 7th September 1849.
43 Samuel Hull (1775-1856). Builder of Duke Street.
44 Sarah Hull (1777-1869).

The portrait

Unlike many of his contemporaries, William Flint's likeness was captured in oils and happily still exists. His left hand at his temple highlighting the creative mind from which designs flow and sitting straight-backed with an elbow leaning on a leather-bound volume; there is a sense of capability, prosperity and vision. On the table before him is his plan of the West Bridge and in the background, as though through an open window, the General Newsroom and two other buildings, as yet unidentified, although the Leicestershire Banking Company's building is probably one of them. This puts the date of the painting sometime after mid-1839, by which time the banking house would have been completed and also the design for the West Bridge agreed. Flint was about 38 years old and his face has an open and kindly appearance. He looks rather smart with his muttonchops, frilled shirt and split cuffs, and thus dresses as he builds: with style and elegance but rather safely.

It is not known how the portrait came to be auctioned at Golding, Young and Mawer's auction house in Bourne, Lincolnshire in 2009. It is

'Uncle William' in about 1840. Artist unknown in oil.

Portrait detail showing the General News Room.

now owned by Sandy and Alan White and hangs (all six feet by four feet of it) in their family home where he is affectionately known by their family as 'Uncle William'.

Where did William Flint live?

He spent most of his childhood at least in King Street. An advert in the *Chronicle* in 1827 suggests he may have lived for a time in a messuage *'...fronting into a yard in Union-street...'*[45] with a garden shared with his neighbour, Nathaniel Corah,[46] which faced Marlborough Street just off King Street. He was still registered as a voter there in 1838. He was certainly back in King Street by 1841. Borough of Leicester records show that Flint moved to Regent Street in the new South Fields in 1845, probably as a result of his marriage, and an auction at the Lion and Lamb

---

45 *Leicester Chronicle*, 21st April 1827.
46 Nathaniel Corah (1777-1831). Hosier and father of a dynasty of hosiers in what would be a worldwide firm.

on Gallowtree Gate advertised two, seemingly connected, residences in Southfields in June 1853, which might be this address:[47]

'All those TWO modern and well-built FAMILY RESIDENCES, situate in Southfields, Leicester, each containing entrance hall, dining, drawing, and breakfast rooms, large kitchen, scullery, cellar, six bedrooms, water-closet, greenhouse, excellent walled garden, and other appurtenances, in the respective occupations of Mr. W. Flint and Mr. G. Thorp.'[48]

Could it be that this address is one of the three houses that later made up the Fielding-Johnson Hospital? It is difficult to prove it. That said, the 1851 census records the Flints at 70, Southfields and the 1885 Ordnance Survey map shows the first house of these three, the one nearest Holy Trinity, is called 'Southfields'. When Flint's coat was stolen from his house in 1857, the address was given as 'Southfields Place'. Wherever their first home was, the Flints moved to 76, Regent Road by 1861, which

Southfields, a house befitting an architect.

47   *Leicester Chronicle*, 4th June 1853.

48   George Thorp (1817-1894). Elastic webbing and glove manufacturer with a mill on Friday Street.

The most likely candidate for 76, Regent Road and where Flint died.

was the first house after the railway bridge going towards Victoria Park and now occupied by Enkalon House. It was demolished before 1960. It looks like a Flint building and is perhaps a more modest residence than might be expected for an architect but, yet again, it is simply expressed in grey brick and has little adornment save for a Greek circular design above the portico.

Partners

From 1849, he was in partnership with Charles Wickes and together they redesigned the Market Hall and erected a row of grand houses in Museum Square amongst other commissions. However, they parted ways in 1853 with the customary notices in the newspapers:

'Notice is hereby given, that the PARTNERSHIP heretofore subsisting between the undersigned WILLIAM FLINT and CHARLES WICKES, in the profession or business of Architects and Surveyors, and carried on at Leicester under the style of "Flint and Wickes", was this day dissolved by mutual consent.

Dated this twenty-ninth day of June, one thousand eight hundred and fifty-three.

WILLIAM FLINT

CHARLES WICKES

N.B. – The business will be conducted in future by Mr. FLINT.' [49]

Not long afterwards, Flint set up business with Henry Shenton, their first commission being for the Leicester Gas Light Company[50] and this partnership lasted until his death.

Business in the 1850s

Houses and factories characterise this phase of William Flint's professional life. House building, whether grand or humble, took up much of the middle years with large humble commissions in Mowbray Street, Infirmary Square and Lancaster Road and a grander row in New Walk in 1852. Also at this

Museum Square: an early commission with Charles Wickes.

49 *Leicester Chronicle*, 2nd July 1853.
50 *Leicester Chronicle*, 25th February 1854.

time, Flint was laying down new streets such as the 'Holme' Streets (Great and Little et al) near West Bridge. The 1850s end with the Italianate and now sadly lost Curzon Street Methodist Church in 1859. During this decade, Flint took on at least three pupils, starting with James Frank Smith and Charles Baker (who would become his assistant) in the early years, perhaps 1851, and then Isaac Barradale in about 1857. His former pupil, William Millican, with him since 1846, left to start his own business in 1851.

Politics

Politics in Leicester during Flint's adult life are more than usually rowdy for the time and this reflects a national picture of agitation and change. Rather surprisingly to a modern eye, votes were not secret and poll books were published revealing who had voted for whom. In the General Election of 1832, the Poll Book records that Flint voted for the two Whig candidates. The Whig party believed in free trade; the supremacy of parliament over monarchy; greater suffrage; religious freedom and the abolition of slavery and became more commonly known as the Liberal Party as the century progressed. The electorate at this time represented about 14% of the total male population. In 1835 and in 1837, both he and his father (eligible to vote because they were £10 occupiers) also voted Whig (although the Conservatives triumphed). The 1841 Poll Book shows that he voted Whig again and qualified due to his land in Southampton Street and St George's Street. In 1847, he voted for Whig candidates Sir Joshua Walmsley and Richard Gardner[51] He did not register a vote in 1852, but in 1857, 1859 and finally in 1861, he voted for John Dove Harris – a Liberal.[52]

Business in the 1860s

New roads and alterations to properties kept Flint busy in the few months of the 1860s in which he lived. He also sometimes revisited old projects,

---

51 Richard Gardner (1812-1856), several times MP for Leicester who died in office.

52 John Dove Harris (1808-1878), variously Mayor of or Liberal MP for Leicester. For obituary see *Leicester Mercury*, 23rd November 1878. Son of Richard Harris Sr.

such as the British School for girls in 1861, which he had built in 1834 and there is a sense of life and craft turning full circle.

William Flint died on 11th January 1862 at his home in Regent Road of 'General Debility and Syncope'.[53] He was buried in Welford Road Cemetery on 16th January and his headstone bears an inscription from Proverbs verse 10, chapter 7: *'The memory of the just is blessed'.* The *Leicester Chronicle* published a warm obituary two days later:

'THE LATE MR. FLINT. – In recording the demise of this gentleman, some reference is due to his talents and character. Mr. Flint had been established among us as an architect for thirty years. He received his professional instruction in the office of Mr. Parsons; and soon after the new municipal body took office, he was appointed architect and surveyor to the borough. He also carried

Flint's grave in Welford Road Cemetery.

53   Syncope is loss of consciousness, often due to low blood pressure.

on an extensive business as a professional architect; several of the public buildings and private dwellings of the inhabitants having been designed by him during the last quarter of a century. Mr. Flint's architectural ideas and principles were all imbibed before the revival of Gothic Architecture took place, and therefore all his works were in Classical styles or in modifications of them. The General News Room, Granby-street, was one of the buildings of which he devised the plans and drew the elevation. Many of the private houses in the suburbs of Leicester, built of white brick with stone facings, which have a light and pleasing effect, were erected from his designs, and in his day and generation he kept pace with the taste of his contemporaries. Some of the younger architects following Mr. Flint seem bent on "improving" the Gothic, by inventing what they call "Victorian" architecture, which to our thinking is a mistake. Mr. Flint did not attempt this, being content with adaptations from received styles, and not being so presumptuous as to conceive he could invent a new one. In private life Mr. Flint was amiable, unassuming, and esteemed, and his decease will be regretted by many friends and acquaintances.'

Warm words were also publically expressed by the Leicester Freehold Land Society:

'During the last year a vacancy has occurred in the office of Surveyor to the Society, by the lamented death of Mr. Flint, who had held the office from the commencement of the Society, and discharged the sometimes difficult duties with great ability and to the entire satisfaction of the Board of Management.'[54]

At the Society's meeting immediately after Flint's death, fuller tribute was made:

'Resolved that the Board of management deeply regretting the decease of Mr. Flint decide to send their appreciation of the valuable services rendered by him; and their belief that the distinguished position he held in the profession, combined with

---

54 *Leicester Chronicle*, 22nd November 1862.

persevering industry and an impartial consideration of the various interests entrusted to him, have contributed very essentially to the prosperity and success of the society from its commencement.

That a copy of the above resolution be forwarded by the secretary to Mrs. Flint.'[55]

He was replaced by his partner, Henry Shenton.

The usual notice to creditors appeared in the *Leicester Journal* on the last day of February with business being handled by Stone[56], Paget[57] and Billson[58], and on 14th March, Flint's effects were auctioned off. The notice of sale in the *Journal* makes fascinating reading:

'SALE THIS DAY
Valuable Household Furniture, Regent-street, Leicester.

JOHN HOLLAND[59]
Has received instructions
TO SELL BY AUCTION,
This day (Friday), the 14th of March, 1862,
A PORTION of the Excellent Modern HOUSEHOLD
FURNITURE, about 22 dozen of Port, Champagne,
and other Wines, upwards of 300 vols. of Valuable Books,
superior Oil Paintings and Engravings, Fishing Tackle,
Bedding Plants, and Effects, of the late Mr. Wm. Flint,
Architect, on the premises, Regent-street, Leicester.
Catalogues are now ready.
Sale to commence at Eleven o'clock precisely'.

---

55 Leicester Freehold Land Society Minute Book 23rd January 1862 LRO 18D70/67

56 Samuel Francis Stone (1834-1915). Solicitor of London Road and son of same-named Town Clerk.

57 Alfred Paget (1810-1904). Solicitor of 2, West Street, sometime town councillor for East St Mary's.

58 William Billson Jr (1829-1901). Solicitor and a near neighbour of Flint's at 80 Regent Street, married to Stone's daughter, Mary.

59 John Holland Jr (1818-1869), auctioneer of London Road with premises on Market Street.

That he had a substantial library and also fine prints and engravings (not to mention a substantial cellar) is not perhaps surprising, but the revelation that he was a keen gardener and fisherman adds a little colour to Flint's personal life and highlights what little is known of him as a man.

The Flints never had children and, in his will, dated the day he died, he left everything to his wife, with a twenty pound annuity to his widowed sister, Elizabeth Whitewood. William Billson (the younger) was the executor, whom Flint describes as 'my friend' and lived 2 doors down at 80, Regent Road. The estate was valued as 'Effects under £2,000'. Ann Flint died on 5th October 1875 at her home 24, Evington Street, which is one of four alms-houses designed by William Jackson[60] and endowed by Miss Lawton[61] '...*to allow such deserving persons as she may select to live in them rent free*' [62]; which may give some indication as to Ann Flint's wealth and

Miss Lawton's Alms Houses, home of Ann Flint in widowhood.

---

60 William Jackson (1829-1894). Architect of Portland Towers, Knighton. Designer of St Margaret's Works for Corah and Sons.

61 Martha Ann Lawton (1793-1872). Benefactress of Belvoir House, London Road. Scion of the Bankart family who also left a legacy of £100 to her friend Elizabeth Parsons, widow of the architect.

62 *Leicester Chronicle*, 13th August 1864.

Flint Street in the 1950s.

status in widowhood. Rather confusingly, she is listed in some directories as 'Mariah' Flint. She is buried with her husband with the epitaph: *'Trusting in Jesus'*. To complete this part of the story, Elizabeth Whitewood was buried with her brother and sister-in-law on 31st October 1876.

Flint was commemorated by having a street named after him in the form of Flint Street, which was situated off Humberstone Road opposite the Humberstone Road Railway station. Fittingly, the next street along was Shenton Street. Like much of their work, the roads were demolished, in this case in the 1970s. Welford Road Cemetery also commemorates him with a memorial plaque, an honour he shares with Isaac Barradale.

What happened to the practice?

It has generally been thought that Flint's practice was taken on by Henry Shenton and he certainly inherited Flint's post at the Leicester Freehold Land Society, for example. It seems, however, that the firm may have gone in two directions. Days after Flint died, the following announcement appeared in the *Leicester Journal*:

'TO THE NOBILITY, GENTRY & INHABITANTS OF LEICESTER, AND ITS VICINITY.

IT is the intention of Mr. JAMES FRANK SMITH to commence, on the 2nd of March next, a Practice as an

ARCHITECT, CIVIL ENGINEER and SURVEYOR. And he trusts that from the long practical experience he has had (11 years) as Assistant to his uncle, the late Mr. Flint, and by his efficiency and diligence in his profession, to merit a share of the patronage so liberally bestowed upon the late Mr. Flint.

Temporary Offices, No. 2 Princess-street,

Adjoining Mr. Hickling's.'[63]

It is almost certain that this is the same J. F. Smith that was *'in attendance'* at Flint's death and who also registered it. Was this a deliberate break with Shenton? After all, Smith was a pupil of Flint's during Shenton's partnership with him. It was Shenton who carried on the 18, Friar Lane

Flint's memorial plaque at Welford Road Cemetery.

---

63 William Hickling (1803-1878). Accountant of Princess Street and later London Road; father-in-law of James Frank Smith. Henry Shenton's son-in-law, Henry Kemp, was one of his executors.

address and also took on another of Flint's pupils as his partner, Charles Baker. Their paths only seemed to cross once again, a few months later, when they co-wrote a letter to the *Journal*[64] about a memorial to J. F. Hollings.[65]

Whatever the situation, Henry Shenton and James Frank Smith, not to mention William Millican, Charles Baker and Isaac Barradale, all sustained businesses in the profession and this is Flint's other legacy, as will be seen in the chapters ahead.

64 *Leicester Journal*, 20th February 1863.

65 James Francis Hollings (1806-1862). Printer and Publisher of the Leicestershire Mercury and sometime Mayor of Leicester who committed suicide at the Stoneygate residence of his brother-in-law John Biggs. For inquest see *Leicester Chronicle*, 20th September 1862.

CHAPTER 2

The Masters: John Edwyn

John Edwyn apprenticed William Flint as an eleven-year-old boy on 10th July 1812. He had become a freeman of the town the same day. Flint stayed with him for a little over six years until 10th October 1818 when he was bound to William Parsons.

Edwyn was born 4th October 1783, the son of local carpenter Thomas Edwyn[66] and his wife Ann Warner[67] (who died in 1787, when John Edwyn was only four years old). He was baptised the next day at St Mary de Castro and it is likely he is connected to the Edwyn/Burnaby family of Baggrave Hall. Thomas Edwyn was a well-known local carpenter, based in High Cross Street, with entries in local trades directories from at least 1791. He had been apprenticed to Alderman William Oldham[68] and in turn was master to several pupils including Hinckley builder William Ashby[69] in 1782. He remarried twice more and died in 1803 aged 48.

John Edwyn combined work as a carpenter, surveyor and architect in common with many in the profession at the time, including Flint. He appears to be the local dealer for Roman Cement and also dealt in stone such as marble.[70] Pre-Flint, he is dealing in timber trees and bed posts[71] and handling the sale of anything from the Lion and Lamb Inn[72] to a '... *a very genteel residence situate in High Cross-street, Leicester, in the occupation of Mr. Wm. Forrester...*'[73] He was not solely confined to Leicester and was

---

66   Thomas Edwyn (1755-1803). Carpenter from Beeby.
67   Ann Edwyn (1759-1787).
68   William Oldham (1737-1814). Alderman and sometime mayor of Leicester, architect of Braunstone Hall.
69   William Ashby (c. 1767-1844). Builder.
70   *Leicester Journal*, 31st July 1812 and also see *Leicestershire Architects 1700-1850* (Bennett 1968).
71   *Leicester Journal*, 26th January 1810.
72   *Leicester Journal*, 15th February 1811.
73   *Leicester Journal*, 13th December 1811; William Forrester (1767-1833). Brewer.

engaged in the sale of the Old Bishop Blaze Inn at Melton Mowbray in 1811 and also 16 messuages and tenements, including framework knitter shops in the centre of Earl Shilton in 1812.[74] He first describes himself as *'Architect and Surveyor'* (rather than just *'surveyor'*) towards the end of 1811, not long before he apprenticed Flint and, from 1812, he is selling land on the newly laid out Bishop Street. He lived in Horsepool Street, now Oxford Street, and maintained offices in Hotel Street.

His first known activity in the time Flint was his pupil was a sale of a dwelling house with brew house in St Nicholas Street and the sale of buildings in Red Cross Street.[75] Business appears to be going well and he had no less than four adverts in the 7th May 1812 edition of the *Leicester Journal*. In 1814, he was (at first jointly with Joshua Harrison[76]) awarded roofing contracts for the restoration of St Margaret's Church with contracts for lead, timber and stone work to follow.[77] Flint's earliest mature work was clerk to the works at St George's and he probably gained much useful experience for it at this time.

It is difficult to attribute architectural work to John Edwyn. Whilst his business as what we now think of as estate agent is relatively straightforward, it is almost impossible to disentangle what might be his work from the work of other builders and architects for whom he was acting. This is also often the case with William Flint. There are some adverts in the press which are concerned with newly erected houses, such as '... *a substantially built modern house'* in Gallowtree Gate or *'Two houses near the High-cross, Leicester extending in front about 59 ft...'*[78] but whether or not they are buildings he constructed or designed may never be proved. With Flint, there are many surviving buildings, photographs and plans which make attribution of his work so much easier. There is no known body of work for Edwyn and his early death meant he never had the opportunity to develop as an architect with more important commissions. It is a sad fact that the only remnant of John Edwyn's work are the few bricks that form the doorways and front walls of houses

---

74 *Leicester Journal*, 24th April 1812.

75 *Leicester Journal*, 11th September 1812.

76 Joshua Harrison (1772-1837). Carpenter and builder of Granby Street and grandfather of architect Stockdale Harrison.

77 *Leicester Journal*, 11th June 1814. The solicitor was a Beaumont Burnaby of Church Gate, possibly his cousin.

78 *Leicester Journal*, 15th March 1811.

Possible remains of All Saint's Open and Edwyn's only surviving work.

on High Cross Street next to what used to be called All Saints Open, just opposite the church. Even here, however, doubt exists as to whether Edwyn was definitely the architect.

His life was a short one and the manner of his death was tragic indeed:

'On Friday night. Mr. John Edwyn, architect of this town, while labouring under an attack of apoplexy, precipitated himself from his room window into the street. When found, the unfortunate deceased had no other covering upon him than that of his shirt. He had bled copiously from bruises occasioned by the fall, and was actually frozen to the ground.'[79]

He is buried in St Mary's churchyard. By the *Journal's* dating, the date of death is Friday 29th December 1820, however letters of administration granted to his sister Anna Dumelow[80] in January 1832 put the date of death two days later on 31st December 1820. It is not clear why the letters of administration were needed so long after his death, but they reveal that

79 *Leicester Chronicle* 6th January 1821
80 Anna Maria Dumelow (1784-1835), wife of Joseph Dumelow (1772-1849), tailor of Union Street.

John Edwyn was unmarried and that his estate amounted to less than £5.

William Flint is agent for the sale of *'An old established Timber Trade …
well adapted for a Carpenter and Builder.'*[81] in 1833 and it is just possible that
this may be his old master's business.

---

81   *Leicester Journal*, 22nd September 1833.

CHAPTER 3

The Masters: William Parsons

The son of Edward Parsons[82] and Katherine Barwell[83], William Parsons was born on 14th December 1796 and baptised at Scraptoft on 17th January 1797. His father was a surveyor of turnpike roads and this is an area that his son would eventually monopolise in Leicestershire to the point where he would ultimately have the living of a network of roads of over 150 miles controlling all of the county's approach roads and stretching into Warwickshire.

Educated at Billesdon, Parsons was articled to William Firmadge[84] in 1809, who was by then making the transition from builder and stonemason to architect. He built Worcester Gaol with him before he went into business on his own by 1819. The same year he succeeded his father (on his death) as Steward to the Corporation, a post he retained after the reformed Town Council came into being in 1836. In 1823 he started work as County Surveyor, a post he held until his death in 1857. He married Elizabeth Berridge[85] in 1820 and they lived at 21 St Martins

William Flint joined him as a

21, St. Martin's, the home of William and Elizabeth Parsons.

---

82 Edward Parsons (1760-1819), surveyor and steward to the Corporation of Leicester.
83 Katherine Parsons (1761-1823).
84 William Firmadge (1755-1836). Leicester architect, alderman and magistrate.
85 Elizabeth Berridge (1800-1887).

Alms Houses at Barrow-upon-Soar.

pupil in 1818 after six years with John Edwyn. It is likely that Flint stayed with him as an assistant after 1821, by which time Parsons had taken on another pupil, Abraham Gill.[86] He was very busy during the time 1818-1826, when Flint was with him. Flint must have learnt a lot from his master and must have been involved with the erection of a fever house at the Infirmary in 1820; the House of Correction in Loughborough in 1824; an alms house for elderly women in Barrow-upon-Soar in 1825 and Stoney Bridge in Stoney Stanton in 1826. These mirror commissions Flint would take on when he went into business on his own, for example, a fever house (at Melton in 1847); a workhouse (in Leicester in 1837 and in Barrow in 1839); a gaol (alterations to the town gaol in 1849) and the West Bridge in 1837.

Significant works for Parsons and his pupil were St George's Church starting in 1823, where Flint was clerk to the works and the rather astonishing County Gaol on Welford Road, starting in 1825. St George's was reckoned to be the most expensive parish church of the century and was the first built since the Reformation.[87] Its original style was medieval in the form of Gothic Revival, but it has suffered from lightning strikes

---

86 Abraham Gill (1803-1834). Leicester architect and later Parsons's partner.
87 Bennett op. cit.

The commanding and audacious County Gaol of 1825.

and fires which has left it with a rather different look. Conversely, the County Gaol is almost entirely unchanged after nearly 200 years. With Parsons as County Surveyor and Flint as unofficial but ever-present surveyor to the Corporation, it is little wonder that the two architects dominated Leicester and its buildings for such a long and important time of growth from the 1830s.

Abraham Gill became a partner in 1832, but his death tragically young in 1834 meant that Parsons operated alone until about 1848, when he took Messing John Dain[88] into partnership; it was he who took the business over when Parsons died and, indeed, lived in his house, taking over his positions as County Surveyor and surveyor for several turnpikes. It does not appear to be as busy a practice as Flint's as judged by the few plans that survive in the Record Office and by the comparatively smaller number of adverts in the press. One still standing in Stamford Street is a very pleasing warehouse for James Jacques,[89] which they built in 1851. Another architect, Thomas Willson,[90] worked closely with Parsons and Dain,

88 Messing John Dain (1810-1886), architect of New Walk and later Richmond, Surrey, designer of Bradgate House for the Earl of Stamford.
89 James Jacques (1804-1865). Woolstapler of Birstall Hill House.
90 Thomas Willson (1814-?). Architect later of London.

Mr. Jacques' wool warehouse in Stamford Street.

but there is some confusion as to whether or not he was a partner in the firm with Dain.

In 1841, Parsons became a magistrate and stayed on the bench until his death. William Parsons died in early January 1857 at 21, St Martins and he is buried at Scraptoft in the same churchyard as his former master, William Firmadge. Elizabeth Parsons died in 1887 and in her will she left a (now lost) portrait of her late husband to his nephew Frederick Parsons[91] and his watch to another nephew, Percival Moses Parsons,[92] who would later achieve national recognition as a civil engineer.

The Theatre Royal of 1836 on Horsefair Street.

91   Frederick Parsons (1838-1885), chemist of 30, Gallowtree Gate.
92   Percival Moses Parsons (1819-1892), civil engineer and inventor.

The original Midland Station at Campbell Street.

William Parsons did not have a particular style in the same way perhaps that Flint did. There are some classical designs, for example the Theatre Royal (demolished in 1956) in Horsefair Street with its Grecian portico and, most obviously, Campbell Street Railway Station (demolished 1890) with its giant Doric columns, but Parsons was to some extent a freer agent than Flint who kept to his rule of simplicity and classical influence, the mechanics of which he must have learnt from his master.

William Parsons' grave at Scraptoft.

CHAPTER 4

The Buildings of the 1830s

Baptist Church
Charles Street
April 1830
Extant

This early commission is approaching two centuries old and stands as a monument to Flint's taste and talent. Though internally there are several alterations, the façade has undergone few changes and looks much as it did when it was first built. Pevsner describes it as having:

> *'A very attractive front, mildly Grecian with its two recessed Greek Doric columns (not too sturdy) on the rusticated ground floor...'*[93]

'Mildly Grecian' may well serve as a useful description of several of Flint's works and shows that he settled on his style early.

In late 1829, and in spite of some opposition from the existing Baptist Church at Harvey Lane, a small group led by church deacons Richard Harris, Spence Broughton[94] and John Carryer[95] as well as James Cort[96] moved to set up a new Baptist church on the site of a wool warehouse in what was then Upper Charles Street. The warehouse had been used by a congregation of Kilhamites, a group of breakaway Methodists, who named their place of worship 'Bethesda'. Sheila Mitchell, in her history of the Baptists in Leicester, suggests that it is likely that the site was purchased (for £955 12s) as it had potential for easy conversion into a

---

93 *The buildings of Leicestershire and Rutland* (Pevsner, 2003).
94 Spence Broughton (1771-1840), doctor and preacher.
95 John Carryer (1782-1846). Jeweller and silversmith of New Walk.
96 James Cort (1771-1851). Iron founder; owner of the Britannia Works, living in High Cross Street who died in a carriage accident – see *Leicester Journal*, 23rd May 1851.

Charles Street Baptist Church: a proud statement of faith in the Baptist and in Flint.

chapel, however this proved impossible due to the walls being unable to support the gallery.[97] As a consequence, Flint was selected as architect for a purpose-built chapel and set about construction. Advertisements for contracts to erect the church, vestries and school went to the press on 1st April 1830[98] and by Christmas Day the same year, the church was ready to open to receive applications for the purchase of pews. In the same edition of the *Leicester Chronicle*, Flint receives his due praise:

> 'A commodious well built structure… It has galleries on the front and sides with a school room behind the pulpit, and altogether presents a neat, chaste appearance, reflecting great credit upon the taste and skill of the architect, Mr. Wm. Flint.'[99]

The Chapel opened permanently on 19th January 1831; it had cost £3,759 11s 4d.[100] There was a remodelling in 1861 and another during the 1880s,

---

97 *Not disobedient … a history of the United Baptist Church, Leicester, 1760 – 1983* (Mitchell, 1984)
98 *Leicester Journal*, 1st April 1830.
99 *Leicester Chronicle*, 24th December 1830.
100 Mitchell op sit.

during which the school was rebuilt and the graveyard closed. 1983 saw further changes and a screen erected to create a bigger vestry and simplify the pulpit area layout. The church is still in use today as Central Baptist Church Leicester and it retains a light and peaceful atmosphere; no mean feat for a city centre church.

Clearly visible on the original entrance gates, the ceiling roses and various other internal decorations as well the main frontage is what will become Flint's trademark: an anthemion and palmette honeysuckle ornament; in this case on a running frieze across the balconies or the frontage – see chapter 13 (What Might a House Have Looked Like?).

Meeting Hall and Library
Wellington Street and Belvoir Street
June 1831
Extant

This Flint building has undergone many changes, not just of use but also of design. The overall shape and idea of what Flint built still survives but there is much that is altered or added (e.g. the porch entrance on Belvoir Street) and, as a result of significant and regular changes of use, almost nothing original survives internally.

The call for public meeting rooms arose because the local Conservative Corporation would not allow any Radicals (later Liberals) to meet in any of their controlled buildings. The Who's Who of Radical Leicester therefore became subscribers to a new meeting hall and raised £3,100 through 107 shares. Nathaniel Corah and John Biggs[101] were among shareholders. William Flint won the competition to design it and superintend its erection '...*without delay*'[102] and by June placed newspaper advertisements for contractors desirous of erecting '...*a Hall, News Room, Library, &c.*'[103]

In late 1833, the Leicester Mechanics' Institute took the upper floor and then the lower floor from 1848-1858, when the Radicals left. In these nationwide institutes can be found the origins of working men's

---

101 John Biggs (1801-1871). Hosier and MP for Leicester commemorated by a statue in Welford Place.
102 *Leicester Chronicle*, 28th May 1831.
103 *Leicester Chronicle*, 11th June 1831.

Wellington Street New Hall later library, another Classical masterpiece.

education and thus they represent the nucleus of the Open University. The emphasis on evidence-based scientific reasoning fits perfectly into Radical Non-conformist Leicester. During this time, it was also home to The Leicester Literary and Philosophical Society.

By 1835, the 'Green Hall' (so called because of the Liberal Party's colours) had become the 'New Hall' and it was used as a trade hall, for example, showing a *'Splendid Foreign Bazaar'* of French, Swiss and German fancy goods.[104] A spell as a concert hall follows, Liszt performed there in 1840. Then, in the 1860s, it was transformed into the Wellington Dining Hall, a working men's eating place.

In 1869, the Corporation purchased the Hall and it became the 'Free Library', opening in 1871 after a great deal of modification during which much of Flint's work was lost. The library moved to Bishop Street in 1905, at which time Brown and Son[105] took it and converted it into an auction room for corn and seed. Pollard and Co.[106] even seem to have bottled ale there during this time.

---

104 *Leicester Journal*, 29th May 1835.
105 George Fowler Brown (1829-1897) and George Fowler Carrington Brown (1874-1927). Solicitors and auctioneers of Newtown Unthank.
106 John Horatio Pollard (1849-1922). Beer bottler of West View, London Road.

The New Hall as it originally looked without portico and with its original side entrance.

In 1935, the library came back to the building and this is when the new porch entrance (until then access had been via Wellington Street) and gallery were added. After 76 years, the Library merged with Bishop Street and closed in 2011. The building is now a photography gallery.

Architecturally, the building is another obvious Flint creation. It is a Greek Revival design stuccoed with large Doric pilasters. The panels are blank throughout with very simple windows and it is still an impressive construction. The railings are the original ones installed by Flint over 180 years ago.

Kibworth Beauchamp Church
Restoration of Tower
1832
Extant

St Wilfrid's Church can trace its rectors back to 1239. The nave and majority of the church building, except the tower, date from the rebuilding in the Fourteenth Century. In 1825 a disastrous lightning strike completely destroyed the tower and, in 1832, Flint was commissioned to rebuild it: it took four years.[107] The church guidebook suggests that Flint modelled it on

---

107 Archbishop Bonney's visitation accounts, LRO.

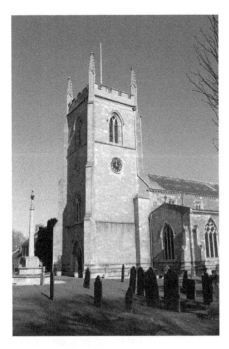

the Gothic St Peter's Church, East Carlton in Northamptonshire by John Wing.[108] The Tower is simple in design with stone ashlar in three parts finished with a crenelated parapet and four pinnacles.

Kibworth Church Tower: a foray into Gothic.

Catholic Chapel and Presbytery Ashby Road, Loughborough November 1832 Rebuilt 1923

The Catholic Emancipation Act of 1829 removed most of the restrictions on social and political activity for British Catholics, giving them almost equal rights. Flint's work for the church is only three years after this and at a time when

St. Mary's Loughborough with its post Flint entrance at 90 degrees to the original.

---

108 John Wing (1728-1794), of North Luffenham. He also designed King's Norton Church – another church with a spire repaired by Flint.

anti-Catholic hostility and anti-Catholic prejudice were common; this is especially true in Loughborough. This is perhaps a daring commission.

According to the church's own account of its history, Father Benjamin Hulme[109] saw the urgent need for a chapel at Loughborough after an Irish Catholic woman of the town had to travel to Leicester to have her newborn child baptised. Evidently, William Flint was chosen as the architect and November 1832 saw the first advertisement to tender for the various 'departments'.[110]

The original Neo-Greek style church, as Flint built it, was smaller and was 71 feet long and 26 feet wide with entrance gained through Hastings Street to what is now the Day Chapel. It was dedicated to St Mary and the cost of building both the church and its associated presbytery in brick and rendered with stucco was £5,000. The large internal fluted columns with palmette capitals are characteristic of Flint and variations of them are to be found in Charles Street Baptist and Market Harborough Congregationalist churches.

The church was remodelled in 1923-1925 when the impressive portico was added and the church extended over the graveyard and rotated so that the present nave is at right angles to the old church. The matching priest's house was incorporated into the building, although the three-bay frontage was retained. Internally, the square columns in the present nave represent the footprint of the original church. The entrance is now on Ashby Road. Flint's classical style was retained throughout, internally and externally.

Factory
Braunstone Gate
Richard Harris
1833
Extant

In the early days of this building's existence, there were two significant events associated with it. The first was a celebration for the Coronation in 1838, where it was the scene of the largest party in the town and provided

---

109 Fr Benjamin Hulme (?-1850). Catholic priest.
110 *Leicester Journal*, 16th November 1832.

Flint's first work for Richard Harris in Braunstone Gate.

dinner for 340 of its workers with Richard Harris himself presiding.[111] In 1846, there was a disastrous fire which caused £4,000 to £5,000's worth of damage. The firm was only insured for £3,000.

The factory produced sewing cotton and linen thread to its own patent and by 1846, Septimus Hamel[112] became a partner, joining Richard Harris's son William Smith Harris[113] to run it.

This is an early business commission for Flint and the start of a long association with Harris firms. The *Chronicle* evidently rated the building:

'An extensive, neatly-built pile of building has recently been erected nearly opposite Earl Howe's Arms in Braunstone-gate. It is intended for a brace manufactory, and being very lofty and stuccoed in front, gives quite an improved appearance to the entrance of the town from Hinckley. The proprietors are Messrs. Harris and Co. The architect Mr. Flint.'[114]

111 *Leicester Mercury*, 30ᵗʰ June 1836.
112 Septimus Hamel (c.1810-1854) of West Street, Braunstone Gate and Woburn Square, London, thread manufacturer. He married Richard Harris's daughter Fanny Dove in 1831.
113 William Smith Harris (1817-1853) of West Street, Braunstone Gate, thread manufacturer and councillor for West St Mary's. Son of Richard Harris and brother-in-law of Septimus Hamel.
114 *Leicester Chronicle*, 20ᵗʰ July 1833.

Earl Howe's Arms lasted as a pub until 1980.

The factory still exists and is now living accommodation for de Montfort University students. Its frontage has been painted and there is almost nothing on the building by way of decoration and, whilst some of this is due to alterations over the years, Flint's design would likely have been very simple. It has three storeys, the first of which has been turned into a bar/restaurant.

Lime Shed
Soar Lane Wharf
Leicester and Swannington Railway
April 1834
Demolished 1863

Railways came early to Leicester, with the Leicester and Swannington Railway being the fifth oldest in the country. This is Flint's only known building in connection with the railways; as such commissions seemed to have been out of his reach. Certainly, William Parsons had strong links with the industry and John Ellis was locally prominent in their management. The nearest he comes to railway work again is the selling of land contiguous with the Soar Lane Station in 1837,[115] although he conducts two surveys for the Corporation in 1837 and 1848. This is ironic in as much as Flint was the reputed designer of Campbell Street Station until Parsons was revealed as the architect in the last thirty years. However, it looks like he got the 1837 report wrong and has to appear before the Corporation to explain his 'misapprehension',[116] so it's perhaps not quite so surprising. The railway opened in 1832 as an urgently needed means of transporting coal from the Leicestershire coal fields whose road and canal transport links were limited. Robert Stephenson,[117] son of *the* George (renowned as the 'father of railways'), was the line's engineer. Notice to tenders was published in April 1834.[118] Little is known about the lime shed, but C. R. Clinker[119] in his book about the line records that

---

115 *Leicester Chronicle*, 18ᵗʰ November 1837.

116 Council minutes, 13ᵗʰ December 1837.

117 Robert Stephenson (1803-1859), railway engineer and later conservative MP for Whitby.

118 *Leicester Chronicle*, 3ʳᵈ May 1834.

119 Charles Ralph Clinker (1906-1983).

it was demolished in March 1863 and the materials, which had originally cost £200, were sold for £45.[120]

British School for girls
Hill Street
May 1834
Demolished

The British and Foreign School Society for the Education of the Labouring and Manufacturing Classes of Society of Every Religious Persuasion was a charity (which still exists) to provide free education for all regardless of religion. In that way, 'British Schools' offered hope for those ineligible for the established church's *'National* Schools'. Boys already had a British School in Sandpit Lane and Flint sought tenders for a corresponding girls' school on 23rd May 1834[121] at the corner of Lower Hill Street and Victoria Street (which was an extension of Hill or Upper Hill Street). No plans, sketches or photographs exist to show what the school might have looked like. The school was demolished after at least 1891 when it auctioned with the boys' school, which by then had moved to the corner of Upper Hill and Eldon Streets. Flint's last recorded work, a fence wall for the school in 1861, may still exist (see chapter 10: The Buildings of the 1960s).

10 Houses and 5 houses
Upper King Street
1835 and c. 1844
Extant

There are two blocks of houses in the same style but not built at the same time. Maps reveal that numbers 1-7, originally three two-storey semi-detached dwellings, which resemble more closely the row on King Street, were not put up until the 1840s. Numbers 9-29 including number 8 Tower Street are a terraced row of three-storey town houses.

---

120 *The Leicester and Swannington Railway* (C. R. Clinker, 1977).
121 *Leicester Journal*, 23rd May 1834.

A stucco terrace with pilasters in Upper King Street.

Pevsner[122] quotes a 'Mr Ashby' as the source that cites William Flint as the architect of this set of houses. It's an unusual entry and the foreword reveals Mr Ashby to be Douglas Ashby,[123] but where his evidence came from is not disclosed. The houses first appear on maps in 1835 and for the next few decades they enjoyed a variety of names, being called plain Upper King Street; Upper King Street Place or Crescent Buildings, Upper King Street.

The row was designed for a new class of professionals and people of independent means: the new middle class. The 1841 poll book lists the following residents who would all have connection with William Flint:

Cornelius Herbert, builder[124]
James Hollings
Samuel Westfahll, later client[125]

---

122 Pevsner op cit
123 Douglas Ashby (1928-2002), authoritative local historian.
124 Cornelius William Hill Herbert (1796-1870), builder with premises on Welford Road. See *Leicestershire Historian 43* (2007) for a useful history of the firm by Caroline Wessel. His great grandson, Albert Herbert, would continue Flint's practice with Charles Baker after Henry Shenton retired.
125 Samuel Christopher Westfahll (1804-1893). Variously wine merchant and draper, later bank manager.

Side house of the Upper King Street terrace. Flint would use this design several times in the future.

William Parsons's assistant (and possibly partner), Thomas Willson, also lived there in the 1850s (in the house once owned by the author). When one of the houses was offered to let in 1859, the rent was £18 per annum.[126]

The buildings use and augment the same anthemion decoration used at Charles Street Baptist Church. The pilasters, use of stucco, the lugged architraves, stringcourse, blind panels and fanlights taken together with the whole simple and elegant classical look make Flint the only architect in real contention. Numbers 21-29 have an additional parapet missing on the others. Did these retail for more? Each house had a large cellar which acted as a kitchen with a range, pantry, coal chute and wood store. The ceilings are made of thick slabs of Swithland slate and these help regulate the temperature for the storage areas very well. Water was supplied via a sink and tap at the top of each cellar stairs and there is a serving hatch into the dining room.

Between 1878 and 1882, numbers 11-29 had new kitchens, water closets and wash cycles built behind them facing into Trinity Lane. A further bedroom above the kitchen was planned but evidently not carried out. The architect was Upper King Street based Henry Herbert,[127] father of Albert Herbert.[128]

More drainage work followed in 1909 and the contractor was Chambers of Belgrave Gate.

Families started moving out of the city at the start of the 1920s and

---

126 *Leicester Chronicle*, 5th November 1859.
127 Henry Herbert (1842-1917), builder and member of the Herbert dynasty of builders and architects.
128 Albert Herbert (1875-1964). Architect with a national and international reputation and son of Henry Herbert.

gradually the houses changed from residential to business use, including theatrical lodgings, so that by 1978 they were all used by businesses. They began to reflect the cultural diversity of the town with the arrival of Abdul Keejam[129] in 1960 who bought number 17. By 2018 half of the houses were in residential use again with number 17 the first in 2001. The rest are used by a diverse range of businesses from a rape crisis centre to a surveyor and web designer. The houses are equally varied with two let to university students and one (number 11) turned into three flats.

Whatever their use, they are a rare William IV survival, having escaped the fate that was planned for them in the 1960s. Along with Crescent Cottages and The Crescent itself, they were identified for demolition as the site was required for the new Ring Road.[130]

Chapel
Northampton Street
c. 1835
Demolished

The details of this building are few. There are two clues as to it being a Flint design. The first is an advertisement in the *Leicester Chronicle* in 1844 offering the

> '... spacious and lofty building, 15 yards, situate in Northampton-street, and lately used as a chapel.' [131]

It had been used by followers of the Catholic Apostolic Church or Irvingites since at least 1836[132] and it was to be sold with vacant possession. The leader of the congregation was Davenport Cartwright,[133] a hosier's warehouseman. (A congregation wasn't established again until 1863

129 Abdul Keejam (fl.1960s). Property owner.
130 'Leicester Today and Tomorrow' by W.K. Smigielski, City Planning Officer, 1968.
131 *Leicester Chronicle*, 10th February 1844.
132 *Leicester Chronicle*, 20th February 1836.
133 Davenport Cartwright (1815-1879), prominent in the movement to get factories to close at 6pm.

The corner of Northampton and Fox Streets c.1920. Could this be Flint's work?

when followers found a site in Cank Street.) It seems that Flint is concerned about a decent sale, as the advert highlights the potential to convert it into school rooms or a warehouse due to its proximity to the station. The second reason to suggest it was a Flint building is that it was offered for sale again in 1846, at the White Lion in Market Place, and although we learn that it is *'A substantially Brick-built CHAPEL, about 50ft. by 30ft.'*,[134] the same conversion potential to school or warehouse is highlighted. All of this suggests that Flint either built or purchased the building and that it took some time to find a decent sale. It was demolished sometimes after the 1920s.

2 tenements
1836
Alfred Street
Demolished c. 1960

Alfred Street was probably demolished in around 1960 and its site is occupied by the Lee Street car park and Lee Circle. Nothing is known about the tenements and it is by no means certain that Flint was their architect. They are interesting because they *may* demonstrate that Flint was undergoing some financial difficulty at the time and put the tenements up speculatively. His sales pitch hangs on the fact that they are only £250 and he promises a good return:

'To be sold by Private Contract.
Two newly-erected Tenements, situate in Alfred Street, near the British Schools. The premises have every convenience, and the

134 *Leicester Journal*, 17th April 1846.

price being only £250, offer a desirable investment for small capital. They will be sold to pay a clear profit of about 8 per cent. Apply to Mr. W. FLINT, Architect and Surveyor, Friar Lane, Leicester. *January. 26ᵗʰ, 1837.'* [135]

What they looked like or who bought them is unknown.

Crescent Cottages
King Street
1836
Extant

Situated opposite William Firmadge's Crescent in King Street, this unusual two-storey terrace with its pleasing bowed end is almost certainly by Flint. Pevsner thinks the terrace to be by him and describes it as having *'considerable charm'*.[136] There are seven houses rendered in Flint's preferred stucco and separated by pilasters with anthemion capitals. Very unusually for Flint, and perhaps unusually for the time in Leicester, there is the name of the building and a date in a cartouche on the final bowed house

Crescent Cottages, similar to the terrace in Upper King Street.

135 *Leicester Mercury*, 28ᵗʰ January 1837.
136 Pevsner *'Leicestershire and Rutland'* in ibid

situated on the corner of King Street and Regent Road. There is also a rather crudely designed copy and clearly later addition tacked on to the end of the row furthest down King Street.

There are several pointers to suggest that Flint was the architect. The first is the general look and choice of materials, e.g. classical with stucco. The lugged architraves are a feature he often used, as are the pilasters and anthemion device. The gratings to the cellar windows are similar to ones he has used elsewhere and so are the fanlights.

Crescent Cottages' unusual main building in about 1900.

The houses closely resemble the terrace in Upper King Street and houses known to be by Flint in Asylum Street and probably by him in Curzon Street. No plans are known to survive and the local press reveals nothing further, however J. D. Bennett was able to secure evidence from previous residents, Gordon White and Hood, an architectural firm that Flint was the architect.[137]

One early occupant of the bowed end building was Miss Booth[138] who plied her trade from this address in 1836:

> 'Elocution
>
> *Miss S. Booth takes leave most respectfully to announce, that it is her intention during her stay at Leicester, to give instruction to a limited number of Pupils in the above art. Terms may be known on application to Miss S. Booth at Crescent Cottage'.*[139]

The terrace is gradually returning to residential use and has been a set of legal chambers for many years. The final bowed building is still the base

---

137 Letter to the author.

138 Sarah Booth (1793-1867). Nationally renowned actress '... *a great favourite of the inhabitants of Leicester in days gone by...*' (*Leicester Chronicle*, 17th September 1836).

139 *Leicester Chronicle*, 22nd October 1836.

for a legal practice and before that was a well-known bookshop for many years. It was also, for a time, a piano shop. The row was listed in 1950.

General News Room
Granby Street and Belvoir Street
November 1836
Demolished 1898

The General News Room was Flint's masterpiece. The fact that it was demolished for road widening at the end of the Nineteenth Century is even now, over a hundred years later, a continuing cause for regret and lamentation. It must have amazed and must have shouted its presence on the main road towards the town centre with its classical confidence and its sheer size.

The design was decided by public competition and the result was revealed in the *Mercury* on Bonfire Night 1836.[140] 34 plans were sent in and three went before the shareholders. Each was given a name: '*Spero*' for Flint's plan; '*Wreath*' for John Weightmans's[141] and '*K*' for William Parsons's effort. The committee of 13 split nine for Flint and two apiece for the others.

The Rooms were evidently built on land occupied by warehouses and other buildings as tenders for demolition appeared later the same month.[142] It couldn't have been a long job because further tenders appeared in February 1837 for contracting for the different trades.[143]

The *Mercury* reported that nearly 150 subscribers attended the first meeting at the new building and go on to describe their approval of Flint's work:

'... all of whom seemed to concur in the opinion that the building, in every particular, reflected the highest credit on the taste and skill of the artist, manifested, not merely in the building itself, but in the adaptation of every part to the purpose it is destined...'

---

140 *Leicester Mercury*, 5th November 1836.
141 John Grey Weightman (1801-1872). Architect of Salford Cathedral and pupil of Charles Barry.
142 *Leicester Mercury*, 19th November 1836.
143 *Leicester Mercury*, 11th February 1837.

The General Newsroom and Flint's lost masterpiece.

The paper also quotes from the British Almanac for 1838 and adds to the praise:

'It is gratifying to find not only that Leicester is beginning to rival some other provincial towns, but that for many of its improvements and embellishments it is indebted to a talented resident Architect, MR. W. FLINT.'

A lengthy description follows and we are lucky to have such a clear picture of how Flint intended for it to be built:

'...faced entirely in Roman Cement: whereas the stylobate is of stone and the part above is cement, with stone dressings. The building stands at the angle of Granby and Belvoir streets, the entrance or east front being towards the former, the south front to the latter. The first of these, which is only 49 feet, has a recessed loggia, a distyle in antis, with one window on a floor on each side of it; within this loggia are three doors with niches over them. The order is the rich Ionic of the Minerva Polias at Athens, and is continued along the south front in four three-quarter columns and

antae. In the five centre intercolumns thus formed are as many windows,
with panels over them, which latter forming a continuous line of sculpture
between the columns will be filled with reliefs designed and modelled by
Mr. W. Pitts,[144] an artist well known to the public by his two magnificent
compositions the shield of Eneas and that of Hercules. The extremities, or
end compartments, have, like those of the other front, two windows, – one
on the lower the other on the upper floor. The order is placed on a stylobate
5 6' high, which depth of surface, being without windows, contributes
in no small degree to the classical air of the ensemble. *The architect has*
arranged his interior very judiciously, and likewise with a careful regard to
effect. In the portico are two entrances, one, through a vestibule in the news
room; the other to the staircase which gives access to the library, forming
the upper part of that room. This apartment is 60 feet by 34, and 30 high
to the ceiling, or to top of the lantern 41 feet. The lowerpart of the room
is lighted on its south side by five centre windows towards Belvoir-street,
beneath the library gallery on that side, which is at the height of 13 feet
from the floor. This gallery is supported by twelve splendid Corinthian
columns, and the walls above it are decorated with bold pilasters, between

John Fulleylove's painting of the library at the General Newsroom.

144 William Pitts (1790-1840). Silver chaser and sculptor of Pimlico.

which will be the shelving or book-cases. Above the architrave of this upper order, is a coved and enriched ceiling. From the centre of the lantern there is an ornamental bronze chandelier, with 15 gas-light burners; and the room is warmed and ventilated by Price and Manby's[145] apparatus. Besides this there is a reading room on each floor at one end of the building and at the other the librarian's apartments &c.'

Opening hours were 8am – 10am and 1pm – 5pm and there was a small row about Sunday opening, led by William Parsons, but this was roundly defeated and it stayed shut.

The Pitts panels were put in place by August 1838 and the *Mercury* covered their unveiling with a description:

Central panel: The Muses with Melpomene in the centre flanked by Terpsichore, Urania, Euterpe and Clio on her right with Thalia, Erato, Calliope and Polyhymnia on her left.

Eastern Panel: Eminent men of Greece and Rome with Homer crowned with angels central supported on his right by Cicero and Virgil and on his left by Socrates and Demosthenes.

Western panel: Milton surrounded by angels with Shakespeare and Newton to the right and Bacon and Chaucer to the left.

Eastern end panel: Africa and America featuring figures from Caffaria,[146] Egypt, Barbary,[147] Mexico, Peru and Pennsylvania, (in the form of William Penn).

Western end panel: Europe and Asia featuring figures from Russia, France and England, Persia, Japan and China

and concludes:

---

145 Henry Cruger Price (1794-1856) and Charles Manby (1804-1884), eminent civil engineers. Their company traded until 1843.
146 Caffaria is now South Africa.
147 Barbary was situated in parts of Morocco, Algeria, Tunisia and Libya.

"The figures are grouped in an admirable manner and the coup d'oeil of Mr. Flint's elegant building is much improved by their addition."

William Pitts was a silver chaser and sculptor and in 1830 had some of his designs incorporated into Buckingham Palace. He did not survive long after his Leicester commission. He appeared to have financial difficulties (could this be why the panels went in seven months after the January opening?) and committed suicide on 16th April 1840, at his home in Pimlico, apparently temporarily insane.

Ill feeling from subscribers about estimates and expenditure made the press throughout 1838 and in January 1839, Flint felt obliged to write to the *Chronicle* in defence of his costings. The overspend was only £114 on top of his original £3,000 estimate and it appears that it was sanctioned by the Committee but rather poorly communicated to members.[148] Such complaints are not uncommon and examples of contractors for all sorts of events and buildings are often defending increases in spending in the press of the time. In 1846, the Committee spread out before the *Chronicle* that they were £50 14s adrift from expectations over the previous year and blames the death of members for the deficit![149] The same edition also reveals that Flint became a Committee member on 1st January.

The News Room never really seemed to do well financially, so that there is almost a sense of relief when it is chosen for demolition in order to widen Granby Street for traffic. The furniture and fittings were auctioned in March 1898 at the General News Room itself and items included eight oak reading and writing tables; 49 chairs; a marble wall fountain and hearthrugs![150] It must have been demolished very shortly afterwards as Henry Goddard's[151] less attractive but still impressive replacement was erected the same year. This too didn't last long as a News Room and was sold for business use a few years later. It still stands converted to retail and residential use.

---

148 *Leicester Chronicle*, 5th January 1839.
149 *Leicester Chronicle*, 10th January 1846.
150 *Leicester Chronicle*, 26th March 1898.
151 Henry Goddard (1813-1899). Member of the Goddard dynasty of Leicester architects and who worked extensively in Lincolnshire.

Bridge
West Bridge
Leicester Corporation
December 1836

As with several other large projects, it took the Corporation a considerable time to make up its mind about what it wanted and give authorisation to proceed. Flint's involvement with the new West Bridge started in late 1836 with the Town Council reporting that the bridge was in '...*a very dilapidated state, so as to expose the public to great risk and danger*'[152]and that Flint was looking into repairs to make it safe at the behest of the Estates Committee. Flint duly reported and then, notwithstanding the safety of the public, the matter goes quiet for some time, although the Mayor, Thomas Paget[153], was forced to explain to the council that '...*finances were not in a condition to enable to them to effect repairs at present*'.[154] Another investigation is asked for

The new West Bridge and another touch of Classical elegance.

152 *Leicester Journal*, 16th December 1836.
153 Thomas Paget (1778-1862). Banker of Humberstone Hall and briefly Whig MP for Leicester. First Mayor of the reformed Corporation.
154 *Leicester Mercury*, 24th June 1837.

and there is almost a sigh in Flint's report to the Estates Committee on 2nd August 1838 where he writes that nothing has changed since his January 1837 report and that, given the bridge is of *'ancient date'* and constructed of rubble faced with ashlar:

> 'I am of the opinion that the state, construction and strength of the structure are not adapted or sufficient to sustain for any lengthened period the constant, heavy, and increasing action over it and if the bridge be widened, whether on one side or both, a considerable expense must be incurred not only in the enlargement, but also, I apprehend in securing the piers. I am therefore of opinion that it would be unwise to incur any expenditure in altering or attempting to improve the present bridge.'

The Committee decide:

> 'Resolved: That Mr Flint be requested to make an estimate of the expense of erecting a new iron bridge.'

And for the 23rd August 1838 meeting Flint provides an estimate for:

> 'A cast iron bridge one span with a waterway about 42 feet clear and a road or platform 30 feet in width between the balustrades and parapets; abutments of brick work faced with stone, cast iron balustrades over the arch, stone parapets to the remainder of the road...'

The estimated cost was £2,400 with a further £190 or £110 depending on size for the temporary wooden bridge needed whilst construction was to take place. Goahead was given provided the Lords of the Treasury were able to help the Council secure the necessary funds by letting them sell Corporation land. A letter from the Treasury appeared in December and the answer was a resounding 'no'.

The matter rests for a while and then on 27th November 1839 the West Bridge Committee is formed as a sub-committee of the Estates Committee, but it quickly becomes clear that it will not be plain sailing.

John Kirby[155] and John Baxter[156] own property needed to be removed for the bridge's construction and they are more than aware that they have the Corporation over a barrel. Neither will budge and by March 1840 the Corporation believes that the only way to break the deadlock is to put the bridge into their proposed Act of Parliament for the Improvement of the Town of Leicester.[157] However, the Committee keeps going and by November, Kirby agrees to sell. With a typical lack of self-awareness, a motion is put before the sub-committee on 16th November 1840:

'Moved: That another opinion be taken in conference with Mr. Flint as to the necessity of erecting a new bridge.'

It is immediately countered:

'Moved: That the erecting of a new bridge be proceeded with. Carried.'[158]

Flint is reappointed as architect and the project starts to get off the ground. At the 21st December 1840 meeting, Flint reports in a very long letter about his plans for the new bridge; a temporary bridge and improving the approaches to the new bridge. The total cost is now £2595 and will be £380 more if stone is preferred. Iron is chosen and an attempt to get eminent bridge builder Tierney Clarke[159] to look at plans before they proceed is *'negatived'*:

'...the Committee were of opinion that they might rely with confidence on the reputation and ability of Mr. Flint, and that it was on the whole better that he should have the entire and undivided responsibility of the undertaking'.

155 John Kirby (1781-1848). Possibly hosier of Friar Lane with premises on Millstone Lane.
156 John Baxter (1774-1853). Probably baker of Red Cross Street and sometime assessor of West St Mary's.
157 The proposed bill, which eventually came to nothing, envisaged new powers for street cleaning; improving the Market Place; widening the North Gates and abolishing the Whipping Toms amongst other measures.
158 West Bridge sub-committee minutes 16th November 1840.
159 William Tierney Clarke (1783-1852). Civil engineer and builder of the first suspension bridge (Hammersmith) across the Thames.

A double-edged sword, perhaps. The Committee also decided that plans must lie at the Library for the whole Council to see until the next Tuesday. Things now start happening as the *Mercury* records:

> 'The West Bridge – Our readers will be gratified by observing that preparations are being made for the long-desired improvement, a new West Bridge. Tenders for a new Iron Bridge, a Temporary Wooden Bridge &c. &c. are to be sent to Mr. Flint Architect. – See advert.'[160]

There were three sets of tenders in all ranging from excavators to painters. In July 1841 the *Chronicle* reported that several four pound cannon balls from the siege of Leicester had been found during the excavation work.[161] James Wykes[162] is the contractor and the building process overcomes several issues; some from the Canal Company about access rights and fencing; some to do with the levelling of the roadways and some about the tow path with Wykes having to be effectively directed to 'just get on with it'. By December, the bridge is open and the *Chronicle* recognises the work gone into it:

> 'THE WEST BRIDGE is now open, and is not only a great public convenience, but a decided improvement to that part of town. It is a neat, substantial structure, and does great credit, to the architect (Mr. Flint) and the workmen and contractors, employed in its erection.'[163]

The bridge was still not finished and the sub-committee continues to meet to discuss various property disputes and finishes etc.; it is not until September that the accounts are audited and Flint receives his payment of £362. 5. 2 ½. And it is still not over, as on 14th October 1842 James Wykes writes to complain about the way Flint has treated him and wants '...*a competent person to go into the business...*' to be appointed.[164] The Committee refuse and back Flint.

---

160 *Leicester Mercury*, 6th March 1841.
161 *Leicester Chronicle*, 10th July 1841.
162 James Wykes (1800-1876) Builder of Freeschool Lane and Guardian of All Saints for over 30 years.
163 *Leicester Chronicle*, 4th December 1841.
164 West Bridge sub-committee minutes, 14th October 1842.

The West Bridge shortly after opening.

It had been quite a journey with many frustrations, although in the end the eventual build was quite speedy and it had the desired effect of easing access to an increasingly prosperous Leicester. It was evidently something to be proud of as the *Leicester Almanack and Directory*, published by Cook[165] of King Street, makes certain to tell *Chronicle* readers[166] that his new book contains a lithograph of the West Bridge drawn by Mr Palmer[167] of Princes Street. It served its purpose for nearly 50 years, by which time the population in Leicester had grown so much that a new bridge was needed and Flint's elegant, almost Venetian, masterpiece was demolished to make way for it in 1891.

Workhouse
Sparkenhoe Street
Leicester Poor Law Union Guardians
September 1837
Demolished 1850 and 1977

The Poor Law Amendment Act 1834 organised the expensive and haphazard system of single parish relief by combining groups of parishes to create Poor Law Unions with the plan being for each to have its own workhouse and abolish 'out-relief'. Thus began a constant source of shame and fear for the poor and the destitute that continued until the

---

165 Thomas Cook (1808-1892). Bookseller and printer of King Street and later globally renowned travel agent.
166 *Leicester Chronicle*, 8th January 1842.
167 Edmund Seymour Palmer (1809-1859) and his wife Fanny Flora Bond (1812-1876) jointly ran a printing business as printer and artist respectively. They later emigrated to America where Fanny achieved international recognition.

The Jacobethan Workhouse after 1858.

1930s in fact and until the end of the last century psychologically.

Leicester's newly created Board of Guardians appointed Flint as architect for their planned workhouse at their board meeting on 27th September 1836 with a salary of 3% of the construction cost. His appointment was not without controversy. Whilst the new Leicester town Council was a bastion of new Liberal politics, the new Board of Guardians was dominated by Conservatives, one of whom was Flint's old master William Parsons who clearly saw himself as eligible for the post, as did most of his political allies. When his ineligibility due to his conflict of interest was pointed out, he stood down, but not without rancour, and the Conservative chairman incorrectly tried to use his casting vote to influence the outcome. There were noisy letters in the press.

It didn't end there, and the 6th December meeting saw a motion carried to cancel the building project. More bad temper followed in the newspapers. In April 1837 fresh Guardian elections took place and several of them were not re-elected, although the Board retained its Conservative majority. In August 1837 a proposal to build a workhouse was finally carried and Flint was reappointed as before with the bonus of permission for a clerk of works, who would turn out to be William Millican's future partner, John Kellam.[168] Flint submitted the final design in October 1838 based on building to start in November for an envisaged summer 1839 completion. Tenders for its construction were sought and decided in favour of:

Messrs Smith and Waterfield, bricklayers	£4,200 10s 9d
Mr S. Hull[169], stonemason	£943 0s 0d
Mr John Crick[170], carpenter	£1,860 0s 0d
Messrs C. Jarratt[171] and Co. ironfounders	£760 0s 0d
Mr R. Catlin[172], plumber and glazier	£726 0s 0d
Mr Mowbray[173], painter	£80 0s 0d

The *Mercury* reports that the land would cost £1,500 which, added to the contractors' and Flint's fees, would lead to a total cost of at least £10,000[174].

The Guardians envisaged a building based on Sampson Kempthorne's[175] popular *Model Workhouse*, which was revolutionary in that the spaces between wings became exercise yards that were then easily segregated. It was popular with Commissioners precisely because it added another dimension of deterrent discomfort as married couples and children were easily and effectively isolated from each other. This variation had a 'Y' shaped set of buildings surrounding by a hexagonal ring of other buildings such as stables, coal sheds, bake house, infirmary and laundries so that each internal exercise yard could be easily separated. The *Chronicle* gave its opinion of Flint's efforts:

'The front elevation is particularly judicious, having a neat, homely, English appearance and nothing of the character of a Bastile [sic]' [176]

---

168 John Kellam (1805-1861), architect of Sparkenhoe Street.

169 Samuel Hull (1775-1856), marble mason of Granby Street.

170 John Crick (1796-1847). Master builder of North Luffenham; sometime Borough Assessor and contractor of the railway to Syston.

171 Charles Jarratt (1802-1875), with premises in Bridge Street linked to Messrs. Stevenson. Later prominent citizen of Milwaukee where he died.

172 Richard Catlin (1794-1863), plumber and glazier of High Cross Street.

173 Henry Mowbray (1815-1896). Painter and property owner, formerly of King Street and future client.

174 *Leicester Mercury*, 13th January 1838.

175 Sampson Kempthorne (1809-1873). British architect known for his workhouse designs.

176 *Leicester Chronicle*, 4th November 1837.

There was a Boardroom in the entrance block and at the end of the complex were inmates' wards; there were day rooms, work rooms and the dormitories were on the first floor above these. The workhouse also had its own chapel. It was built to house 600 inmates.

The building appears to have been virtually finished by the end of July 1838 and the *Mercury* was impressed:

> *'The new Union workhouse is rapidly approaching its completion, being very nearly covered in. It is not only much larger than the generality of Union Workhouses, being calculated to accommodate 650 persons, but also one of the best-looking buildings of that description we have ever seen, reflecting great credit on Mr. Flint, the Architect. Standing on high ground it forms a prominent object in the view from various parts of the county.'*[177]

The design itself has been frequently described as *'Jacobethan'*; a term coined by John Betjeman to describe a particular brand of English Renaissance Revival style that incorporates Elizabethan Gothic features and Jacobean Classical ones.

Stonebreakers' granite at Leicester Workhouse.

Workhouses were unpopular with some newspapers and this coupled with the vicious political attacks make for an ill-humoured press continuing during the building's construction. There are arguments about money; queries about whether the master and matron are entitled to a maid and there are also detailed discussions about heating it with Dr Arnott's Thermometer Stove[178] chosen as:

'...it appeared that there was not anywhere a workhouse equal in the size to the one in

177 *Leicester Mercury*, 28th July 1838.
178 Neil Arnott (1788-1874). Scottish physician, co-founder of the University of London and Physician Extraordinary to the Queen. His stove won the Rumford Medal of the Royal Society in 1854.

Leicester. Mr. Flint was going from home and perhaps he would obtain information from various sources.'[179]

Where was Flint going?!

The building itself must have been ready by September 1838 as tenders appeared for 14 Arnott stoves, 21 fire grates and *'Steam cooking apparatus sufficient to provide for 500 persons'* at the end of the month.[180] A tender for digging and laying a drainage culvert followed the next month and even this led to acrimony and bitterness as played out in the newspapers. In the end, the workhouse did not open properly until early 1839 and, even then, only admitted about 160 people, mainly the children and the elderly, but also a few *'...young men of weakest intellects...'* In April, Flint handled the sale of the now redundant St Mary's Workhouse, which was situated between Welford Road and Infirmary Square.[181] The *Chronicle* gives an idea of what life was like in the new setting and includes dietary details such as beef for the elderly four times a week for dinner; milk porridge for children in the afternoon and the fact that inmates were allowed out on Sundays to attend a place of worship.[182]

Parsons and Dain rebuilt most of the workhouse in 1849 creating an 'H' shaped set of buildings and demolishing most of Flint's original design behind his retained striking main building. Even this process turned sour, but this time it was Flint who felt aggrieved and felt the need to write to the *Journal* in an open letter protesting about the fact he had felt excluded from the competition for the re-building.[183] The irony could not have escaped either Parsons or Flint. The entrance block in Sparkenhoe Street was retained, as were several outer perimeter buildings and Flint worked for the Guardians again in 1858 with Henry Shenton when the firm built the machine room and porter's lodge. When the workhouse closed in around 1930, the buildings were turned into Hillcrest Hospital before that too closed in 1974, after spending its final years as a refugee hostel. The site was demolished in 1977 and was replaced by Moat Community College. When the author worked there from 2003-2006, the original cellars still existed. Part of the kerb, gates and fence wall still exist on

---

179 *Leicester Chronicle*, 21st July 1838.
180 *Leicester Journal*, 28th September 1838.
181 Leicester Journal, 16th April 1839.
182 *Leicester Chronicle*, 9th March 1839.
183 *Leicester Journal*, 28th December 1849.

Sparkenhoe Street in 2018 and also, by the looks of it, the perimeter walk following Hutchinson Walk as far as the staff entrance to the school.

Barrow-upon-Soar Workhouse
Lingfield Road
Mountsorrel
November 1837
Partially extant

Perhaps as a result of his design for the Leicester workhouse, Flint was commissioned by the Barrow Union to produce designs for their new workhouse in Mountsorrel (which was in Rothley Parish) – it was a slow process. On Boxing Day 1837, the Guardians of Barrow Union resolved:

> '…that a competent person be employed to survey the workhouse and report to the Board the proposed cost of rebuilding, altering or enlarging the same on the plan generally adopted for Union workhouses… It was resolved that Mr. Flint of Leicester do survey the workhouse.'[184]

Entrance building to Barrow-upon-Soar Workhouse now in Rubicon Close.

184 Minute Book, Barrow Union, 26th December 1837.

As with the Leicester Workhouse, the Guardians wanted a building based on Sampson Kempthorne's Model Workhouse.

Flint reported back to the Board on 23rd January with a clear message that the existing workhouse, designed by John Winfield,[185] would cost too much to rebuild. The next month, the Board resolved to treat for a new workhouse to be built. They considered five options and plumped for the third:

"Two acres and a half thereabouts situate at the corner of the lane leading to the turnpike road to Rothley Plain was offered by Mr. Wale[186] at £150 per acre. This has frontage toward the turnpike road and also the lane. This site is elevated and of a salubrious character and near the stone quarries of Mountsorrel."

The Board estimated a two-year building time[187] and Mr John Snelson Shenton[188] handled the purchase in September 1838.[189]

A little earlier, tenders had been sought and, in the end, 13 were received. At the end of November, Flint won the contract and once again defeated his former master William Parsons as he had done with the Leicester workhouse:

'The building committee having selected from the plans for a new workhouse those of Messrs Parsons, Flint, Railton[190] & Scott[191] and Moffat[192] as being best adapted for the purposes of the Union. It was resolved that the plans of Mr. Flint be adopted.'

---

185 John Winfield (1766-1813), surveyor.

186 Mr Wale – Robert? Likely the same man who supplied the existing workhouse with its bread.

187 Minute Book, Barrow Union, 5th June 1838.

188 John Snelson Shenton (1789-1862), probably connected by marriage to Mr Wale. No connection has yet been established with Henry Shenton, if there is one.

189 Minute Book, Barrow Union, 4th September 1838.

190 William Railton (1800-1877). Architect of Beaumanor Hall and more prominently Nelson's Column in Trafalgar Square.

191 Joseph Scott (1784-1859), Architect, surveyor and timber merchant of Market Harborough.

192 William Bonython Moffatt (1812-1887). London architect; assistant and later partner of George Gilbert Scott (1811-1878) of Carlton Chambers, Regent Street.

Poor Law Commissioners agreed to Flint's plan and their assent is recorded in the Minute Book on 8th January 1839. Three weeks later, the Board authorised a spend of £4,545 and it is careful to note that Flint is told this.[193]

As with a surviving letter from Flint about the Congregational Chapel in Market Harborough, there is some evidence that he is thinking of others as he works. At the 5th March meeting, Flint brings a request from the builders who ask if they may make bricks from the clay that can be procured from the site. However, the Guardians give an unequivocal and stereotypical 'no'.[194]

Notices to contractors appeared in the local press throughout January and February 1839 inviting applications to William Flint by slaters, bricklayers, plasterers, carpenters and glaziers, amongst others.[195] By May 1840, the workhouse was clearly nearly ready and insurance was sought for £4,000 at the County Insurance Office.[196] Also, applications for tenders were again invited, this time for 35 iron bedsteads and two double gates of wrought iron ('...*without ornament [and] of ample width...*'),[197] which serves to demonstrate the breadth of an architect's business activities in early Victorian England. The first board meeting was held at the new boardroom on 3rd June 1840.

After a spell as Glenfrith and then Mountsorrel Hospital, the workhouse was demolished in around 1960. Only the entrance block still survives in Rubicon Close off Lingfield Road and, unusually for a Flint building, there is a panel on the gable over the main door bearing the date of erection.

Cells at Barrow workhouse just before demolition in about 1960.

193 Minute Book, Barrow Union, 29th January 1839.
194 Minute Book, Barrow Union, 5th March 1839.
195 *Leicester Chronicle*, 2nd February 1839.
196 Minute Book, Barrow Union, 19th May 1840.
197 Leicester Journal, 1st May 1840.

Banking House
Granby Street
December 1838
The Leicestershire Banking Company
Demolished

The Leicestershire Banking Company engaged Flint to build them their new banking house in 1838. Late that year, he was advertising tenders for diggers, bricklayers, slaters, plasterers, stonemasons, carpenters, joiners, iron founders, plumbers, glaziers and painters to be delivered to the Bank's headquarters in Friar Lane in late January the next year.[198] The company advertised again in late March and this may be because the designs had been enlarged due to the purchase of Messrs. Pickford and Co's[199] premises in Granby Street, which the company intended to knock down in order to erect their own building '...*replete with all necessary convenience*'.[200] The Company became known as Pares' Leicestershire Banking Company then Parr's Bank before being absorbed into the National Westminster Bank. It has not been possible to find out when it was demolished.

Lancaster Place
London Road
September 1839
Trinity Hospital Trustees
Demolished 1890

Lancaster Place started life as Trinity Hospital Houses: a proposal for four villas built on land owned by Trinity Hospital. Tenders for 21-year leases were invited in February 1840 advertising '...*Ornamental Ground in front and separate spacious gardens at the back...*'. Each house was to have three sitting rooms and five bedrooms with usual kitchens, closets and cellar.[201] Trustees had advertised for 200,000 bricks in the previous September and

---

198 *Leicester Journal*, 28th December 1838.
199 Pickford and Co. (then a 'van office') are still operating today as Pickford's removal company. They were already nearly 200 years old in 1838.
200 *Leicester Chronicle* 30th March 1839 report on the company's ninth Annual General Meeting.
201 *Leicester Mercury*, 29th February 1840.

it is likely that they were intended for these houses.[202] They were situated next to St. Paul's New Connexion Methodist Church, more or less where the Thomas Cook statue is found now.

Three letters from Flint about the project survive at the LRO. The first, on New Year's Day 1840, authorises payment of £245 to carpenter and builder, John Gamble.[203] It appears that the decision about three or four houses was made in August 1840 when Flint offered Trustees the choice between accepting Gamble's tender of £1269 4s 0d for four or £951 18s 0d for three. They went for three houses.

The *Leicester Chronicle* sheds light on the reason for the name change:

'LANCASTER PLACE. – The handsome pile of buildings recently erected adjoining the railway bridge on the London-road, has been designated "Lancaster-place", out of compliment, we presume, to the founder of the institution to which the property belonged – Henry, Earl of Lancaster,[204] who founded Trinity Hospital, so far back as the year 1330.'[205]

The association with The Trinity Hospital land in this part of Leicester lasted at least another 20 years as Flint and Shenton were engaged in selling 6,242 square yards of land with extensive frontage onto London Road on the southward side of Lancaster Place in 1860.[206]

Demolition took place in 1890 to allow for the widening of the Midland Railway. The building materials reclaimed were sold in situ at 11am on the 27th February of that year[207] by Warner[208], Sheppard[209] and Wade.[210]

---

202 *Leicester Journal*, 20th September 1839.
203 John Gamble (1801-1841), builder and joiner of Colton Street.
204 Henry, Earl of Lancaster (c. 1281-1345). Grandson of Henry III and benefactor to the poor, who died at Leicester Castle.
205 *Leicester Chronicle*, 1st January 1842.
206 *Leicester Journal*, 9th March 1860.
207 *Leicester Chronicle and Mercury*, 22nd February 1890.
208 Robert Warner (1825-1877). Horsefair Street auctioneer and local councillor.
209 Thomas Sheppard (1826-1890). Horsefair Street auctioneer and long-serving Blaby Union Guardian.
210 George Tempest Wade (1848-1919). Horsefair Street auctioneer.

Fish Market alterations and a new Conduit
Market Place
December 1839
Leicester Corporation
Rebuilt

At its 6th December 1839 meeting, the Estates Committee asked Flint for a report on the 'sufficiency' of the newly reconfigured Fish Market. Evidently work had recently taken place to improve it but had been found wanting. At the Corporation meeting in October 1839, Councillor Paget admitted that *'...the Fish Market was an unfortunate business'*.[211] Nothing much happens again until May when he makes a valuation to replace some market buildings with thatched roofs and then the Estates Committee set up a Fish Market sub-committee in September 1840. In November he submits a report and advises on plans for the best positioning of fish stalls and associated drainage works. There is more delay and then in April 1841, Flint submits a new plan involving paving, with asphalt, slating, building a warehouse and creating a urinal and privy – all for £250. There is a plan for a new associated building to be rented to existing tenant Mr Berridge[212] and provision is for 18 fish stalls supplied with water from the conduit. At the same time, his plans for a new conduit are agreed.

The council are concerned at the next meeting in May about whether there will be *'... effluvium from the use of asphalt and no odour from it'*.[213] Evidently Flint's reassurances cut no ice and they opt for Yorkshire stone to pave the site. Berridge's building is ready in October and Flint has to account for why the area was not yet paved – rather obviously it is so building work does not disturb the stonework! In the same letter to the Council he tells them that Messrs Willsons (sic)[214] will have finished their casting of the new conduit by the start of November.[215] By December, it is up and running:

---

211 *Leicester Chronicle*, 19th October 1839.
212 Mr Berridge (fl.1840s). There are several Berridges in the Market Place at the time, so it has not been possible to identify which one this project concerned.
213 Estate sub-committee minutes, 25th May 1841.
214 Richard Wilson (c.1787-1869) and William Wilson (c.1791-1869). Iron and brass founders and millwrights of Charles Street.
215 *Leicester Journal*, 22nd October 1841.

'THE CONDUIT was lighted the first time on Thursday evening, but owing to the lamp being too small, the light was not so brilliant as could be wished, and therefore a reflector is to be introduced to increase it. The edifice has a very neat appearance, and meets with very general admiration.'[216]

At the same time, stalls are now being let in the Fish Market. The *Chronicle*[217] praises Mr Warren Lindley[218] for the work on the conduit. However, it is not his work and a cheerful and generous but accurate Flint writes to the editors in the following week's edition:

'DEAR SIR, – I am surprised by the terms of the paragraph in this morning's Chronicle, relating to the Conduit, which states that "the models for the embellishments of this handsome fabric proceeded from the head and hand of Mr. Warren Lindley." This implies that he designed the ornamental parts, but the truth is that the whole design is my own; excepting that, for some arrangement of the lead works I am indebted to Mr. Lewin, the plumber. With that exception, I supplied drawings the full size of, or as large as, the objects, for all and every part of the structures, its details and ornaments: and from these drawings the modeller and founder worked. I agree with you that Mr. Lindley is entitled to every praise for his talents as a modeller, and I may add, that I have been the first to elicit and encourage them: but the observation to which I refer is beyond the truth. These remarks will also apply to part of your notice of the West Bridge. I would not trouble you on this subject, but you will perceive that, in cases like the present, incorrect representations of the kind I refer to restrain professional exertions, by taking away the chief compensation for them.

I remain, Sir, yours faithfully,
William Flint
Friar-Lane, Leicester
Dec. 4, 1841.

---

216 *Leicester Chronicle*, 4ᵗʰ December 1841.
217 *Leicester Chronicle*, 4ᵗʰ December 1841.
218 Warren Lindley (1802-1874), stoneworker and grave cutter later with John Firn of Humberstone Road.

[We cheerfully give insertion of the foregoing letter, in justice to Mr. Flint, and to Mr. Lindley, who has called to candidly state as much as it contains himself. We believe the statement furnished to us by a third party was erroneous, owing to his want of knowledge of the details of the subject, and not to a desire to misrepresent anything. – ED. L. C.][219]

The Conduit shortly before demolition in Wigston.

The octagonal conduit building was removed and sold for £6 1. 6. and it eventually ended up in the grounds of what is now Wigston Academy[220] before it was demolished to make way for the school.

Flint's Fish Market was replaced in 1881 by the (still extant) cast iron canopied work of his pupil James Frank Smith.

---

219 *Leicester Chronicle*, 11th December 1841.
220 Where the author is Executive Head teacher – see chapter 14 The Pupils: William Millican.

CHAPTER 5

The Buildings of the 1840s

Vestry
Baptist Chapel
York Street
May 1840
Rebuilt 1866

York Street's Baptist Zoar Chapel was opened in 1818. In May 1840, Flint was taking bids from contractors to erect a vestry to his design.[221] The Chapel was rebuilt by Peculiar Baptists in 1866 and, after a period as a Spiritualist Church, remains open as Gospel Hall church. It is possible that the vestry survived the rebuilding.

Three Houses
Regent Road
c. 1840
Partially extant

When the two Leicester City Council office blocks in Welford Place were demolished in 2016, the demolition site was surrounded by fences on which large pictures of Leicester buildings were attached. The three houses on Regent Road, now number 80 and known as Regent House, were one such picture. Architects were listed underneath each building with the date of construction. In this case, both were left blank demonstrating that the City Council is unable to determine who designed it and when. A contemporary engraving shows that they were built by 1846 and each house had a name: Southfields was nearest West Street; Arnold House was the middle house and Southfields House the last one. They were

---

221 *Leicester Mercury*, 27th May 1840.

The three separate Regent Road houses as they were built.
Flint's home was the one furthest left.

separate houses until they were joined to form the Fielding Johnson[222] Hospital in 1925. In their time, the buildings have been homes, offices, the headquarters of the YWCA, and an electro-therapy centre. Flint almost certainly lived in one of them. Various sources give Flint as the architect but other than look and reputation, there is no direct evidence to prove it.

However, a clue may be an advertisement in the *Leicester Journal* in April 1844. Flint is handling the sale of:

'THE *Newly-erected and Beautiful SUBURBAN VILLA, in Regent-street, Leicester, the Residence of WILLIAM BETTS, Esq.*[223]

This most commodious House is replete with modern conveniences, has a Southern aspect to the Pasture Lands, called the South Fields, and commands an extensive and uninterrupted view of the Valley of the Soar, with a cheerful prospect of the Midland Counties Railway'[224]

William Betts's wife Elizabeth[225] had died in September, hence perhaps

---

222 Thomas Fielding-Johnson (1856-1931). Businessman who named the hospital in honour of his parents. His mother was a daughter of Samuel Stone, Town Clerk.

223 William Betts (1791-?). Railway contractor. Shenton and Baker handled the sale of his estate comprising a considerable number of houses in Southfields in 1874.

224 *Leicester Journal*, 26th April 1844.

225 Elizabeth Hayward Betts (1796-1843).

the move. The long list of rooms includes a housekeeper's room; two servant's bedrooms; a 22 feet by 18 feet breakfast room and library; a large bathroom; seven excellent bedrooms and the whole of the premises:

> '... fitted up in the most careful and scientific manner, and with warm and cold water circulations.'

It was three storeys high and had a large basement. There was also a detached wash and brewhouse, stabling for four horses and a double coach house. With vinery, conservatory and planted gardens, the plot amounted to 2,100 yards of land.

Betts sold his furniture by auction at the premises in October 1844 and this is the first concrete link between the house above and the three Flint houses as the *Chronicle* calls the house 'Southfields House.'[226] Whilst it still does not entirely prove that Flint was the architect, there is at least now some circumstantial evidence to suggest it. Through the marriage of one of Betts's daughters[227] and the 1841 census, it is possible to date the houses to either late 1840 or early 1841. Before they were joined, each had a similar entrance porch to the one still extant and Southfields and Southfields House had side entrances on West Street and Hastings Streets respectively.

In 1948, the hospital was subsumed into the NHS and served as a maternity hospital. Closure came in 1989 shortly after which the houses

Only the frontage remains from Flint's time after conversion to offices in the 1990s.

---

226 *Leicester Chronicle*, 28th September 1844.
227 Elizabeth Meadows Betts later Giles (1819-1896), married on 21st August 1841 at St Mary de Castro.

A surviving outbuilding from the Regent Road houses.

were demolished, although the frontages were retained behind which a large block of offices was constructed. One of the original outbuildings survives and some of the railing and walling is original. The houses are designed in the Classical style and resemble the simplicity characteristic of Flint's style.

2 houses
Princess Street
December 1841
Extant

The evidence to suggest that this is a Flint construction is the rather unusual advertisement in the *Leicester Journal* in December 1841:

> 'Two houses situate in Princes-street, Leicester; each house containing cellars, kitchen, scullery, two sitting rooms on the ground floor, drawing room on the one pair floor, and four bedrooms, with a small hosier's warehouse attached. The premises have been recently and substantially erected and are completely fitted up.
> For particulars apply to Mr. Flint, Architect, Friar Lane, Leicester. December 2nd, 1841.
> N. B. This advertisement will not be repeated.' [228]

228 *Leicester Journal*, 3rd December 1841.

Bold and unfussy elegance in Princess Street.

The last line has all the signs of desperation and perhaps Flint was pressed for money. The lack of third party involvement is another factor in attributing them to Flint.

The most likely contenders for this commission are numbers six and eight at the Crescent end of what is now Princess Road West. Number eight has a small industrial building attached to it, which could easily be the *'small hosier's warehouse'* outlined above and they are certainly *'substantially erected'*. In look, it is easy to imagine this is a Flint design with its bold and unfussy neatness and, additionally, 1841 seems to be a lean year for Flint in terms of substantiated commissions.

Congregationalist church
Leicester Road
Market Harborough
November 1842
Extant

In November 1842, Flint travelled to Market Harborough by gig to inspect a seventeenth century meeting house in Bowden Lane to see if it could

Market Harborough Congregational Church on Leicester Road.

be repaired and enlarged for wider use by the town's Congregationalist worshippers. He billed the church for the journey claiming 23 shillings.[229] Evidently it could not, so Flint was engaged to create a purpose-built chapel and there is an inscription on a parapet bearing the unspecific legend 'Independent Chapel'.

In March 1843, Flint advertised for no less than six separate tenders to erect a new independent chapel on the corner of Bowden Lane and Leicester Road in Market Harborough.[230] Tender number one was looking for diggers, bricklayers, slaters and plasterers; number two for stonemasons; three for carpenters and joiners; four for iron founders; five for plumbers and glaziers and the sixth for painters. The capacity was 1500 worshippers. Construction was relatively swift and was complete enough to be described by the *Chronicle* in June 1844: '*It is a fine building and does great credit to the architect, Mr. Flint, of Leicester.*'[231]

The *Mercury* describes the opening which took place on a 'fine' day on 11th July 1844. It gives details of the building:

229 Letter LRO N/C/215/152/21.
230 *Leicester Journal*, 31st March 1843.
231 *Leicester Chronicle* 29th June 1844

'This handsome structure, and admired and truly spacious place of worship... The edifice is highly creditable to the architect, (Mr. Flint, of Leicester)...and stands at the north entrance of the town, to which locality it forms no slight ornament' [232]

Unusually, a series of letters from Flint to the Building Committee survives.[233] The correspondence reveals details of costs and contractors: the Derwent Iron Foundry carried out the metal work; George Smith[234] was the plumber and glazier; John Norman;[235] Thomas Yates[236] completed the stone work; Henry Bell[237] the painting and John Burditt[238] the carpentry and demolition of the old building. Occasionally there are scribbled designs such as a Corinthian column sketch; financial calculations and information about features such as the plan for a Boccius Burner (this is a large and very elaborate gas light and there is some doubt if the church went ahead with installing it).

An unhappy commission: a letter where Flint describes himself as '...much pressed and not very well.'

However, one subject dominates: money. Evidently the church had invested in Messrs Goddards's Bank, which had failed, meaning that a collection at the opening service was necessary, raising over £1,100 and more than enough to redeem the new chapel from any debt;

232 *Leicester Mercury*, 27th July 1844.
233 LRO N/C/215/152/1-26.
234 George Smith (1813-1852). Plumber and glazier of Welford Road.
235 John Norman (1819-1885) of John Norman and Son builders of High Cross Street, imprisoned for debt in 1861.
236 Thomas Yates (fl.1840s). Stonemason of St Mary's Road, Market Harborough, went bankrupt in 1847.
237 Henry Bell (1811-1880). Painter and stainer of Southgate Street.
238 John Burditt (c.1806-1876). Timber merchant and builder of Market Harborough.

although during construction, Flint is frequently asking Thomas Heygate,[239] treasurer to the Building Committee, to advance sums to his contractors. For example, in June 1844, Flint reports that:

> 'Mr. Norman is anxious to settle some money of obligations arising on this building: and he will be much obliged if the Committee will favour him with this amount of one hundred and sixty-seven pounds.'

He does something similar for Mr Burditt the same month to get him the £64 5s 8d owed him for taking down the old buildings and, in August 1844, he reports that he has had to lend Bell £5 until the Committee pays him. In December 1844 he writes that:

> 'Mr. Yates has written to me today to say that he is much pressed for money: and asking me to solicit you to advance him ten pounds further on account of the Harborough Chapel. This I beg to certify you may do.'

Indeed, in this letter, Flint says that: *'I am very much pressed…'* It carries on into the next year so that in January 1845 Flint points out that Mr

Corinthian Column: Flint used these in almost all of his grander buildings.

239 Thomas Heygate (1806-1894). Surgeon of High Street, Market Harborough.

Norman is suffering from '...*a privation of money*' and underlines the word '*contract*' in his request for £80 10s on his behalf. In the same letter he talks of having '... *a little unsettled discussion with the Derby People* ...' suggesting trouble ahead, but he does not elaborate. His final letter has a blunt final sentence: '...*allow me to add that I am very short of money*'.

In spite of its financially troubled start, this is an enormously attractive building. It is another Greek Revival style Flint building and is built of white brick with Ionic and Corinthian columns. Internally, the church resembles his 1830 Baptist Church in Charles Street with a gallery supported by iron Corinthian columns and the raised pulpit. In this case there is also a magnificent archway that frames and focuses the pulpit and leads to the vestry. It is another bright and airy space that is simple and peaceful and totally in keeping with his style.

4 retail shops and houses
Market Harborough
The Harborough Charity Estate
William Flint and William Holloway
August 1844
Existence uncertain

This is an interesting commission because it appears to be the only example of Flint working in tandem with someone other than Charles Wickes or Henry Shenton. The only certain fact about the project is that it was advertised in the *Leicester Journal* in 1844.[240] The Harborough Charity Estate existed for the:

> '... *maintenance of aged and decayed house-dwellers and tradesmen, for keeping the streets in repair, putting poor boys out to apprentice, &c.*' [241]

J. D. Bennett suggests[242] that William Holloway[243] was connected to Holloway and Son, the Market Harborough auction house. Little is

---

240 *Leicester Journal*, 16th August 1844.
241 *Leicester Chronicle*, 1st June 1844.
242 Bennett op cit.
243 William Holloway Jr (1800-1880) of Braybrooke; builder, auctioneer and valuer connected to Holloway auctioneers in Market Harborough.

known about him or why the project needed two architects to carry out the works or what Flint's connection to the charity was or indeed where the buildings were. It is possible that it was connected to the work he was doing at the Congregational Church in the town at the same time.

St Mary de Castro Church
Chancel and other repairs
October 1844 and 1846
Extant

Flint was advertising for stone masons and others to contract for '... *the reparation of the walls, windows and other parts*'[244] at the church of his christening in late 1844. He had been a £5 subscriber to the fundraising appeal that July.[245] The 1840s was a busy time for fundraising at St Mary's and Flint contributed another £5 in March 1846.[246] By January 1845, Flint was looking for building contractors for the reparation of the chancel and it may be that he had discovered the need for this further work during the October repairs.[247] It was a considerable commission. The walls were repointed and the roofs repaired and there were new windows and a new arch built to replace the existing elliptical one in the chancel. The organ gallery and children's gallery were taken out, as were some pews, all by May 1845. The contractors were Waterfield and Smith. In the spring of 1846, work continued and the 1795 vestry was removed; new stained windows were created and more seating put in. Finally, the chancel was refloored. The cost was £524.[248]

The *Journal* rated his results:

'... *the beautiful restorations of St. Mary's Church were taking place under the direction of our highly talented architect and respected townsman, Mr. Flint.*'[249]

---

244 *Leicester Journal*, 18th October 1844.
245 *Leicester Journal*, 26th July 1844.
246 *Leicester Journal*, 6th March 1846.
247 *Leicester Chronicle*, 18th January 1845.
248 *Bringing them to their knees* (Geoffrey Brandwood, 2002).
249 *Leicester Journal*, 6th March 1846.

The controversial window at
St. Mary de Castro.

Praise was not universal: in the months after the work was finished, articles appeared in *The Ecclesiologist* and *The Gentleman's Magazine* and they were unimpressed by Flint's efforts; more heat was added by the untimely death of the vicar.[250] Such was the condemnation that Flint felt the need to write a long letter of self-defence to the *Journal* and he doesn't hold back:

'I am aware that those that do not belong to the 'ecclesiological clique' are objects of its mendacious spleen and, therefore, am not surprised by the personal attack.'[251]

He signs off:

> 'Can it be doubtful whether the work of Church restoration will be more promoted by the influence, exertions and examples of men like Mr. Brown, or by the unfounded and intemperate notices, and the indecent haste to insult the dead and the living of the Ecclesiologist.'

This is ironic and unjust given his report in January 1845 where there is a real sense of respect and acknowledgement from Flint for the architects of centuries gone by:

> *'... but I would add that both externally and in the interior, the chancel is rich in beautiful details of Anglo-Norman architecture; and that I do not propose to destroy these details for the purpose of renewing them... But*

250 Rev John Brown (1792-1845). Northern Irish vicar of St Mary's. For obituary *Leicester Mercury*, 20th December 1845.
251 *Leicester Journal*, 20th November 1846.

to protect them as far as may be by repairing the adjoining ashlar and water tablings.' [252]

The Parish Council obviously didn't have any issue with Flint's work and asked him to go back in 1850 to report on the damp in the walls.

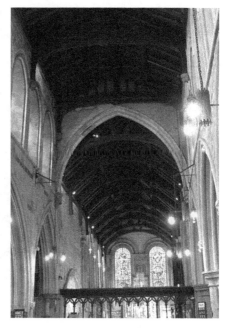

Flint's nave arch at St. Mary de Castro.

The church was founded in 1107 and rebuilt in 1160 and has twice lost its spire; the first time before shortly before 1783 and the second time as recently as 2013. Pevsner rated parts of the church very highly.[253] It is grade 1 listed and is still a centre of (Anglo-Catholic) worship under the episcopacy of the Bishop of Richborough, as a church that does not accept the ordination of women priests. It is also actively fundraising (when hasn't it been?) with the aim of restoring the missing spire.

Cotton mill and warehouses
King Street and Marlborough Streets
Richard Harris
c. 1845, 1850, 1851, 1856 and 1859
Flint & Wickes and Flint & Shenton
Extant

The Harris building still exists and stands proudly in warm red brick on the corner of King Street and Marlborough Street finishing in Duke Street. It is another Flint building in a simple Italianate style and has three storeys and a basement. There are rusticated quoins and string courses with regular fenestration and the building is almost square. The original

252 Estates Committee minutes, 7th January 1845.
253 Pevsner in ibid.

*The Harris warehouse on King Street: the scene of much work
for Flint over several commissions.*

entrance on King Street survives, although the 'R. Harris and Sons'
engraving has been crudely and obviously filled. The other doorway is a
later Shenton and Baker addition.

It remains unclear when the mill was built. Noted Local historian Dr
Joan Skinner[254] puts it at 1840 and attributes it to Flint; the listing entry
for it also cites Flint but suggests 1845 for its construction. The earliest
existing plan is by Flint and Wickes and dates to 1850 and is concerned
with the conversion of privies into water closets to be supplied by water
from the Leicester Water Works Company.[255] In 1851 (and the plan has
the same number as the 1850 plan[256]), the factory appears to have been
extended by about one third on the end furthest from Belvoir Street and
a proof cesspool built at the Duke Street/Marlborough Street corner of
the building. Flint returned in 1856, this time with Shenton to extend

254 Dr Joan Skinner (1923-2006). Victorian Society campaigner and industrial
    historian.
255 LRO 1851/108/1. The actual plan is dated 1850 and seems to be linked to the
    1851 plan.
256 LRO 1851/108.

the cellarage under the Duke Street end of the factory[257] and their final visit was in 1859 when they converted several cesspool privies into water closets and laid drainage.[258] Shenton and Baker came back in 1866 and 1867 to put in a new window to the basement and the new entrance. Finally, Albert Herbert carried out basement and drainage work in 1916.

Richard Harris started his business in 1802 and he soon acquired a factory in Braunstone Gate in the year 1833, built by Flint. He appears with premises in King Street from at least 1027 making braces and cravats.

The Harris company failed in 1887 due mostly to the burden of Richard Harris's complex will and its need to provide for unmarried daughters and younger sons, although John Dove Harris junior did manage to buy the original Braunstone Gate West Street premises through a partnership with Orson Wright[259] to form Harris Wright and Company. After Harris and Sons, the building was used as a warehouse for Pool,[260] Lorrimer[261] and Tabberer[262] until about 1970 and a few iron gutter pipes still exist in Marlborough Street with their ornate PLT design. The warehouse was given grade 2 listing in 2000 and turned into student flats in 2002.

Warehouse (later Post Office)
Granby Street
1845
Corah and Sons
Demolished c. 1887

In between the General News Room and the Leicestershire Banking Company building, Flint built a third edifice: a warehouse for Thomas Corah.[263] The rapid growth of trade in Leicester in the early 1840s had

257 LRO 1856/773.

258 LRO 1859/1162.

259 Orson Wright (1853-1913). 'The father of South Wigston', influential builder, responsible in part for the Grand Hotel and sometime town councillor.

260 Joseph Pool (1803-1884). Hosier of Langham House, Highfield Street.

261 John Lorrimer (1827-1891). Hosier and sometime town councillor of Park Hill House, Aylestone. For obituary see *Leicester Chronicle*, 15th August 1891.

262 Osmond Tabberer (1836-1907). Hosier and magistrate of the Holt, Stoneygate.

263 Thomas Corah (1807-1870). Son of Nathanial, hosier and liberal town councillor. For obituary see *Leicester Chronicle*, 5th March 1870.

*Confusingly built before the first Post Office but as a warehouse for Corah's.
It became Leicester's second Post Office.*

prompted the company to expand from their Union Street premises to a purpose-built one nearer the railway station. The site had been used by Pickfords for their fly vans, it was about 480 square yards and purchased at £1 per square yard. The cost of the new building was £3,500 and it was put up in 1845. It was situated on the block between Belvoir Street and Bishop Street.

In 1865, Corah's needed to expand again and built their long-lived and much-loved St Margaret's works. They sold the warehouse for £4,500 to the Post Office who converted the warehouse into Leicester's main branch. The Post Office had moved about quite a lot in the previous thirty years and this was its fourth (but by no means last) relocation, which was to last until 1887. James Williams[264] altered the warehouse at a cost of £1,000. The builders were W. Neale and Sons[265] who disposed, *'To be sold cheap'*, of a large quantity of iron columns not needed for the building's new purpose.[266]

It was a three-storey building and a surviving photograph in the Post

264 James Williams (1824-1892). Whitehall-based Post Office architect who designed Derby Post Office amongst others.
265 William Neale (1815-1886), builder, mason and saw mill proprietor of Southgate Street and Peacock Lane.
266 *Leicester Journal*, 18th January 1867.

An 1848 painting showing the General New Room and the boldly simple Corah three storey warehouse in the exact centre of the picture.

Office phase of its life reveals it to be a typical Flint design. It is stuccoed and elegant in its simplicity with few adornments, although there was a decorative Italianate balcony to the windows on the middle floor. It was demolished around 1887 when the new Post Office opened.

Ironically, this future Post Office was built before the first permanent office, which Flint would start work on in 1846!

Post Office
Granby Street
July 1846
Postmaster General
Demolished

The first purpose-built Post Office in Leicester appears to be rather overlooked (and hard to follow in the contemporary press) William Flint building. The only advert with a named link to Flint occurs in the *Leicester Mercury*:

> '*NEW POST OFFICE AT LAST. – at last it appears Leicester is about to have a decent Post Office. The site, we believe, will be between*

Leicester's first Post Office – Flint at his Classically simplest in 1845.

the *Leicestershire Bank and the Crowns. Tenders were to be sent in to Mr. Flint, the architect, yesterday (Friday) afternoon.'*[267]

The Leicestershire Bank is also a Flint design and the Three Crowns was demolished to build a bank, which is now the National Westminster Bank, a William Millican design.

The building opened in the August of 1847 and didn't meet with universal acclaim:

'THE NEW POST-OFFICE, Leicester, was opened on Thursday, when great numbers of the inhabitants indulged their curiosity by walking into the building and examining its arrangements. The new office is very convenient, though, we imagine, hardly so commodious as it might have been. It comprises a large apartment for the receipt and sorting of letters, a room for the Postmaster, a room for the deliverers and messengers, a sitting apartment, offices, and a wide passage for the shelter of the public. In the latter are windows where applicants for stamps, letters, and money orders may be waited upon.'[268]

There was much discussion in the papers about its clock and how it should be regulated to the new system of railway time.

The Post Office building resembles his style and has a look of Flint's original Corn Exchange about it. A plan for it survives and is reproduced in John Soer's history of the Royal Mail in Leicestershire and it is uncertain when it was demolished.[269]

---

267 *Leicester Mercury*, 11th July 1846.
268 *Leicester Chronicle*, 14th August 1847.
269 *The Royal Mail in Leicestershire and Rutland* (Soer, 1997)

Museum alterations
New Walk
October 1846
Leicester Corporation
Extant

The roots of this work are in the Museums Act of 1845, which gave town councils the powers to establish museums. In late 1846 the Corporation's Museum Committee asked Flint to look into purchasing the Theatre in Horsefair Street with a view to its conversion into a museum to house the burgeoning collection of the Leicestershire Literary and Philosophical Society.[270] William Parsons had only comparatively recently built the theatre in 1836, so perhaps business wasn't good, as theatres have never really prospered in non-conformist Leicester. The Committee then briefly looked at the Three Crowns Hotel in the same street before they rejected it to look instead at the Proprietary School on New Walk.

After lots of committee work considering heating and lighting (including a glass roof) the Museum Committee approved the plan by William Flint to adapt Joseph Hansom's[271] Propriety School on New Walk into a museum, lecture room and school of design.[272] They had recently purchased it for £3,300 and accepted Flint's plan for £400, although recommended postponement of the further costs of £160 for lecture room and £145 for school of design. The Council evidently couldn't raise the purchase price, so the project was delayed until August, by which time a further plan from Flint for all three phases of the alteration was approved for £500, although the means of heating the establishment was left undecided. There were several delays, but work was eventually completed by June 1849 with the first day open to the public being scheduled for Thursday 21st June. The same edition of the *Journal* reveals that Flint's fee for the work was £34 10s and 6d.[273]

---

270 Estate Sub-committee minutes, 27/10/1846.
271 Joseph Hansom (1803-1882). Gothic Revival architect and designer of the eponymous cab.
272 *Leicester Journal*, 4th October 1848.
273 *Leicester Journal*, 15th June 1849.

Fever House
Thorpe Road Workhouse
Melton Mowbray
July 1847
Melton Mowbray Union Guardians
Demolished 1869?

Not much is known about this commission and the only real evidence that Flint was working in this area is a notice in the *Leicester Journal* advertising for tenders and directing them to view the plans and specifications at Flint's Friar Lane offices.[274] Minute books for the Union have almost all been lost and none of the remaining years cover Flint's work. The Workhouse itself was designed by Charles Dyer[275] and built in 1836 and was used as a hospital well into the 20th Century. It is possible that the Fever House was demolished in 1869 when Robert Johnson[276] built an infirmary on the site. Most of the workhouse still survives awaiting a new purpose or the demolition ball.

Cattle and Sheep Market
Horsefair Street
December 1847
Leicester Corporation
Demolished 1872

The Leicester Improvement Act of 1846 required a reorganisation of the town's markets and a removal of the most inconvenient and unsanitary animal ones to create a new cattle and sheep market in Horsefair Street on the site of what is now Town Hall Square.

In late December 1847, the *Leicester Journal* published Flint's advertisement for tenders addressed to 'Paviours, Builders and Others'.[277] It was clearly a large construction project encompassing sloping, paving, forming roads, drainage, fences, gates, cattle standings (to be made of oak), sheep pens and wrought iron works.

---

274 *Leicester Journal*, 16th July 1847.
275 Charles Dyer (1794-1848). Prominent London and Bristol architect.
276 Robert Winter Johnson (1832-1884), Melton Mowbray based architect.
277 *Leicester Journal*, 31st December 1847.

Now the site of the Town Hall, Flint's re-ordered cattle market of 1847.

The market lasted on this site until 1872 when a purpose-built and much larger version opened at Freeman's Common. Demolition came swiftly the same year in order to erect Leicester's much anticipated (and still much admired) Town Hall.

Worsted spinning mill
West Bridge
Ellis and Whitmore
July 1848
Extant

Proof to absolutely link Flint and this factory has not been available. As with several industrial buildings of the time (e.g. the Turner Factory redesign on King Richard's Road), the contemporary local press is tight-lipped as to the identity of the architect. However, there is a significant source that leads to an attribution to Flint. The LRO holds a manuscript of a history of the mill and site written by A. M. Mackness[278] in 1948.[279] Mackness clearly

---

278 Albert Melling Mackness (1908-1977).
279 LRO DE 2043 *'Patons and Baldwins Ltd. Story of West Bridge Mills Leicester 1839 – 1948'*.

had access to an extensive archive of bills and plans, presumably retained by Patons and Baldwins. Their whereabouts is now unknown and it is thought that the archive may have been destroyed in the fire at the site in 1979. There is a considerable Patons and Baldwins archive held with Clackmannanshire Libraries and although they have extensive records of almost all the firm's other factories and buildings, there is nothing from Leicester!

The *Chronicle* carries the first mention of the factory in 1848:

'NEW WORSTED FACTORY. – Workmen are now engaged in excavating the earth for the foundation of a new worsted manufactory, near the West-bridge, intended for Messrs. Ellis and Whitmore. The building will be erected upon a large scale, at a cost, we understand, of £6,000.'[280]

Mackness records that the builders were Waterfield and Coleman;[281] the stonework by Lindley and Firn[282] and the ironwork by Andrew

Altered but still dominating the West Bridge landscape:
The Whitmore Ellis worsted spinning mill.

280 *Leicester Chronicle*, 22nd July 1848.
281 Samuel Coleman (1784-1871). Builder of Newtown Street. Partner of William Waterfield before Thomas Smith.
282 John Firn (1812-1873), stoneworker and grave cutter of Humberstone Road.

Now offices, this was a spinning floor – note the vaulted roof.

Handyside.[283] The boiler for the engine house arrived via the canal from the Haigh Foundry Company in Goole!

Pevsner describes the building as *'A narrow six storey block with little eaves detail to relieve the severity'*.[284] It is a rectangular building of purple brick and has a slate hipped roof. For many years there was an unusually narrow chimney that adjoined the boiler house. It evidently began listing and had been for at least 50 years when Mackness was writing in 1948.

The mill opened in June 1849 and in style, leading to a rather startling newspaper headline: *'Monster tea party in a factory'*. The *Mercury* was on hand to record proceedings:

'On Wednesday afternoon a tea meeting, on an unusually large scale, was held (by permission of the worthy proprietors) in the noble factory just erected by the West Bridge for Messrs. Ellis and Whitmore… The tea-tables were laid out in the fourth storey, the pillars and walls of which were liberally decorated with evergreens. Nearly 1500 persons partook of tea…'[285]

Guests were treated to oranges and strawberries brought from London and there was dancing accompanied by Mr Brown's[286] band before games of 'Jack-in-the-ring'. Some guests had come on specially laid on trains, not so surprising, as this was a temperance event in all but name; and

---

283 Andrew Handyside (1805-1887). Eminent Derby iron founder and early producer of pillar boxes.
284 Pevsner op cit.
285 *Leicester Mercury*, 30th June 1849.
286 Mr Brown (fl.1840s) was a journeyman mechanic and amateur violoncellist.

inevitably Edward Ellis[287] gave a speech on the evils of drink. Beverages at the event were provided from a 'monster tea urn'. There was even a balloon which was viewed by guests from the fifth floor!

The company was an 1844 partnership between John Whitmore,[288] John Ellis and his eldest son, Edward Ellis who took quarter shares each with Whitmore taking the half share. It did not fare well financially and made losses in 1851, 1853, 1857, 1859 and 1862, although there were boom years such as 1863 and 1864 when wool was in demand as a result of the Cotton Famine caused by the American Civil War.

The mill sits on an island on Bedehouse Meadows and for much of its early life was prone to flooding. It has lime concrete foundations which harden in water. It has six floors of which only five were originally intended for spinning; it was not long, however, before the sixth was put into use. For most of Ellis and Whitmore's time, the mill was used as follows:

Ground floor:	Wool carding and combing
1st floor:	Reeling, preparing, balling and spinning
2nd floor:	Preparing, spinning, doubling and winding
3rd floor:	Spinning
4th floor:	Spinning
5th floor:	Spinning

The site had been used by Bankart and Sons[289] and was acquired by Ellis and Whitmore in around 1844 during the 'Hungry Forties'. Expansion was clearly on their mind early on as bricks started to be stockpiled for the new factory as early as 1846, when there were already 220,000 on site.[290]

Over 1875 and 1876, Shenton and Baker carried out an extensive rebuilding project at the site and it would appear the work was not as good as the master's:

---

287 Edward Shipley Ellis (1817-1879), local politician, benefactor, businessman and property magnate.
288 John Whitmore (1806-1881) of Elmhurst, London Road, leading Leicester industrialist and sometime local councillor.
289 Thomas Bankart (1757-1836) and Samuel Tuffley Bankart (1791-1862). Carpet manufacturers.
290 Mackness op cit.

The remains of huge washers or boilers at the bottom floor of the mill.

'It must be admitted that Shenton and Baker did not design in the tradition of William Flint. Their buildings have developed many cracks and faults, though they were not to know that a railway would one day be built alongside.'[291]

After Ellis and Whitmore came J. and J. Baldwin of Halifax in 1904 and then Patons and Baldwins Ltd in 1920, a huge company at the time and so large that it was an original FT 30 company. It ceased trading in 1961. Peck's moved in during 1948 and occupied some of the building before taking it over completely.

Peck's closed in 1977 and the main building and others on the site were left empty. In 1979 a fire destroyed all the surrounding buildings but the mill itself was saved and Douglas Smith Stimson Partnership were chosen to restore it. Glasswork to create a new entrance and also surround the building was completed to much acclaim. The site was chosen as a renovation site by City Challenge in 1994. It remains a beautiful building and the restorers clearly understood and honoured Flint's sense of proportion and style. From 1998 it has been used as the Land Registry building and the glass additions on the canal side are designed to look like a steamship in full steam.

---

291 Mackness op cit.

Borough Gaol alterations
High Cross Street
November 1848
Demolished 1897

There was a place of detention in High Cross Street (the medieval Centre of Leicester) from the 13th Century. In more modern times, John Johnson[292] designed the Borough Gaol in High Cross Street around 1792. It was confusingly situated next to the *County Gaol*, designed by George Moneypenny[293] and kept for a time by Daniel Lambert.[294] The construction of William Parsons's County Gaol on Welford Road led to a decline in the fortunes of this prison and it was demolished in 1836/1837.

The Borough Gaol is featured in John Flower's lithograph of the High Cross dating to about 1830 and it was a rather elegant and classical

John Flower's Old Jail (sic) painting of 1830.

---

292 John Johnson (1732-1814). Architect of the Royal Infirmary, Consanguinitarium and Assembly Rooms.

293 George Moneypenny (1768-?). Prominent prison architect and ironically first inmate at the County Gaol where he was imprisoned for insolvency.

294 Daniel Lambert (1770-1809) Gaol keeper and, for much of the last two centuries, the world's fattest man.

building with much to commend it. It needed rebuilding in the 1840s and Flint secured the contract due to his close links with the Council who engaged him to alter and enlarge the Gaol in 1848[295] and his plans won the enthusiastic backing of the *Leicester Chronicle*:

'Mr. Flint, we think, has shown great skill and judgement in his re-arrangement of a portion of the prison. He has not proposed to reconstruct the whole, but to substitute for a part now little used a plain building – plain as the loudest declaimers against expensive gaols could desire. In this he would find separate cells, of the proper dimensions, for thirty-nine persons, male and female. The remainder of the building would then accommodate forty-six prisoners – seventeen females and twenty-nine males, in wards where they would be partially associated. Under the proposed alterations, therefore, the prisoners would be subject to the operations of the two systems, and the old gaol would not be so completely pulled to pieces as it must be if the Separate System be entirely adopted. The architect has evinced considerable ingenuity

Facing stones and a portion of the retaining wall still survive in High Cross Street.

295 Estate sub-committee minutes, 9th November 1848.

and thought upon the preparation of the plan, which deserves public attention.'[296]

The usual advertisement for contractors went to press on 20th July 1849.[297] Regrettably, demolition took place in 1897 and now only a small and part-rusticated section of wall survives in High Cross Street commemorated by a City Council plaque. Some foundations may also remain.

Cottages
Knighton Hill
September 1849
Flint & Wickes
Demolished c.1885

There is an advert for tenders in the *Leicester Journal* and this is the primary source of evidence for this piece of work early in Flint and Wickes' partnership.[298] Headed Freemen's Allotments and addressed to builders, contracts are invited '... *to erect the intended Knighton Hill Cottage'*. No more is known about the commission, but it is likely that the work was connected to Freemen's Cottages on Welford Road, which were alms houses for freemen and their widows. They don't seem to retain any obvious work from Flint's time and were rebuilt in 1856 and enlarged in 1885 and then again in 1893, both times by Stockdale Harrison.[299]

2 houses
Princess Street
Mr Shuttleworth
November 1849
Flint & Wickes

The *Leicester Mercury* reports the fact that the Council approved

---

296 *Leicester Chronicle*, 14th April 1849.
297 *Leicester Journal*, 20th July 1849.
298 *Leicester Journal*, 14th September 1849.
299 Stockdale Harrison (1846-1914). Popular and busy Leicester architect.

Flint's plans for two houses for Mr Shuttleworth in Princess Street in November 1849.[300] The plans do not survive. Princess Street has many surviving buildings that could not only be this commission but also as yet unidentified Flint commissions. Whoever Mr Shuttleworth was, he did not live in the houses and seemed to live outside Leicester.

300 *Leicester Mercury*, 17th November 1849.

CHAPTER 6

The Partners: Charles Wickes

Charles Wickes was in partnership with William Flint between about 1849 and 29th June 1853. Architect, artist, author, confidence trickster or jailbird: Charles Wickes was all of these things. His life story could have been written by Dickens.

He was born in Dover on 4th May 1828, baptised there on 9th June 1828, the son of William Wickes[301] and his wife Mary Anne.[302] In 1841, Wickes is living with his parents and brother Frederick[303] in Magdalen Street in the St Giles area of Cambridge. The whole family is described as being of 'independent means'. By 1851, the family are in Leicester and are residing in Regent Street, not far from William Flint, and his father lists his profession as 'fund holder'. Another move to New Walk and then the family leave Leicester around 1855 and head for Woodland Road, Spring Grove, Isleworth.

In partnership

Although he claims credit for the Corn Exchange in the Market Place, no single design can be attributed exclusively to Charles Wickes. During his partnership with Flint, the practice was doing steady business and there are several shop fronts and houses; a terrace on New Walk; the houses in Museum Square and the enlargement of Holy Trinity Church. However, there is no *great* commission as there had been in the 1830s and early 1840s. If Wickes was in practice alone, he is not listed in any directories; no plans exist of any work undertaken and there is no trace of him in

---

301 William Wickes (1792-1866). Fund holder and native of Dover.
302 Mary Anne Wickes (1791-1863).
303 Frederick Wickes (1821-?). According to court records an architect, but no designs have been found.

the local press. The first work recorded by the partnership is the rather sketchy Knighton Hill Cottage 1849 and the last is the Newarke Street Frisby and Chawner warehouse in March 1853. The partnership was dissolved on 29th June 1853.

As an author

Charles Wickes was the author of three books:

- *The spires and towers of medieval churches of England (1851), published by J. Weale (volume two in 1854 and a third in 1859 with the complete edition in 1859 by Thompson and Co.)*
- *Memorials of English Medieval churches (1857), published by Thompson and Co.*
- *A handy book on villa architecture (1862), published by Lockwood and Co. (see chapter 15 The Pupils: Charles Baker)*

The *Leicester Journal* carries an advert for his first book in its 11th April 1851 edition and details the different local publishers and finishes. A very positive review appears in The Builder in 1853:[304]

SPIRE OF ST. JAMES'S CHURCH, LOUTH.

This engraving of St James in Louth comes from his 1851 book on church spires and towers.

'*What we have said will show that we consider Mr. Wickes's book a very creditable production, notwithstanding the author did commence it beardless,* imberbis adhuc, *as he expresses it, and we hope it will prove the corner-stone on which he may build up fame and fortune.*'

---

304 The Builder, 31st December 1853.

Wickes' designs for residential houses are still stylish today.

During his time with Flint, Wickes designed a display cabinet that went to the Great Exhibition: another piece of work for Richard Harris, this octagonal brass sash-barred and crimson skirted compartment displayed shawls, polkas, hoods, gloves and boots and *'is very creditable to the taste of Mr Wickes'*.[305] Unaccountably, he was also a 10 shilling subscriber to the Church of England Scripture Readers' Association for Leicester the same year![306]

As for his post-Leicester public life, it was colourful. Charles Wickes's personal life was no less colourful and he claims to have been married with two children. He lived with Matilda Kipps[307] at Swanage

Wickes' displays for Richard Harris's wares at the Great Exhibition made the front page of the Mercury.

305 *Leicester Mercury*, 14th June 1851.
306 *Leicester Journal*, 21st March 1851.
307 Matilda Kipps (1839-1908).

and they were man and wife in all but ceremony. In 1871, she is living in Islington with a child, Charles Wickes,[308] who is 10 years old and was born in Bath. No marriage or register of birth has been found. By 1881 she is calling herself Matilda Wickes and she is the landlady of the Duke of York in Stamford Hill. She describes herself as widow and the 20-year-old Charles is a compositor and listed as her son. In 1891, they are back in Islington, but in 1901 are to be found together in Northwold, Norfolk at the Brook Glen Fruit Colony, a smallholding and self-sufficiency charity. Charles describes himself as a *'poultry and fruit farmer'* and is unmarried. This is where Matilda probably died in 1908, registered in Thetford under the name Matilda Wickes. No further trace of Charles has yet been found.

After Leicester

The *Aberdeen Journal* carries a warning to bankers June 1863:[309]

> 'CAUTION TO BANKERS. – An imposter, who gives his name as Charles Wicks [sic], a church architect – varied occasionally to Wilks, Beach and Wellingham – 5 feet 9 in. in height, light complexion, has succeeded in defrauding some bankers in England. The police have a warrant for his apprehension for defrauding Messrs Jemmet, Pomfret, & Co., Ashford to the amount of £50.'

A little more light is shed on his activities in The Illustrated Weekly News:[310]

> 'EXTRAORDINARY CASE OF SWINDLING
> THE Police Gazette notifies that one Charles Wickes is "wanted" for frauds upon bankers, in Cambridge, Bedford, Ipswich, Tunbridge-wells, and elsewhere, and warrants are out for his apprehension. The young man, however – for such he is – manages not only to allude the vigilance of his would-be captors, but also to continue to impose successfully upon bankers. A few days

---

308 Charles Wickes (c.1861-?). Compositor.
309 Aberdeen Journal, 10th June 1863.
310 Illustrated Weekly News, 20th June 1863.

ago a "young gentleman" called at the Bilston District Bank in Wolverhampton, and presented a letter of introduction, professedly from a clergyman living in the neighbourhood; and the address and deportment of the bearer of the letter were such as excited no suspicion. He said that he had come into the neighbourhood with the view to purchase an estate, which he named, at Chesterton, near Bridgenorth; and for the purchase of which, he added, he had agreed. In short time he should take up his residence on his newly-acquired property, for he had married a lady of fortune, whose family lived near to the estate. Of all the banks in the district he should, under advice, prefer the Bilston District Bank at which to have his account, and he now desired to open it by having a check for 2,000/ drawn upon the Southampton Bank, placed to his credit. With this check as security, no difficulty was experienced by the "young gentleman" in obtaining the means of supplying his immediate expenses; for he "had not supplied himself with cash." Readily, therefore, the small sum for which he asked – only 40/ – was handed to him, and he shortly left the bank. The answer from Southampton, when the "handsome check" was presented was that the "gentleman" in question had possessed himself of one of their check-books, but that was all they knew about him; he certainly had "no effects" in the Southampton Bank. The matter is now in the hands of the local police. The "young gentleman" who is supposed to be about thirty years of age, on arriving at Wolverhampton took up his quarters at the leading hotel. Here, after a time, he ordered out a carriage and pair to drive him to the residence of the clergyman whose good nature he correctly calculated upon as a means to the end designed. The driver, however, appeared without white gloves. This was unbearable. He was quickly instructed to assume them, for he (the visitor) "could not think of his attempting to drive him without white gloves". On the step of the carriage "the gentleman" paused to instruct the coachman to stop at the most fashionable hatter's in the town, where the visitor handed in his hat to have a mourning band put upon it. Duly arrived at the residence of the clergyman, he sent in his card with a mourning border. The card announced him to be "Mr. Charles Wickes, Woodlands, Spring-grove and Carlton Club,

Pall-mall". This address obtained him a ready audience. Now face to face with the Rev. Gentleman, the latter was quite prepared, from the features of his visitor, to believe him when he said that he was the son of an old parishioner whom he (the clergyman) knew when he had a living at Cambridge. The young gentleman had embraced the profession of architect, and furthermore was an author; for it was he, he asserted, who had written the work, published by Weale and by Ackerman, on the "Towers and Spires of England". He was in that neighbourhood sketching the Collegiate Church of Wolverhampton, with a view to the publication of his sketch in another work which was preparing; but he was without ready cash, and desired an introduction to one of the banks in the district. He not only obtained the note of introduction, but also an invitation to dinner on the following day. It is, however, needless to say that, having obtained the £40, he was not of the Rev. Gentleman's dinner party on the morrow, nor was he to be found at the hotel'.

From later newspaper reports, it is clear that Wickes and Kipps were in cahoots and began their life of crime in 1858. Although Wickes's real name was publicised widely in 1863, he avoids capture and the trail goes cold until 1868 when he is revealed as using the alias Howard and apprehended in Wareham, Dorset. The Edinburgh Evening Courant describes their capture:

'WHOLESALE FORGERY OF CHEQUES. At the Bow Street Police Court on Saturday, Charles Wick [sic], alias Howard, and Matilda Howard, alias Kipps, were charged with forging numerous cheques upon the London and County National Provincial and other banks, and the woman with uttering one of the forged cheques. It appeared that the male prisoner had for years carried on in a methodical manner a wholesale system of forgeries on banks in London and elsewhere. His plan was to open a fictitious account with a bank, and obtain a cheque-book, afterwards using the cheques to open other fictitious accounts at other banks by depositing large cheques and then obtaining change of small ones. He carried this system on with marvellous success till February last, when, with the female prisoner, who had been living with him at Clarence Cottage, Swanage, he made an attempt to leave the neighbourhood. Two policemen seeing the prisoners walking from Swanage to Wareham, at one o'clock, on the morning of February 15th, and carrying a trunk between them, watched them go to the Red Lion, at Wareham, and then gave information, in consequence of which they were apprehended. Upon the female prisoner were found a number of cheques, books of various banks, bearing upon the counterfoils of the used cheques memoranda in the male prisoner's handwriting of the circumstances under which they had been used, and a series of diaries extending over ten years, from 1858 till 1868. The diary contained a minute account of the prisoner's conduct from day to day giving a detail of the various frauds committed on banks. Various charges were gone into, and they were remanded'.

At some point the case against Matilda Kipps was dropped and she did not appear in court with him. Wickes was remanded in custody on 20th March 1868 to Newgate prison. His custody records reveal further titbits of physical description: he had a scar under his right eye and another on his left thumb.

He was tried on 7th April 1868 at the Old Bailey with ten indictments of feloniously forging and uttering cheques with intent to defraud. The Courant describes his trial a month later:

'EXTENSIVE FRAUDS ON BANKERS

AT the Central Criminal Court yesterday, before the Common Sergeant, Charles Wickes, a middle-aged man of gentlemanly appearance was brought up for judgement. The prisoner pleaded guilty to ten indictments, which charged him with forgery and uttering forged orders.

MR SLEIGH[311] (with whom was Mr. Poland[312]) stated the facts of the case. The prisoner, he said, was a man of education. He was

---

311 William Campbell Sleigh (1818-1887), lawyer and politician.
312 Sir Harry Bodkin Poland (1830-1928), lawyer and politician.

the son of an architect who had set him up in business; but he abandoned it, and took to that which could not be characterised by any other terms than a clever system of obtaining money from bankers by false pretences. The prisoner had defrauded bankers in various parts of the kingdom; but the banks to which he (the learned counsel) particularly referred were the National Bank, the London and County Bank, and the National Provincial Bank. It was the habit of the prisoner to call upon bankers and say that they had been introduced by Mr. So-and-so, naming one of the directors; that he had an account at his bankers in the country, but that he was going to have a residence in the town and that he proposed to open an account with the bank to which he had been introduced. Upon this he would hand them a cheque for £1000, and receive a cheque book. He generally complained that his cheque book was too small for his large business. He would then put his hand in his pocket and say "Oh, by the way, I have a cheque paid me by one of my tenants: will you be good enough to send it to the counter to get it cashed?" it seemed that the courtesy of the London bankers was very great – (A laugh) – for in most instances they were kind enough to accommodate him. He must say that it showed not only great courtesy, but great credulity, for, as he said, in most instances they cashed the cheques. The prisoner had a peculiar fancy for £55 5s. The next day it was found that the cheques were forgeries. However, some bankers were sufficiently sharp not to be taken in. The prisoner had been in the habit of keeping a diary in which he had duly entered full particulars of the various frauds of which he had been found guilty. By this diary they traced him from the year 1863. His diary stated that in 1863 he visited thirteen banks, from which he obtained £1000. In the month of October 1867 he got no less than £600 from four banks; and it seemed that in the four years he had got as much as £1832 3s 5d. The way in which he detected was this. He and the woman with whom he lived were at Swanage, in Dorsetshire, but as he failed to pay, there was a threat that proceedings would be taken against him for obtaining goods under false pretences. He then suddenly disappeared. One of the county constabulary, with an amount of cleverness and ingenuity which he (the learned counsel) did not think the metropolitan force would exactly make use of took it upon himself to stop them on a highway, and as he was not satisfied with their answers he took them into custody. He did not know on what charge the officer arrested them, and probably the officer didn't himself. (A laugh.) However, he was told that it was between one o'clock and two o'clock in the morning. It was a wise discretion, for it resulted in enquiries being made, and the present prosecution instituted.

Mr. F. H. LEWIS[313] briefly addressed the Court on behalf of the prisoner. He thought that if the case had come before a jury that they would have recommended him to mercy, on the ground of the peculiar temptations which had been thrown in the prisoner's way by the bankers. He had two brothers in the Church.

The COMMON SERGEANT said it was quite idle to say anything to the prisoner, because he was a man of education and fully understood the position in which he was placed.' [314]

He got no mercy and was sentenced to 15 years penal servitude. On 28th April 1868, he was sent to Millbank Prison. The architect of this prison was Sir Robert Smirke,[315] the brother of the Sydney Smirke whose Trinity Church he and Flint had altered in 1853. The prison register for 1868 shows that he was entered in the Governor's Journal of Misconduct Book at least eight times, it reveals that he had contact from his putative mother-in-law and also had a visit from one of his brothers. Rather ominously it records that the visit was 'stopped' and it may be that he was exhibiting signs of mental illness. He transferred to Woking Convict Invalid Prison on 11th February 1869 and was then sent to Parkhurst, on the Isle of Wight on 22nd February 1870. He stayed there for some years and by 1876 was back at Millbank, which he left on 12th June to return to Woking again.

---

313 Frederic Hyman Lewis (1834-1889). Barrister and leading proponent of British chess.
314 Edinburgh Evening Courant, 9th April 1868.
315 Sir Robert Smirke (1780-1867), nationally acclaimed architect and leader of the Greek revival movement and architect of the British Museum, Custom House and Covent Garden Theatre amongst other buildings. Brother of Sydney.

Charles Wickes' death certificate.

It looks like by then he was a very sick man as he was one of three admissions that day; the other two on their way to Broadmoor Lunatic Asylum.

He died at Woking Prison on 22nd April 1878, the cause of death recorded as: *'Sudden effusion of serum on brain';* a symptom of which can be mental confusion or disturbance. He is described as: *'convict formerly an architect'* and with that, the story of this talented architect, artist and author comes to an end.

CHAPTER 7

The Buildings of the 1850s Part 1

Alterations and drainage
Hotel Street
William Stretton
March 1850
Flint & Wickes
Demolished

From the plans,[316] these look like rather grand premises with rather grand staircases on Hotel Street owned by William Stretton.[317] They were not a symmetrical pair and were probably of two storeys with basements. The council gave approval for the alterations to go ahead on the 'give and take' principle, in other words, a system in which a reasonable user can make reasonable changes without doing any damage to the enjoyment of an adjoining property. The work involved bow windows to the first floor 12 feet above the basement and drainage work including new vaults for the privies. Their use and location have yet to be identified but they were probably on the on the opposite side of the street to the Assembly Rooms.

Rectory
Emmanuel Church, Forest Road
Loughborough
March 1850
Flint & Wickes
Extant

The LRO holds a series of plans[318] for the improvement or construction

---

316 LRO 1850/36 and 1850/36A.
317 William Weston Stretton (1798-1888). Worsted manufacturer and magistrate of Danes Hill House.
318 LRO 1D69 1-37.

of rectories in the county. There are a few for William Parsons (e.g. Blaby and Markfield) and also Emmanuel Church's new building by Flint and Wickes. The incumbent was the Rev Robert Bunch,[319] Fellow of Emmanuel College, Cambridge in whose gift was the Parish of Loughborough Emmanuel.

There are four architectural drawings which reveal the rectory to be a building of some size and luxury. It had a large drawing room; a library; a business room and a butler's pantry on the ground floor as well as an attached but separate knife house; wash house; piggery and coach house, etc. On the first floor were six large bedrooms and associated linen room and dressing rooms and seventh bedroom on the attic floor. In a letter attached to the plans, Flint records that the cost of building it was £1,601 13s and swears by oath that '...*tenders have been made by respectable and competent persons...*'

The design of the house bears a very strong resemblance to Charles Wickes's Design 4 in his '*Handy guide...*' book so this may point to the

The Emmanuel Rectory, Loughborough.

319 Rev Robert James Bunch (1811-1870). Church of England vicar who died in France.

Loughborough Emmanuel Rectory today.

design being a Wickes project more than Flint's. The rectory was known as Glebe House for many years and has been Hardwick House School since 2013.

Warehouse
Welford Place
April 1850
Messrs. Henry and Co
Flint & Wickes

Approval was reported in the *Mercury* on 4th May 1850 and the company put the warehouse up for auction in October 1853 describing it as: *'That SPACIOUS and CONVENIENT WAREHOUSE, in Welford-place, occupied by Messrs. A. & S. Henry[320] & Co.'[321]* This was a firm of textile merchants and, including a short time operating from York Street, the company were not in Leicester for long and left by about 1854. The company survived

---

320 Alexander Henry (1783-1862), later MP for South Lancashire and his brother
    Samuel Henry (1775-1840), American born textile merchants.
321 *Leicester Journal*, 28th October 1853.

until 1983 when it was placed into the hands of the receivers. It has not been possible to locate exactly where the warehouse stood.

Fence
The Newarke
April 1850
Flint & Wickes
Trinity Hospital Trustees
Demolished

A small job, but it illustrates the scope of Flint's work. The fence was for the green in the Newarke behind the Chapel and cottages and enclosed some land from the road. Plans were given approval by the Town Council on 17th April 1850.[322]

Warehouse alterations
Albion Street
John Biggs
May 1850
Flint & Wickes
Demolished

This is a run of the mill job altering an established warehouse and such commissions were a staple of Flint's business. This one on Albion Street was given approval on 22nd May 1850.[323] John Biggs and Sons was yet another Leicester hosiery firm and the plans show that it was a simple extension to the existing building carrying on the pilastered frontage to Albion Street.

Warehouse
St Nicholas Square
June 1850

322 LRO 1850/45.
323 LRO 1850/57.

Thomas Rust and Co.
Flint & Wickes
Demolished c. 1920

This was a worsted warehouse which was situated contiguously with St Nicholas Square and St Nicholas Churchyard. Either address is given in various trade directories. It was a large site at the edge of which Flint built the Rev. Clarke's cottages in 1851. Certainly, the site was already being used by the company in 1850 and Flint retained several existing buildings and either extended them or incorporated them into his own design. Thomas Rust[324] had not long dissolved his partnership with Henry Hull,[325] which may have been the impetus for expansion.[326] In 1895, the company was embroiled in a scandal about the sale of Jewry Wall (which they owned) to the Manchester Sheffield and Lincolnshire Railway (from 1897 the Great Central) who wished to put their railway through it and there were mutterings of defamation involving clergy at St Nicholas before it was all sorted out.[327] The company disappears from trade directories after 1904 and demolition came some time before 1930 when archaeologists uncovered the Roman baths complex.

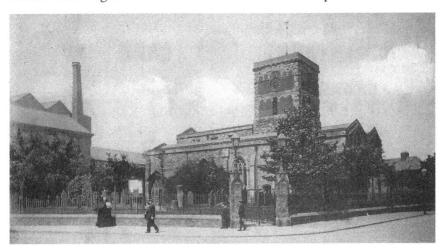

A glimpse of the Rust's mill (left) in this postcard from 1905.

324 Thomas Wills Rust (1805-1871). London born worsted spinner of London Road.
325 Henry Hull (fl.1840s). Hosier of New Walk.
326 *Leicester Chronicle*, 8th July 1848.
327 *Leicester Chronicle*, 20th April and 15th June 1895.

Corn Exchange
Market Place
July 1850
Leicester Corporation
Flint & Wickes
Extant

Leicester Town Council debated the state of the market building at their meeting on 26th June 1850.[328] Councillor Hardy[329] was vociferous in his view that a new one was needed:

> 'What on earth is it kept for? Down it must come, for it [is] the most useless building in Leicester.'

The *Chronicle* reports that the Council agreed to ask Flint to produce a plan of the new Market House, '… to project sixty feet from the Bull's Head, and to hide the buildings behind.'[330]

William Millican's painting of the Exchange Flint was about to replace.

328 *Leicester Mercury*, 29th June 1850.
329 William Hardy (1818-1861). Tailor and woollen draper of Hotel Street and Conservative councillor for St Martin's.
330 *Leicester Chronicle*, 6th July 1850.

The next month, Flint wrote to the council to describe his plan and this was reported *verbatim* in the *Mercury*.[331] These are Flint's own words about one of his buildings and as such are something of a rarity:

"The design consists of a ground floor Market-House, 100ft. long and 52 ft. 6 in. wide within; the area being 5250 ft. divided into three parallel avenues, each 17 ½ ft. in width, having separate entrances from the Market-place at the ends, and a transverse communication with the centre of the front. The external height 35 ft. from the pavement of the Market-place to the top of the general parapet, or as high as the chimney of the adjoining houses... The roof is a triple one, supported by twelve light cast-iron columns, in two rows, and glazed on the eastern slope of each... The basement or vaults to be constructed under the whole area of the Market-house... The total area of the vaults would be about 5000 ft.

Specification. – *The walls of the building to be constructed of brick-work, stucco, and cement, with stone copings, window-sills, strings, steps to the Market and kerbs, and jointed and coloured internally. The paving of the Market-house to be of stone. The roof to be wrought, and the glass of the three eastern slopes therein to be cast-plate about 3/8 in. thick*"

Flint's original but short-lived Corn Exchange. It has a strong similarity to the original Post Office.

---

331 *Leicester Mercury*, 10th August 1850.

A contemporary engraving shows that it was a curious-looking building. It had plenty of windows and the architraves were more ornate than usual for Flint with a trio each side of the door alternating triangular and segmental pediments. The top of the building finished in a parapet surmounted by Grecian urns interspersed with six blind panels and, above the doorway, two columns either side of a clock with a larger urn on each. The clock was evidently a finishing touch as a letter dated 3rd February 1851[332] survives from Flint to clockmaker, Edward Loseby.[333] It asks for a tender for a two dial clock, one internal and one external and explains that it could be an adaptation of the old one or a new one. Flint informs him that he is also writing to other resident clockmakers.

On 27th January 1851, Charles Wickes gave a lecture (*'The Romance of the Arts'*) to the Leicester Literary and Philosophical Society. In the society's centenary book,[334] an interesting conversation about the Exchange is recorded:

Frederick Ordish's redesigned Corn Exchange in about 1900.

---

332 LRO MISC 52.

333 Edward Loseby (1785-1867). Hotel Street watch and clockmaker, silversmith and jeweller.

334 *Centenary Book of the Leicester Literary and Philosophical* Society (Lott, F.B., 1935) p.56

The Corn Exchange today.

'Dr. Barclay[335] referred to the bad style in which Mr. Wickes was building the new Market House, and thought it was a disgrace to Leicester, that it could not afford something better than stucco. Mr. Wickes explained that he was not responsible for the Market House. He was told to work up a large quantity of old material, as it was only a place for selling butter and eggs.'

Evidently, it was not a popular building and as quickly as 1855, it had been significantly altered by Frederick Ordish[336] who added not only a second floor but a very unusual external staircase. This wasn't particularly popular either and it took until well into the twentieth century before it was appreciated. The sheer size of the windows is still surprising in its boldness.

Grade 2★ listed in 1950, the building, by now long since a pub, became the focal point of the Leicester City's Market Place Conservation Area in 1974. It is still a pub and is now at the centre of the Council's "Market Masterplan", which plans to open up the space around the Market Place.

Warehouse alterations
Free Lane
October 1850

---

335 Dr. John Barclay (1823-1877). Physician of Friar Lane.
336 Frederick Webster Ordish (1821-1885). Architect of Bank Buildings on Gallowtree Gate in partnership with J. C. Traylen. He was crushed to death by a train at Syston Station – see *Leicester Chronicle*, 26th September 1885.

Thomas Johnson
Flint & Wickes
Demolished

Situated near the Congregationalist Chapel, this warehouse was used by Thomas Johnson[337] to supply his business on Gallowtree Gate to which he came in late 1850 from Cheapside. Somehow he managed to combine a furnishing business with work as an agricultural ironmonger and, in 1848, the sale of Peruvian guano![338] Although it is possible that Flint built the whole building, the plans look much more like the job was to carry out alterations for drainage and to create a basement.[339] Flint had several contracts similar to this and the plans carry a reminder about how drainage and sewerage were becoming safer and better organised:

> "Drainage, The blue lines CC to shew 6 inch tubular drains, D a 9 inch ditto, to be continued to the Public Sewer, EE trapped Gratings. The basement will not require drainage, or be drained into a cesspool beneath its floor. The Privy to have a vault beneath it built proof to contain excreta only. The Dusthole to be for the reception of dust and be covered, and both paces to be Ventilated."

The building itself had a covered passageway and at the rear some gardens. There are no signs of the warehouse ever having existed now.

Museum Square
5 Houses
November 1850
Thomas Swain
Flint & Wickes
Extant

Plans for developing the field on the north side of the Museum field were considered by the council in February 1850:

---

337 Thomas Johnson (1803-1877). Furnisher and ironmonger of Lansdowne House, Highfield Street and later to become a photographer.
338 *Leicester Journal*, 31st March 1848.
339 LRO 1850/94.

'... that a part of the ground next Victoria-place, New Walk, fronting the north side of the Museum field, be offered for sale in five lots for the erection of five houses – [built according to the admirable elevation by Mr. Flint] – worth from £35 to £40 a year; that, as they would not be prepared for some weeks to make any recommendation as to the mode in which to lay out part of the Course and adjoining land for building, the Race Course should be allowed for the Races and Cavalry exercise this year...'[340]

There followed a great debate about horseracing and fairs, but Flint was not overlooked:

'...Mr. Macaulay said he hoped that the parties purchasing the land would be bound by Mr. Flint's plans, so that they might have some uniformity of architecture – a matter in which this town is notoriously deficient. (Hear).'

The sale of the land was conducted on the Thursday evening before the Saturday edition of the *Mercury* which reports that Mr Swain[341] bought the

Thomas Swain's houses in their guise as 'The Hydro' in the 1920s.

340 *Leicester Mercury*, 16th February 1850.
341 Thomas Swain (1820-1858) Sanvey Gate builder who died in mysterious circumstances in London under an assumed name hours after signing his will – see *Leicester Journal* 2nd April 1858.

whole plot for 9s a yard.[342] The following week's edition reveals that a condition of sale (along with other 'special conditions') was that Flint's designs had to be used and that the site was 1765 square yards in size.[343] Formal plans were given approval in November 1850.[344]

These are stylish houses of three storeys and cellars. They are unfussy and elegant, built of grey gault brick with some use of stucco, in this case the rusticated dressings and the architraves. Early residents were Charles Baker's family. The middle three (1-3 Museum Square) face the museum and the two on each side built at right angles to the rest front Princess Road (number 38) and New Walk (number 47) respectively. The end houses do not quite match as the New Walk facing house has four windows not three as with the Princess Road house. The whole row is grade 2 listed and is owned by Leicester City Council and was converted to commercial rather than residential use in the last part of the twentieth century. However, the twenty-first century will likely see a return to domestic occupation

Museum Terrace today, in business use but ripe for returning to domestic use.

---

342 *Leicester Mercury* 16th March 1850
343 *Leicester Mercury*, 23rd March 1850.
344 LRO 1850/46.

Warehouse
Rutland Street
February 1851
John Corah
Flint & Wickes
Demolished

Flint and Wickes built two separate but joined hosiery warehouses for John Corah[345] in 1851 in Rutland Street. They faced onto Rutland Street with a parlour (and washing place) on the side next to Charles Willey's[346] warehouse. This substantial building was at least two storeys high and only had four water closets: three on the ground floor and one on the first. The plans show that the kerb (or boundary line of the street, as it was described) was re-sited by about four feet to allow for the building's area gratings.[347] What happened to the building and precisely where it was sited is unknown.

Warehouse
Newark Street and Pocklington's Walk
Robert Warner
1851 and October 1855
Flint & Wickes and Flint & Shenton
Demolished

The plans for the 1851 work seem to have only partially survived. There is no record of their approval either, but this may be due to their incomplete status. The plans show:

> *'The site of the intended Buildings is now covered by Buildings. It is proposed to Drain the Basement by a Cesspool sunk to the Springs, into which the pure water beneath the Floor and none other will be conducted. The other drainage to remain as it is.'*[348]

---

345 John Corah (1805-1870). Hosier of Highfields.
346 *Probably* Charles Joseph Willey (1830-1897), grocer, tea dealer and cheese factor with a shop on Granby Street, later of Edinburgh.
347 LRO 1851/126.
348 LRO 1851/129.

Robert Warner[349] of Robert Warner and Co was a hosiery manufacturer and his works were on the corner of Newark Street and Pocklington's Walk.

Flint and Shenton were engaged in 1855 to make additions to the factory by adding male and female water closets; to add drains and erect an eighty feet steam chimney. These plans show what Flint and Wickes must have built in 1851 and reveal an engine house with a boiler room beneath it; a press room and a factory; all led to from a gateway onto Pocklington's Walk. They were demolished in the late 1980s.

King's Norton Church
Restoration of spire
May 1851
Flint & Wickes
Extant

St John the Baptist Church was built in Ketton stone around 1760 by John Wing at a cost of £20,000 in the Neo-Gothic style and this is the second tower repair to one of his churches undertaken by Flint. Wing added the spire in 1775 and it was this that was destroyed by lightning in 13th May 1850 at about half past five in the afternoon. The tower and roof were badly damaged and the font and organ destroyed. The edition of the *Leicester Mercury* accords events a rare illustration by W. F. Miller[350] and carries a description, in the form of a letter by J. F. Hollings, of the '... *course of the electric fluid and entering the details*

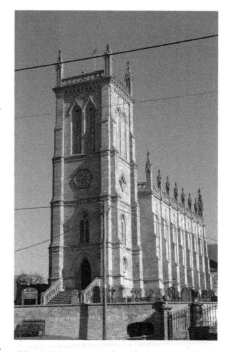

King's Norton: another (but more striking) church tower repair.

---

349 Robert Warner (1817-1856). Hosiery manufacturer.
350 William Frederick Miller (1815-1868) Artist of Asylum Street.

of its destructive effects'. Adverts appeared inviting tenders from builders, stonemasons and others from 23rd May 1851.[351] It would appear that not enough money was raised to rebuild the spire so, as with Kibworth Beauchamp, only the tower and roof were repaired and stand today as Flint left them.

4 houses
Hastings Street
Mr Blackwell
June 1851
Flint & Wickes
Demolished c. 1975

The Corporation sold a 701 feet square plot of land on Hastings Street to Mr Blackwell[352] at six shillings a yard in March 1851.[353] By June, Flint and Wickes produced plans for four houses backing into the railway line and as the railway line comes in to the city at an angle, the gardens got progressively longer further away from the station. The block of houses had shared steps up to the front doors and shared privy and dust pit buildings at the bottom of the garden. They were two storeys tall and had basements in which the kitchen and scullery were to be found. There was a passage separating the four houses from their neighbour nearest to the station, Mrs Payne-Johnson.[354] The passage led to a path that stretched all the way round the back of the houses, probably as a means of collecting rubbish. The plans have faint pencil markings of a name on each house, presumably these were the first tenants.[355] Nearest Mrs Johnson is 'Shoby' then 'Bishop' and the last two 'Talbot'. Like Mr Blackwell, research has not identified who they are. The plans are indexed with 'Mr Blackwell (Midland Railway)' which suggests that they may have been railway employees' cottages.

---

351 *Leicester Journal*, 23rd May 1851.
352 Mr Blackwell (fl.1850s). Railway contractor.
353 *Leicester Mercury*, 15th March 1851.
354 Frances Johnson (1803-1890) of Princess Street; widow of solicitor Richard Payne Johnson.
355 LRO 1851/166/A/B

Alterations to outbuildings and drainage
Granby Street
Benjamin Brookhouse
July 1851
Flint & Wickes
Demolished

The premises were next to Flint's John Coral's warehouse on Granby Street. Benjamin Brookhouse[356] was a landowner and was also, like Flint, a committee member of the General News Room. The job included creating a new gateway from the buildings into Rutland Street as well as the construction of drains and toilets. The plans show that the building was on the corner of Granby Street, roughly where the former Duke of Wellington Hotel is situated. His son advertised the sale of the buildings in 1858 and used Flint and Shenton to deal with the sale.[357]

2 Cottages
St Nicholas Square
July 1851
Rev. Clarke
Flint & Wickes
Demolished c. 1970

St Nicholas Square was a continuation of High Street via St Nicholas Street and is now lost under the A47 by the Holiday Inn. The plans for these two buildings for Rev. Clarke[358] were approved on 9th July 1851 and they describe the buildings as cottages, but the *Leicester Mercury* report on 16th August called them 'tenements'. They appear to be more traditional cottages from the plan. The work involved demolition of existing buildings: '*There are two area gratings in the buildings to be taken down which will be replaced*'.[359] The cottages were asymmetrical with one having a garden and the other not. They also had cellars. The right hand one (which had a garden) backed onto Thomas Rusts's worsted warehouse and factory. They were probably lost at

---

356 Benjamin Brookhouse (1771-1853). Landowner.
357 *Leicester Chronicle*, 25th December 1858.
358 Rev. Clarke (fl.1851).
359 LRO 1851/191.

the time the Holiday Inn was built, but this is not certain and neither is the identity of the clerical gentleman who caused them to be built.

Warehouse and additions
King Street
Robert Overton
September 1851
Flint & Wickes
Demolished

Leicester's hosiery trade was enjoying something of a boom in the early 1850s and this is reflected in the number of additional warehouses built and enlargements Flint and Wickes carried out. This one, for Robert Overton,[360] was on the street where Flint lived for nearly thirty years. A three-storey extension was to be built as well as four side buildings: coal house; frame house; harness house and coach house. He also added several privies, a dust pit and a dung pit. Overton later took Joseph Marlow[361] into partnership and the firm became Overton and Marlow, but it does not seem to have outlasted Marlow's death. The business was located on the site of St Martin's House, a large block of student accommodation opposite Leicester City Council's Pilot House.

Factory and warehouse, drainage and alterations
Marble Street and Newarke Street
May 1852, February 1855 and 1859
Charles Billson
Flint & Wickes and Flint & Shenton
Partially extant

The first surviving plan for Charles Billson's[362] factory dates to May 1852 and concerns substantial alterations and new drainage to an existing

---

360 Robert Overton (1792-1871). Hosier of de Montfort Square and later Elmsleigh.
361 Joseph William Marlow (1840-1880). Hosier of West Street.
362 Charles Billson (1805-1878). Hosiery manufacturer, sometime town councillor.

The Billson warehouse in 1988 shortly before demolition.

factory complex.[363] A new factory with a frontage to Marble Street was built with a new warehouse directly behind it. This was on the corner of the road nearest to the Magazine. The next set of plans is for October 1852 and concerns ventilation to the areas.[364] The original building may have been of Flint's design but, as with the Harris factory on King Street, it is not possible to state this without doubt.

Flint returned with Shenton in 1855 for work to put in a series of drains to the Newarke Street sewer and add a thirteen feet storey to a warehouse as well as construct a new warehouse and glass roof cover. Evidently a modern building, plans clearly show that there are indoor water closets on each floor![365]

The firm's last visit was in 1859 when the Marble Street factory and warehouse look as though they were enlarged to three and four floors (with basements) respectively. The main factory fronting to Newarke Street seems to have been enlarged at the same time gaining a new work room and water closet area. Drains were also put in throughout.[366]

363 LRO 1852/302.

364 LRO 1852/370.

365 LRO 1855/658.

366 LRO 1859/1127. The index does not record them as by Flint, but the plans do.

The 1859 Billson extension still exists as a printing company in Marble Street.

There is some confusion as to the commission's patron. Each plan records Charles Billson as the owner of the building or, at least, client. However, also on Newarke Street (but not Marble Street) was Billson and Hames,[367] a hosiery firm, formerly of Duns Lane. This does not appear to be the same firm as Charles Billson, who was on Newarke Street from at least 1843, but it must presumably have a connection.

The factory complex was auctioned at the Wellington Hotel in 1873 in two lots. The first comprised a range of warehouses in Newarke Street with ale stores underneath, which had been occupied by Billson until his eventual business difficulties left him bankrupt that year, and also Walter Whitmore,[368] with some of it untenanted. The second lot was for a three-storey warehouse fronting Newarke and Marble Streets occupied by J. S. Rice and Co,[369] and also a three-storey factory with yard and outbuildings fronting Marble Street and occupied by Messrs. Toone and Partridge.[370]

367 Joseph Hames Sr (1800-1879) of Rotherby Hall, hosier of Billson and Hames in Newark Street.
368 Walter Whitmore (1839-1889). Yarn merchant of New Walk.
369 Jabez Strickland Rice (1825-1877). Hosier of Upland Terrace, de Montfort Street.
370 Frederick Toone (1848-1880) and James Partridge (1822-1883). Hosiers in partnership until 1878.

Grosvenor House, a large block of student flats, occupies most of the site, however a narrow three-storey warehouse building facing Marble Street still exists and is in the occupation of a printing company.

6 Houses
New Walk
June 1852
Joseph Hames
Flint & Wickes
Extant

Numbered 7-17 New Walk (with number seven nearest King Street), this terrace of six three-storey houses still exists. It was built for Joseph Hames (see above) in 1852 and, after some years as business premises, the houses have now returned to domestic use and are at the higher end of the house market once again, just as they were when they were built. Rendered in brick without the use of stucco, the architraves are heavy and match the arched doorways and rustication. There is no adornment save for two string courses between the floors, a few elegant empty cartouches

6 houses for Joseph Hames: typical of rapidly aggrandising New Walk in the 1850s.

on the ground floor under the windows and a portico in the middle of the row. Vehicular access is via a carriageway behind Princess Road. They are similar to the houses for Thomas Swain two years previously. The plans are held at the Record Office but are damaged with the part usually identifying Flint missing, however they bear all the hallmarks of a Flint and Wickes design and obviously so.[371]

3 Houses
Asylum Street
Mr. Brown
September 1852
Flint & Wickes
Demolished c. 1960

Plans were given approval for these three stucco terraced houses on 15th September 1852[372] and they bear a strong similarity to Flint's 1836 Crescent Cottages on King Street, most obviously sharing lugged architraves, blind panels and columns. They were built at an angle to follow the street and seemed to share one privy between them. They were demolished sometime after 1957. The area is now called Gateway Street and forms part of the de Montfort University campus. With such a common surname, it has proved impossible to pinpoint Mr Brown.

Unmistakeable Flint commissions for Mr. Brown. They were demolished in the 1950s.

---

371 LRO 1852/316.
372 Plan LRO 1852/358.

4 houses
Midland Street
John Carrington
September 1852
Flint & WIckes
Demolished late 1960s

The plans for this job indicate that only one house would be built at the time of submission but that the other three were also given permission.[373] The houses followed the same pattern as many of his other commissions; they were built in pairs separated by a common passageway and had two storeys and a basement with attached scullery. What makes these houses unusual is that the scullery building had two floors and a flat roof. The dust pit and privy were attached to the scullery building. The houses fronted Midland Street and were bordered by properties owned by Mr Jones[374] on the right, Mr Nichols[375] behind and Mr Towndrow[376] to the left. John Carrington[377] was a painter of Millstone Lane and probably gave his name to Carrington Street; George Nichols is a likely contender for the name of Nichols Street. Midland Street still exists in the St George's area and runs into Nichols Street by the Phoenix Theatre complex. There is little for the modern visitor to see from Flint's era of its history. Whether the three houses were eventually built is uncertain as a reasonably contemporary Ordnance Survey map does not show the configuration of the plans as submitted. Demolition came to the area in the late 1960s.

Public house alterations
Marquis of Granby Inn
London Road
Leicester Corporation
December 1852

---

373 LRO 1852/356.
374 William Jones (c.1799-?). Builder of Midland Street.
375 George Nichols (1812-1892). Variously architect, washing blue maker and sanitary clerk of Humberstone Road, later Norfolk Street.
376 William Towndrow (1775-1850). Gentleman of Regent Street.
377 John Carrington (1805-1866), painter and gilder.

Flint & Wickes
Demolished

An advert looking for building tenders in the *Leicester Journal* and minutes from the Corporation's Estates Committee reveal that Flint and Wickes had a commission at this establishment in 1852.[378] It was for alterations and enlargements. The Marquis of Granby Toll bar stood at the Southern Edge of Victoria Park and the public house from which it took its name was nearby. It replaced the London Road toll bar by the Marquis of Wellington public house in 1851. It is popularly recounted that the Marquis of Granby[379] has more public houses named after him than any other person on account of his setting up his old soldiers as landlords. Dr Helen Boynton puts the pub's location where Granby House stands, just before the Park Hotel and on the same side.[380] It is unclear when it was demolished, but Samuel Harris won the contract to demolish the five houses at the back of the Inn at the same time as demolishing the toll bar in 1853.[381]

The Marquis of Granby, another Corporation property that Flint worked on.

378 *Leicester Mercury*, 25th December 1852.
379 John Manners, Marquis of Granby (1721-1770). British soldier and commanding officer during the Seven Years War.
380 *The Changing face of London Road* (Boynton, 2001).
381 Estates Committee minutes, 30th May 1853.

Trinity Church
Regent Street (Road)
February 1853
Flint & Wickes
Extant

Trinity Church was designed by Sydney Smirke[382] and opened in 1838 as the church for the newly created parish of Holy Trinity, formerly part of St Margaret's. It was a simple design and complemented the houses in Upper King Street, one of which became its vicarage.

In 1853, Flint and Wickes were contracted to carry out improvement works '... *for the better ventilation and accommodation... which has for some time been generally acknowledged'.*[383] Charles Frewen Turner[384] was fittingly patron for the improvement scheme which created 230 additional seats and he contributed £500 himself for the work and also purchased the land for the enlargement. It

Holy Trinity Church. Leicester.

Teulon's rebuilt Holy Trinity Church at the turn of the Twentieth Century and quite at odds with Smirke and Flint's work.

was Frewen-Turner whose largesse had built the church in 1838. William Neale was appointed contractor and the church evidently closed whilst the work was carried out; re-opening with a variety of visiting preachers on 28th September the same year.[385] A simple affair was planned:

---

382 Sydney Smirke (1798-1877), architect of the Carlton Club in London.
383 *Leicester Chronicle*, 12th February 1853.
384 Charles Hay Frewen-Turner (1813-1878) of Cold Overton Hall. Staunchly protestant conservative MP for East Sussex and Leicestershire landowner and magistrate.
385 *Leicester Journal*, 30th September 1853.

'The promotors of the enlargement of this edifice have declared, that it is their deliberate intention to avoid all unnecessary and symbolical decorations, and to combine simplicity with efficiency, in the enlargement and improvement'.[386]

Flint was ideal for this work as this is very much in accordance with his style of design.

The church acquired the 'Holy' part of its name in about 1878.[387] The church was extensively 'vociferously' (Pevsner) remodelled by S. S. Teulon[388] in 1872 and further remodelled in 1901 and then the 1960s. As a consequence, it is difficult to disentangle Smirke or Flint's work, but that notwithstanding it remains one of the most interesting examples of Gothic Revival architecture in the region.

Warehouse
Newarke Street
March 1853 and June 1858
Frisby Chawner
Flint & Wickes and Flint & Shenton
Demolished

The first commission was for a three-storey warehouse. The first floor was eleven feet eight inches high; the second nine feet nine inches and the third three inches less than the second. There was also a basement. Frisby[389] and Chawner[390] were already operating as hosiers from this Newarke Street address and the plans are clear in recording that there would be no need to alter drainage and that the new eaves cornice will still

386 *Leicester Chronicle*, 12th February 1853.
387 *Holy Trinity and its surroundings 1838 – 1966* (Anon, 1966).
388 Samuel Sanders Teulon (1812-1873), described by Pevsner in his 'Leicestershire and Rutland' as: "… that most assertive and roguish architect of his generation".
389 William Smith Frisby (1822-1882). Leicester hosier and sometime Overseer of St Mary's.
390 John Chawner (1807-1874). Leicester hosier.

be within the existing boundary line.[391] In 1858 Flint returned, this time with Shenton, to put in to the basement of his 1853 warehouse a male and female toilet complex complete with lobby, urinal and area.[392] By this time the company had lost Frisby and become Chawner and Co. There was no access to Newarke Street from the premises and entrance was gained by a gateway to the rear of the property. It is unknown when the factory was demolished.

As a sole trader

The partnership with Wickes was dissolved in June 1853. Was Flint suspicious of his partner's probity? We will never know but, for the next few months, Flint practised alone.

Warehouse
Pocklington's Walk
August 1853
Joseph Whitmore
Demolished

This was a simple two-storey warehouse with a basement. It was accessed via Messrs. Nall and Co.'s yard on Pocklington's Walk.[393] Plans were given approval on 24th August 1853 on condition that a sewer was made within 100 feet of the premises.[394] Joseph Whitmore[395] was a woolstapler and was the elder brother of John Whitmore; his business did not prosper and went bankrupt almost immediately. In 1854 began a series of auctions for the warehouse itself and then its contents and finally his other assets with an auction to raise money for his creditors held at the premises. Mr

---

391 LRO 1853/419.
392 LRO 1858/1035.
393 James Nall (1808-1894), lithographer, printer and engraver whose Queen Street company went out of business in 1854.
394 LRO 1853/495.
395 Joseph Whitmore (1798-1855). Wool stapler and owner of the Black Bull Inn, Applegate Street.

Cooke[396] of Friar Lane conducted a sale of most of Whitmore's assets in November 1854 including the warehouse:

> 'Lot 1 All that newly and very substantially-erected WAREHOUSE, three storeys high, fronting to the Pocklington's-walk, in the Parish of St. Margaret, Leicester, together with the yard and buildings behind the same, now or late in the occupation of Messrs. Nall and Co.' [397]

It is not known when it was demolished.

2 Houses
Regent Street (Road)
August 1853
Nathan Westerman
Demolished c. 1965

These two fine houses resemble several that Flint designed in the 1850s. Nathan Westerman[398] was a wool spinner and he is typical of the new middle class who could afford an architect to build substantial houses for them; in this case as houses to let out as, although Westerman lived in Regent Road, he did not live in either of these houses.

The building consisted of a pair of semi-detached villas. They had a garden at the front and shared a hallway and entrance. Downstairs was a dining room, kitchen, parlour, best closet, pantry and scullery. Outside was a dust pit and privy situated in a walled yard. There was also a shared garden at the back. They had three floors and a cellar.[399]

They were situated on the same side of the road as the former Fielding-Johnson Hospital, but after the railway bridge and probably next to John Flower's House. Flint was a near neighbour and Shenton would also live a few doors away in the 1870s.

---

396 James Cooke (1802-?). Leicester auctioneer and brickmaker of Friar Lane and Welford Road living in Rutland Street, later in partnership with Robert Warner, auctioneer.

397 *Leicester Mercury*, 4th November 1854.

398 Nathan Westerman (1799-1863). Wakefield born lambswool spinner with premises on Millstone Lane.

399 LRO plans 1853/486.

A probable glimpse of Nathan Westerman's pair of three storey houses on Regent Road.

They passed out of the family as shown by the auction held under the terms of Nathan Westerman's will in 1896 and by then they were numbered 92 and 94 Regent Road.[400] After that, they survived until the 1960s when they were demolished.

Palisade fence
de Montfort Square
Leicester Corporation
September 1853
Demolished

The council required a palisade fence to bound the road in de Montfort Square and Flint, operating in between his partnerships, held the contract to design it. His advert for iron founders and smiths went to the press in September 1853.[401] The fence probably went the way of most metal municipal furniture and went for scrap during the First or Second World War.

---

400 *Leicester Chronicle*, 28th March 1896.
401 *Leicester Chronicle*, 10th September 1853.

Warehouse
Wellington Street
Ward and Sons
September 1853
Extant

Daniel Ward[402] and Sons were a firm of printers and the warehouse was at number 6, next to Flint's library. It has three floors (the ground and first floor 11 feet nine inches high and the second floor an inch taller) and a basement. Externally, it is a clean and bright building and, as to be expected with Flint, has little ornamentation. The ground floor has until recently been obscured by signage, but the next two floors retain their original look and the cornices to the hipped roof are very attractive. Ward and Sons moved out by 1867, although they retained premises at 13, Wellington Street, and the building was divided and used by a variety of mainly hosiery firms such as Pollard and Pochin,[403] who left around

Ward and Sons' 1853 commission and a building that has seen many uses from a Curry's warehouse to Adult Education.

---

402 Daniel Ward (1810-1867). Printer of Seymour Street.
403 Fancy hosiery manufacturers William Gamble Pollard (1834-1918) of Oak House, Queniborough and Ivanhoe, Knighton Park Road and John Pochin (1839-1913). For obituary see *Leicester Chronicle*, 19th April 1913.

1891 or A. E. Adams,[404] who were there for fifty years or so. It was also briefly a warehouse for Curry's electrical retailers after the War. The Adult Education Service moved in from about 1960 and they have already celebrated their fiftieth anniversary as tenants. Incidentally, the third floor of the building still houses a printing business. The building is a little-known Flint survival and deserves better recognition.

---

404 Andrew Elworthy Adams (1846-1902) of the Leicestershire Club and also Narborough, hosiery manufacturer.

CHAPTER 8

The Partners: Henry Shenton

Henry Shenton was born on 4th April 1824, the son of Joshua Shenton[405] and Elizabeth Richards.[406] He was one of at least six children and the family lived in London Road. His father was a businessman and was in partnership with

George Legge: Shenton's stepfather and minister of Gallowtree Gate Chapel.

James Pickering[407] as a carrier, but it is likely he had other business projects, including a wine and spirit business in Humberstone Road. It is difficult to be certain as there are several Joshua Shentons trading in Leicester at the time, although he is certainly the same Joshua Shenton who advertised the sale of a grocer and tea dealer's business in 1832[408] and he also seems to have been a cement dealer. The family probably lived on New Walk prior to London Road and William Flint handled the sale of their property in 1831.[409] Joshua died on 27th August 1833 in Hastings and his widow remarried the Rev George Legge,[410] independent minister of Gallowtree Gate Chapel in 1838.

---

405 Joshua Shenton (c. 1794-1833) of London Road.

406 Elizabeth Shenton (1789-1855), daughter of Alderman Richards.

407 James Pickering (1806-1860). Carrier of Humberstone Road and sometime councillor for Middle St Margaret's. Left Leicester for Cheshire in 1837.

408 *Leicester Journal*, 9th March 1832.

409 *Leicester Journal*, 11th March 1831.

410 Rev George Legge LLD (1802-1861). Scottish born Congregationalist minister. For obituary see *Leicester Chronicle*, 2nd February 1861.

Pre-Flint

Henry Shenton was a pupil of D. R. Hill,[411] a public works architect of Birmingham. During his time there, he met and married Sarah Matthews Britain of Vyse Street in Birmingham at Carr's Lane Congregationalist Chapel on 21st June 1848.[412] They had two children: Ellen[413] and Annie.[414] Both married well by the standards of the day: Annie became the second wife of Walter Glynn,[415] a Liverpool shipping magnate, while Ellen married John Dove Harris Jr.,[416] grandson of the Leicester hosier Richard Harris whose King Street factory Flint designed and which he and Shenton would later enlarge.

Shenton's pre-Flint architectural practice does not appear to be extensive. He handled the sale of grazing land near the Willow Bridge in 1849 and there was a bigger auction in 1852 for properties in Archdeacon Lane and Thames and Navigation Streets. He also worked with Flint in 1853 representing St Margaret's Vestry in a valuation dispute.[417] As for building, one commission has been identified for '...*the erection of a house and offices in the Parish of Knighton...*',[418] but research has not unearthed any further details. It is probable that he spent his time conducting valuations and surveys to make a living.

In Partnership

Shenton entered into partnership with William Flint in early 1854, Flint's partnership with Charles Wickes being dissolved in the June of 1853. An

---

411 Daniel Rowlinson Hill (1810-1857). Birmingham Borough Architect notable for several prisons e.g. Birmingham, Lewes and Wandsworth. For obituary see Coventry Herald, 8th May 1857.
412 *Leicester Journal*, 23rd June 1848.
413 Ellen Aycliffe Shenton (1853-1885).
414 Annie Louisa Shenton (1858-1920),
415 Walter Glynn (1837-1905); owner of John Glynn and Sons and managing director of Leyland Lines. For obituary see Manchester Courier, 4th March 1905.
416 John Dove Harris Jr. (1838-1915). Hosiery manufacturer, later of Bosavern House, St Just, Cornwall.
417 *Leicester Mercury*, 28th May 1853.
418 *Leicester Mercury*, 7th February 1852.

early joint enterprise was the Female Infant Orphan Asylum in 1854.

After Flint died in 1862, Shenton carried on the practice, although some of it must have gone with James Frank Smith as he set himself up in business at the same time. Shenton also took Flint's formally informal place as council surveyor[419] (moved by Mr Stafford,[420] seconded by Mr Moxon[421]) and his elected place as surveyor to the Leicester Freehold Land Society:[422]

'A resolution was passed expressing deep regret for the removal by death of the late Mr. Flint, and confirming the appointment of Mr. Henry Shenton as his successor. In supporting the motion, Mr. G. Stevenson[423] spoke in high terms of the valuable services rendered by Mr. Flint from the formation of the society to the period of his decease, and commended his successor as likely to be equally faithful and useful in the position to which he had been appointed.

Mr. Shenton thanked the meeting for the kindness shown him by appointing him surveyor. He could not claim to possess the same amount of experience as Mr. Flint, but could truly say that it should be his earnest endeavour that that the interests of the society should not suffer through being placed in his hands.'

Post-Flint

By early 1863, Charles Baker had joined the business as partner and Shenton and Baker, as the firm became known, were in partnership for 23 years operating, as always, from 18, Friar Lane. The Leicester artist John Fulleylove[424] worked with Shenton for a time in the early 1860s,

419 Common Hall Book, 4th March 1862.

420 John Stafford (1823-1910). Council Alderman and prominent grocer; co-owner of Evans and Stafford.

421 Thomas Moxon (1805-1863). Tailor and woollen draper of High Street and long-serving conservative councillor for St Martin's ward – for obituary see *Leicester Journal*, 9th October 1863.

422 *Leicester Mercury*, 22nd November 1862.

423 George Stevenson (1821-1904). Solicitor and later magistrate of Regent Road.

424 John Fulleylove (1845-1908). Leicester born artist who achieved national recognition.

Shenton and Baker's unsuccessful clock tower design.

when he trained as an architect and may have overlapped briefly with Flint. In 1873, Shenton and Baker took on Albert Sawday[425] as an assistant and his own practice would eventually descend from Flint's via theirs via Baker.

The practice was embroiled in the Clock Tower scandal (see Chapter 14 The Pupils: Isaac Barradale) with their own design which came third. They built the Congregationalist Church in 1865 in Oxford Street, still standing but with the frontage entirely

The interior of what is now the Jain temple on Oxford Street.
Shenton's debt to Flint is obvious.

---

425 Albert Sawday (1851-1923). Devon-born Leicester architect, councillor and sometime mayor, later in partnership with Albert Herbert.

Pickard's worsted spinning mill on Oxford Street in 1977.

transformed with marble and now a Jain temple. Also on Oxford Street is a decorative archway to another commission, for James Pickard's[426] lambswool spinning business. Another church was the Emmanuel Baptist church in New Park and Leamington Streets in 1871 with its unusual octagonal lantern roof (it was demolished after the almost inevitable arson attack in 1978). Shenton also worked on alterations to the Great Meeting in East Bond Street in 1865 and his lovely colour illustrations still exist at the Leicestershire Record Office, perhaps revealing him as something of an artist.[427]

The retained decorative archway from the Oxford Street Pickard mill.

426 James Eastwood Pickard (1815-1894) of The Elms. Lambswool yarn spinner and sometime Liberal town councillor for All Saints.
427 LRO N/U/179/98/5.

Emmanuel Baptist Church in the 1970s after de-consecration and not far from arson and inevitable demolition.

Shenton's greatest work is probably the Water Board offices on Bowling Green Street. This is the earliest example of what became unofficially known as 'Municipal Gothic' and it remains an impressive edifice with much of its original railing and carving to the wooden doors still in place. A similar gothic work is the bootmakers' factory and shop at 74, Granby Street for William Bruin[428] and Sons in 1873. Named Balmoral House, the building is an example of the single factory business with retail premises for its wares at ground floor level. They undertook domestic

Shenton and Baker's Municipal Gothic water Board Offices in Bowling Green Street.

428 William John Bruin (1833-1920), bootmaker of de Montfort Street.

Shenton and Baker's Museum extension is in a totally different style to Hansom's original.

Bruin's workshop and retail premises on Granby Street.

work too, for example a pair of three-storey gabled houses (now 2-4) in New Walk in 1878.

Shenton and Baker added the grey brick Italianate wing with tower to the Museum in 1876 (in 1891, Baker would add more and Baker's future successor Albert Herbert would add, extend and alter the site in 1909). The relocated Gas Works on Aylestone Road was another large and prestigious work in 1878-9. A row of three-storeyed half-timber gabled cottages (known as Gas Works Cottages) of red brick and blue dressings with a manager's house, gate house and incorporated clocktower, the site still exists and houses

An ambitious undertaking for the Gas Board in Aylestone Road.

the National Gas Museum. The firm were also responsible for several substantial industrial sites, for example the St Leonard's Works worsted mill at Frog Island for W. Thompson and Sons[429], erected in 1867 and then extended in 1881. Here there is a strong legacy from Flint with its imposing Italianate palazzo style – a clear descendant of Flint's Ellis and Whitmore worsted Mill of 1848. From 1922 it was occupied by Frisby, Jarvis and Co. and much of the building was destroyed by fire in 2005. Its burnt-out shell still survives: thanks to the Victorian Society, it had been listed in 2003, but this was no protection. For Wale and Sons[430] in 1871, the partners erected the still extant (but changed into flats) four-storey hosiery warehouse in Lower Brown Street.

The partners went into road building in 1864 and laid out several new streets off Humberstone Road viz: Sheldon, Albert (now Alberta) and Cradock Streets. For the Leicester Freehold Land Society, the firm was responsible for surveying their Ninth Estate again in the Humberstone Road area in 1869 and the next decade saw several commissions to lay out new streets. In 1870, they extended Leamington, Dane and New Parks Streets for Richard Harris and the same year they laid out St James Road and St James Terrace off London Road. The end of the decade saw much more work for building new streets. The Clarendon Park Company, one owner of which was Samuel Stone, was created in 1877 and owned almost all of the land in what is now known as Clarendon Park. Shenton and Baker were responsible for creating the Montague Road and Queens Road Extension in 1879 with St Leonard's, Howard and Cecil (now Cecilia) Roads following in 1881. Meanwhile in 1878, the firm was busy with the Leicester Freehold Land Society's Twelfth Estate in Avenue Road Extension, Queens Road and Lorne Road.

The practice benefitted from its pre-Flint work and by (naturally) carrying over business for existing customers. For example: work for Archibald Turner was carried out at his Bow Bridge factory in 1865 and 1868; another shop front was put in for Robin's in the Market Place in 1864; there were several visits to the Whitmore Ellis Factory (1865 for instance); the Harris factory on King Street had more alterations in 1867 and there was also work at Hill Street British school in 1870.

---

429 William Thomas Thompson (1822-1886). Worsted spinner of Ruding Villa, Fosse Road.
430 Henry Wale (1818-1893). Hosier of the Woodlands, Narborough.

A tune from Henry Shenton's book on church singing.

Given the connection via his stepfather, it is highly likely that Shenton was the same Henry Shenton who wrote: *"Congregational Psalmody"*[431] for the Gallowtree Gate Chapel in September 1859. Not only does this book give tunes for hymn singing, it helpfully leaves blank pages for worshippers to add their own words and tunes!

Shenton was a political Liberal and stood for the party for election to the Town Council on 1st November 1865, winning West St Mary's with Charles Harding[432] and defeating George Ellis[433] and William Barfoot.[434] He sat for three years, but retired in 1868, for undisclosed reasons.

In 1879, he was elected Fellow of the Royal Institute of British Architects and was proposed by Joseph Goddard,[435] William Millican and Richard Spiers.[436] His nominations papers give a good précis of his career:

---

431 LRO L285.8.

432 Charles Harding (1825-1878). Councillor, later Alderman for West St Mary's ward and sometime Mayor. Tea dealer of Granby Street.

433 George Henry Ellis (1844-1889) of Southfields Villa, partner in Whitmore Ellis, later town councillor for West St Mary's.

434 William Barfoot (1828-1916). Spinner and woolstapler of Welford Road, Councillor, later Alderman for West St Mary's and sometime Mayor. Partner at T. Rust and Co.

435 Joseph Goddard (1840-1900), third generation of the Goddard architect dynasty and designer of the Clock Tower and Thomas Cook building. For obituary see *Leicester Chronicle* 13th October 1900.

436 Richard Phene Spiers (1838-1916). Eminent and influential architect and teacher.

'Pupil of the late D. R. Hill of Birmingham. Partner of the late William Flint of Leicester from 1854 until the date of his decease in 1862. Now senior member of the firm Shenton and Baker of Leicester. Water works and gas offices. The school of arts and lecture hall. Public and other schools. Chapels. Warehouses and manufactures. Builder of the old and new gas works. Gentlemen's houses and other houses and buildings all in Leicester and the vicinity.' [437]

He would become an enthusiastic proposer to the Institute himself and proposed Albert Sawday to associateship (alongside Millican and Barradale) in 1882, for example. He left Leicester in 1883 and went first to Leamington Spa and then to Liverpool. He died on 9th January 1896 at his home in Rock Ferry, Birkenhead, the funeral took place in Leicester on 23rd January and received coverage in the *Leicester Chronicle* two days later:[438]

'DEATH OF MR. HENRY SHENTON.

The death occurred on Saturday last at Rock Ferry, Birkenhead, of Mr. Henry Shenton, architect formerly of Leicester, and at one time a member of the Town Council. The deceased gentleman was in practice in Leicester, in partnership with Mr. C. Baker, of Friar Lane, until April, 1883, when he retired from the profession. Shortly afterwards, he went to Leamington, where he resided about eight years, and subsequently to Birkenhead. He was elected by the Liberals a member of the Town County for West St Mary's Ward in 1865, and sat until 1868, when he retired, and did not afterwards take an active part in public life. During his short association with the Council, however, he showed considerable ability and aptitude for public work, and he was very generally respected. Deceased was 71 years of age. The remains were brought to Leicester, from Liverpool, on Wednesday morning, and interred at the cemetery. The funeral cortége was met at the cemetery by a considerable number of the deceased gentlemen's friends and former colleagues, including many representatives of the Leicester Society of Architects; of which he was a member.

---

437 RIBA nomination papers F v5 p.146.
438 *Leicester Chronicle*, 25th January 1896.

The mourners were: – Mr. Walter Glynn, of Liverpool (son-in-law); Master Bertie Harris (grandson), and Mr. Charles Baker (late partner). Among others also present were: – Mrs. George Royce, Mr. John Goodacre (President Leicester Society of Architects), Mr. Pick (secretary), Ald. Sawday, Mr. Stockdale Harrison, Mr. Joseph Goddard, Mr. A. H. Paget, Mr. Kempson, Mr. James Tait, Rev. J. Went, Mr. Geo. Stevenson, Mr. Geo. Hodges, Mr. T. Collins, Mr. Roper and Mr. Albert Gimson. The service was conducted by the Rev. C. P. Eden, vicar of Knighton. The coffin bore the inscription, "Henry Shenton, died 19th January, 1896 aged 71 years". Wreathes were sent by the deceased gentleman's "Friends at Richmond House, Rock Ferry", Mr. and Mrs. George H. Hodges, Mr. C. Baker, Mr. Walter Glynn, and the grandchildren, Winifred and Cecil Harris.'

Probate was granted to his widow and also to his friend and former partner Charles Baker; his estate was valued at £4,428 19s. His wife survived him by eight years and died at her daughter's house, Brynhir, in Criccieth on 12th May 1904.

Both he and his wife, as well as one his brothers (Joshua) and one of his sisters (Frances) were re-buried at Welford Road Cemetery when

Henry Shenton's second grave (in Welford Road Cemetery).

Gallowtree Gate Chapel burial ground was demolished in 1921. They lie together with the Rev. Legge and members of his family marked by a tall needle tomb not far from the Harris memorial, where Shenton's daughter Ellen lies. Like Flint, Henry Shenton was commemorated by a street name near Humberstone Road.

Shenton Street was fittingly next to Flint Street.

CHAPTER 9

The Buildings of the 1850s Part 2

Proof gas tanks, sheds, roofs and drains
Gas Street
February 1854, July 1856, December 1858 and March 1860
Flint & Shenton
Demolished

The Leicester Gas Light (later *and Coke*) Company was created in 1821, the same year it lit Leicester's street lamps by gas. It would supply Flint with a decent stream of work in the 1850s and the company's offices were also in Friar Lane. The gas station was in Gas Street, renamed for it in 1821, replacing its original name of Union Wharf Street.

Flint and Shenton did much work at the Gas Works in Gas Street
shown here in the 1960s.

The first contract was to build a proof gas holder tank to contain 240,000 cubic feet and tenders were sought to build this and accompanying sheds in February 1854.[439] In 1856, Flint and Shenton put in culverts at a depth of six feet eight to run into the Borough Sewer on Gas Street. The plans show tanks 1, 2 and 6 and also reveal that there were two houses on the site.[440] In 1858 Flint and Shenton were seeking ironfounders to build the roof of the gas station's new extension with its 57 feet span and a louvre 200 feet long.[441] Finally, in 1860 another brick gas holder tank was required and notice to tenders was published in March of that year.[442] This time, the holder was 133 feet in diameter. The company was wound up in 1878[443] and a new and enormous gas station was built on Aylestone Road. It is still there as are the cottages, gatehouse and adjacent clock tower which Shenton and Baker would build the same year.

Gas Street still exists and runs between Vaughan Way and the canal. A few walls remain from the time, but Flint's main work is long gone. The site was still used as a gas works in the 1960s and was probably cleared along with the last of the area's houses the same decade.

4 Houses
Regent Street and Lower Hastings Street
August 1854
Thomas Swain
Flint & Shenton
Demolished c. 1975

This is undoubtedly a Flint and Shenton design and has often been overlooked as the existing plan[444] is missing its bottom right corner where the partners' details are nearly always recorded.

The four houses were situated at the corner of Regent Road and Lower Hastings Street and backed on to the railway line; the site now totally obliterated by Tigers Way. The first house was a double-frontaged

---

439 *Leicester Chronicle*, 25th February 1854.
440 LRO 1856/828.
441 *Leicester Journal*, 3rd December 1858.
442 *Leicester Mercury*, 3rd March 1860.
443 Like the Waterworks Company, it was later taken over by the Corporation.
444 LRO 1860/601.

Shown in 1973 just before demolition, these houses were demolished for Tigers Way.

dwelling on Regent Road at right angles to the next three and with four large rooms downstairs. The three houses in Lower Hastings Street formed a small terrace and were simpler having only two main rooms downstairs. Each had a garden running down to the railway line.

They reflected Flint's taste in that they were unadorned, without stucco and had a string course, unfussy architraves and no more.

24 houses
16 on Mowbray Street and 8 on Infirmary Square
Henry Mowbray
September and December 1854
Flint & Shenton
Demolished 1957

These houses really do represent 'lost' Leicester. There is no trace of Mowbray Street as it is now submerged under the Royal Infirmary. Similarly, although Infirmary Square exists in name, its houses have vanished. There is a public toilet and some benches and nothing else.

The 16 terraced houses on Mowbray Street came first and they have two storeys and a basement. There was an attached scullery built on the back and a yard gave way to a shared dust pit and toilet for each pair of houses. Each pair was separated by a narrow (three feet) passage. Approval for them was given in September 1854.[445] On the opposite side of the road to the 16 houses, the eight 1855 houses are at right angles to Mowbray Street, fronting Infirmary Square. On the 1885 Ordnance Survey map the houses are known as Rutland Terrace. The two developments are similar but not the same. The later terrace (approved in December 1854)[446] has a set of steps up to the front door and the total height is 6 inches shorter than the 1854 houses. The privies faced away from the houses and were reached after the dust pits.

Henry Mowbray is described in 1861 census as '*Gentleman and proprietor of houses*' and he is living at 2, Mowbray Street but he had been a painter who Flint used on various jobs. The row is occupied by the new upper working class with prison wardens, a police constable, a tailor, and several bookkeepers. Mowbray had made his money as a painter and would use Flint again in 1855 for more houses.

Infant Orphan Asylum
Fosse Road Central
September 1854
Flint & Shenton
Demolished c. 1971

Flint and Shenton had only recently gone into partnership when their plans for an orphanage in Dane Hills were approved on 12th September 1854.[447] The land belonged to William Stretton. The foundation stone was laid amid much ceremony, as the *Leicester Journal* describes:[448]

'INFANT ORPHAN ASYLUM

LAYING THE FOUNDATION STONE OF THE NEW BUILDING.

The committee of the Leicester infant Orphan Asylum having determined to erect a building suitable to the objects of the

---

445 LRO 1854/612.
446 LRO1854/643.
447 Plan LRO 1854/615.
448 *Leicester Journal*, 6th October 1854.

institution on an eligible site on the Dane Hills, the ceremony of laying the foundation stone was performed on Friday last by Lady Hazlerigg,[449] to whose indefatigable exertions, in conjunction with those of other ladies, the orphans of Leicester will be indebted for the home which is about to be built for their reception.

Proceedings commenced with children from St Martin's schools singing the 100th Psalm (old version) led by the Rev E. T. Vaughan,[450] which then led to a speech from Earl Howe,[451] followed by a prayer from Rev Vaughan [which the paper quotes in full].

Lady Hazlerigg then advanced to the stone leaning on the arm of Earl Howe. A bottle was deposited under the stone containing the following inscription:

A very rare photograph showing the Female Orphan Infant Asylum in 1971 shortly before demolition.

---

449 Lady Henrietta Anne Hazlerigg (c. 1784-1868) of Noseley Hall.
450 Rev Edward Thomas Vaughan (1813-1900), vicar of St Martin's Church (now Cathedral).
451 Richard William Penn Curzon-Howe, 1st Earl Howe (1796-1870), British courtier.

The First Stone of the Leicestershire Orphan Asylum was laid on the 20th day of September A. D. 1854, by the Lady Hazelrigg, assisted by the Right Honourable Earl Howe; William Flint and Henry Shenton, Architects; Cornelius William Herbert, William McCracken[452], Richard Catlin, John Law[453], Builders.

Lady Hazelrigg and Earl Howe and some others of the company present also affixed their names. Her ladyship then received a silver trowel from the architect, Mr. Flint, and the stone was lowered in to its place with the usual formalities.'

And then, after singing the Doxology, the ceremony was over. The same article gives a very useful description of the plans for the building:

'The site of the building is exactly at the junction of Watts' Causeway with the Foss [sic] Road, on the north side of Hinckley Road. It will stand on half an acre of ground, so that there will be ample space for gardens and shrubs. The building will be a plain but neat and pleasing specimen of Old English style of domestic architecture. It will consist of a ground floor and a single storey, the frontage to the Foss-lane being 65 feet, and the south front towards the Hinckley-road, at which the principal entrance is situated, 29 feet. The material is red brick, with stone dressings. The design embraces a spacious work room, lighted by a bay window, and (exclusive of the bay) is 19 ½ feet in length by 15 feet in breadth, a kitchen 18 feet by 15 feet, a dormitory 30 ¼ feet in length by 18 ¾ in breadth, a dormitory for elder girls, a matron's bedroom, and every necessary convenience in the way of domestic offices.'

Such was the occasion that the paper's *'own poetical correspondent'*, Mrs Edward Thomas [454] wrote a poem·

---

452 William McCracken (c.1805-1862), stonemason of Stamford Street.
453 John Quincey Law (1798-1864) iron founder and sometime town councillor for East St Margaret's. For obituary see *Leicester Mercury* 16th April 1864.
454 Mrs Edward Thomas of Rollestone Hall fl. 1838-1869

"BEING DEAD YET SPEAKETH"

THE FIRST STONE OF THE NEW INFANT ASYLUM ON THE DANE HILLS WAS LAID BY LADY HAZLERIGG SEPTEMBER 29TH, 1854

LADY – when Time its destined course hath run,
And, from such labours, even thou dost cease;
The righteous Work thou hast this day begun:
Shall, for thy Memory, win a longer lease,
Than all thy other virtues might have claimed:
When, by posterity, a PATTERN'S named.

There is no weeping in supernal spheres,
So calm, so consistent, is celestial joy;
Yet, sainted Mothers must dissolve in tears
Marking how thou thy "TALENT" dost employ
For them, their Orphans, helpless and bereft,
In death, they with much poignant anguish, left.

Rome had her Triumphs, and thou hast thine,
But, how far sweeter is the odour shed
From wreath of Asphodel[455] (which they entwine
To cast a heav'nly halo round thine head)
The hapless infants, rescued now by thee;
Than blood-stained Laurels of antiquity!

And, not alone they triumph of the hour! –
Ages to come, when gazing on that pile,
Shall feel the hallowed, sanctifying pow'r
Of Worth too pure, for Envy to defile;
And add their DISTANT praises to the mood
Of PRESENT homage, for this gracious deed.

Thus – from thy grave, Beneficence will speak
And – from thy ashes, will glad Hymnings break

---

455 Asphodel – The everlasting lily said to grow in Elysian Fields

Proclaiming thou, the destitute and the weak,
Didst of thy mercy chosen objects make;
The "little children" – Christ did symbolise
As types most perfect, of Eternal Skies.

The cost of building was reckoned to be £900. There appears to be one photograph extant[456] taken before demolition in 1971 to make way for road improvements. It reveals a similarity with some of the plans in Charles Wickes's contemporary *'Villas'* book. What became of the time capsule bottle is uncertain. Perhaps it's under the enlarged King Richard's Road that occupies most of the site.

5 houses
Deacon Street
James Wootton
October 1854
Flint & Shenton
Demolished c. 1969

Deacon Street still exists near Jarrom Street behind the Royal Infirmary. Much has changed since Flint's day and this area was almost entirely erased during the slum clearances in the 1960s. James Wootton[457] was a builder based in Oxford Street and this is the first of Flint's three commissions for him, all in the same area.

The houses formed a terrace separated by a passage with the three houses on the left. They had two storeys, had a kitchen and a parlour downstairs and a common dust pit with just two shared privies. Evidently, water was not piped in and was supplied to a large joint cistern (arrived at by a set of steps) by the Leicester Waterworks Company.[458]

---

456 By Dennis Calow and held by the University of Leicester.
457 James Wootton (1817-1885). Builder of Oxford Street who went bankrupt in 1857.
458 Leicester Waterworks Company, private water company taken over by the Corporation in 1878.

Warehouses and buildings
Lower Brown Street
December 1854 and February 1859
William Gimson
Flint & Shenton
Burnt down 1862

No account of any activity in Mid-Victorian Leicester is complete without a member of the Gimson family. For William Gimson,[459] Flint and Shenton built a warehouse for his sawmill business in Lower Brown Street. The site comprised two warehouses (of which one was three storeys high); a wash house; engine house and pit; drying stove room and the increasingly common water closets as opposed to privies. The plans show a particular focus on drainage.[460] It looks like the complex was shared with James Pickard's spinning business (before it moved down the road to Oxford Street); it may well be that this set of buildings replaced another premises that had been destroyed by fire in 1847 and this may also have been a Flint building.

Gimson engaged Flint and Shenton to add another warehouse and factory to the business in 1859. The plans[461] show a large three-storey building with basement and they were proudly named *'Paradise Works'*. This particular part of the company was situated on the corner of Norton Street and Welford Road. From this distance in time it is hard to discern which part of the Gimson business did what as the site was home to all sorts of woodworking, from chair making (for retail in the company's Haymarket shop) to sawing and veneering. In February 1862, the whole premises would be completely destroyed by fire incurring substantial losses, much of which was uninsured,[462] although the firm would live on under the Gimson name until as late as 1988. Gimson's adjacent house on Welford Road was saved by the efforts of the fire brigade and the local public, and this where his son Albert, who would become Charles Baker's assistant, was born in 1863.

---

459 William Gimson (1815-1901). Builder, sawmill owner, father of Albert Gimson and uncle of Ernest Gimson.
460 LRO 1854/645.
461 LRO 1859/1114.
462 *Leicester Journal*, 21st February 1862.

2 houses
New Bridge Street
Henry Mowbray
February 1855
Flint & Shenton
Demolished 1965

Planning consent for these buildings was given in January 1855, only a month after Flint's previous commission for Mowbray. They are next to the eight houses facing Infirmary Square but at a slight angle. The design is very similar again with two floors, a basement and scullery, although this time the dust pit and privy are built as part of the houses. There are gardens and the properties share a 60 foot well for which the plans show there is a pump.[463] Flint would have more work in New Bridge Street later in 1855.

2 houses
London Road
William Rushin
February 1855
Flint & Shenton
Demolished

William Rushin[464] was a builder and commissioned Flint to produce a design for a pair of houses on London Road but he did not live in them, choosing instead a house on nearby de Montfort Terrace, a row of his own construction. He sold[465] one of them to John Wood[466] and the other to his son William Rushin[467] as soon as they were built. A palisade fence enclosed gardens which led to large three-storey houses with entrances from the side. In design they resemble the pair built for Nathan Westerman in 1853. They shared a well in the back yard and the privy was right at the back of

463 LRO 1855/653.
464 William Rushin (1801-1878) of William Rushin and Son, builders, with a yard in Albion Hill. His granddaughter would later marry Arthur Wakerley.
465 Indenture in the author's possession.
466 John Wood (1815-?). Currier of Cank Street.
467 William Rushin (1838-1888), builder.

The Rushin houses appear on the left of this unusual and blurry view of London Road in 1923.

the house, which must have been rather a long walk as the houses stretched quite a distance. For some reason, and this may have something to do with the ground on which they are built, there was a necessity for 'stench traps'.[468] Located between de Montfort and Nelson Streets, the houses look like they were situated where Shimla Pinks Indian restaurant opened in the early Twenty-First Century. From the photograph, which shows them partly obscured by their neighbour, the houses are a typical Flint design: stuccoed, clean and unfussy. It is not clear when they were demolished.

5 houses
Princess Road
Cornelius Herbert
February 1855
Flint & Shenton
Demolished c. 1975

This is another partial plan survival which bears the separate names of Flint and Shenton in faint pencil where the title of the plan is usually to

---

468 LRO 1855/662.

be seen.[469] There is another name, but that part of the paper is missing. In an unidentified hand there is a brief note that '... *the elevation will be nearly the same as the one that was sent before*', however, no plan has come to light.

This was a commission for five linked houses on Upper Princess Street: a double-sized middle house flanked on each side by a pair of smaller dwellings. They were located at the top of Princess Road on the south side of the railway immediately before the extant but now closed railway bridge linking to Princess Road East. Each side house went from two large sitting and dining rooms to a lobby, pantry and kitchen. There was a garden to the front bordered by a pilaster wall and another garden to the rear which led to privies and an ash pit on top of a cesspool. This was presumably similar to the middle house but there is no detail on the plan. They had three storeys and a small cellar.

4 houses
Hastings Street
Jonathan Collins
March 1855
Flint & Shenton
Demolished c. 1973

Hastings Street was situated in between Waterloo Street and Lower Hastings Street. All has been demolished except some of the Lancaster Road side of Lower Hastings Street and has been replaced by Tigers' Way. Flint and Wickes had the contract to pave and macadamise Hastings Street in 1853.[470]

Jonathan Collins[471] commissioned Flint and Shenton to build four three-storey houses with basements. The surviving plans show the houses backed onto the railway at the end of a 42 feet garden reached through a yard housing a scullery, water closet and dust pit.[472] It looks like they were situated after the Regent Road turning just before the Princess Street junction, where another Flint building was situated. Tigers' Way

---

469 LRO 1855/652.
470 *Leicester Chronicle*, 23rd April 1853.
471 Jonathan Beaumont Collins (1808-1889). Builder and Guardian of St Mary's.
472 LRO 1855/669.

was constructed in 1973 when the houses were probably demolished.

Collins lived at 24, Lower Hastings Street as identified by the 1861 census. In 1851 he was living in nearby Tower Street and presumably moved into the house Flint designed for him around 1855.

2 Streets and 4 houses and a public house
Raglan Street and Cross Street
James Wootton
August 1855
Flint & Shenton
Demolished c. 1965

Before Flint could erect any buildings, he had to build the streets for this latest commission for James Wootton, which was just round the corner from Deacon Street and also ran into his recent buildings for Henry Mowbray on New Bridge Street. Permission for the streets was given on 3rd August 1855 and the buildings received theirs exactly one week later.[473] The plans show that Raglan Street was to terminate into Cross Street, which was at ninety degrees to it. It is not clear if the latter was laid out or not; certainly the Leicestershire Freehold Land Society got Flint to lay out Havelock Street in 1858 and it is this street that ran into Raglan Street. It was nine yards wide; had a gradient of 1 in 144 and was culverted at the same time.

The houses formed a terrace that faced New Bridge Street and the public house was on the corner with a frontage to Raglan Street. It was a double-fronted building with a tap room, bar, kitchen, parlour and brew house and also a dust pit and privy outside but part of the building. At number 55, it was called 'The Lord Raglan' and was still trading in 1954. Its first landlord was John Bray[474] and his widow sold the property in 1874.[475] Four houses adjoined the pub and it is likely that they were intended as commercial premises in as much as one (number 51) had a bake house and large oven building and was used as a bakery.

Demolition came in about 1965 and, while parts of New Bridge

---

473 LRO 1855/724 and LRO 1855/727.
474 John Bray (1822-1871). Publican.
475 *Leicester Journal*, 3rd April 1874.

Street survive, albeit truncated, Raglan Street now lies under the Royal Infirmary. Almost all of this part of Leicester has vanished and it is a feat of imagination to think that this was once an up and coming and desirable part of 'New Leicester' with a community who lived, worked and died there.

Water Closet
Wellington Street
Josiah Fleming
September 1855
Flint & Shenton
Demolished

Josiah Fleming[476] and Co. were a firm of engravers, embosser, lithographers and letter press printers at 37, Wellington Street. This was a simple job converting an existing privy into a water closet using six-inch pipes to run into the existing sewer. The work reflects a growing insistence on better sanitation and there are several similar examples of such work as part of commissions for the firm at around this time.

4 houses
Nichols Street
Thomas Coltman
October 1855
Flint & Shenton
Demolished

Thomas Coltman's[477] four houses all had cellars, six rooms and gardens.[478] They are very similar to all the other houses Flint is putting up in rapidly expanding Leicester although, unusually for this type of house, each has a separate privy. They follow the pair separated by passageway pattern. A

---

476 Josiah Fleming (1818-1906) of Parkside House, Aylestone Park, printer and sometime overseer of St Margaret's.
477 Thomas Coltman (1802-1881), carpenter, joiner and builder of Ann Street.
478 LRO 1855/742.

clue to their location on Nichols Street is that there is an existing stable marked on the plan at the back of the first house. Nichols Street with a connection to Midland Street is in the St George's area of the city and was completely demolished in around 1967. The most likely candidate for this particular Thomas Coltman is the Charles Street carpenter and joiner and likely another Flint business contact.

2 houses
Rutland Street
George Anderson
October 1855
Flint & Shenton
Demolished

These houses were certainly grander than most of Flint and Shenton's other houses at this time. Double and not single cellared, they also had breakfast rooms in addition to the usual dining rooms and kitchens, etc. They fronted, as a semi-detached pair, onto Rutland Street and backed onto to the wall of four houses at the bottom of their yards. George Anderson[479] was looking to exchange land in order to build them. Written on the plans are the details:

> "It is proposed to purchase the piece of land containing 7 2/3 yards coloured yellow, and give up to the Public the portion coloured blue, if the Local Board will consent: otherwise Mr. Anderson would be glad to receive a proposition from the Local Board." [480]

Anderson was trading with premises at 80, Rutland Street in 1855 and put this and its neighbour 80½ up for sale in 1864.[481]

---

479 George Anderson (1812-1889), Scottish Draper and later alderman. For obituary see *Leicester Chronicle* 28th December 1889.
480 LRO 1855/750.
481 *Leicester Mercury*, 4th June 1864.

4 houses
Deacon Street
Thomas Norman
December 1855
Flint & Shenton
Demolished c. 1969

These Deacon Street houses for Thomas Norman[482] are larger and of a better standard than the ones Flint put up for James Wootton the previous year. They were separated by a common passageway in the middle, had two floors and each had a brick-built scullery extension. The middle two also had water closets and each shared a garden with its neighbour.

Rather unusually, at the end of the gardens was another set of buildings separated by the same passage with access to Atkin Street. There was a brew house, cow house and shed. The complex also had a dust pit and its own privy. Although animal husbandry was commonly included in a domestic setting, it was becoming rarer, especially in the rapidly growing towns. The plans were approved on 14th December 1855.[483]

House alterations
London Road
Henry Kemp
March 1856
Flint & Shenton
Demolished

Henry Shenton's brother-in-law Henry Kemp's[484] detached house was situated at 33, London Road between John Lorrimer, the hosier, and John Holland, the auctioneer not far from the station but nearer to Granby Street. It had been the Shenton family home since at least the 1830s. Common with almost all London Road houses at the time, there was a

---

482 Thomas Norman (1812-1882). Brother of John, plumber and glazer of High Cross Street.

483 LRO 1855/758.

484 Henry Kemp (1819-1895). Husband of Shenton's sister, Frances. Silk mercer with a business in the Market Place and later Registrar for births and deaths for Eastern Leicester. For obituary see *Leicester Chronicle* 30th March 1895.

front garden which led to a portico and the house itself. The work was to build a dust pit and privy in the backyard and construct a coal shed.[485] There was also considerable drainage work to link the house to the sewer on London Road.

2 Houses
Fosse Road
May 1856
William Stretton
Flint & Shenton
Extant

Much of the land around the part of Leicester where these houses were built formed a triangle comprising Fosse Road, Kirby Street and Stretton Road and much of the land was owned by 'landed proprietor' William Stretton. The ring road now cuts through it and its countryside setting now seems fantastic. Flint and Shenton's orphan asylum of 1854 was in this triangle as were Thomas Bland's houses, which the firm would put

A departure from Flint's usual style at Dane Hills.

485 LRO 1856/786.

up in 1857. These two houses appeared in 1856 but it would appear that Stretton carried on living in the family home, Dane's Hill House.

The houses face onto the corner of Fosse Road and a garden led up to an entrance after which came a large hall. To the left were a separate scullery and kitchen, each of which had bay windows, to the right a large dining room and behind it a large drawing room. In the yard to the rear were the usual privies, dust pit, cess pool and also a liquid manure tank. The right-hand house had a coach house with rooms above it. They are of two storeys and each has a cellar. The plot of land was next to Stretton's paddock.[486]

The houses still exist on Fosse Road Central on the Daneshill Road corner and are surrounded by an attractive stone wall. The design is a departure for Flint as there is more decoration than usual and he has used bricks of several colours.

Commemorative stone for Richard III
Bow Bridge
October 1856
Archibald Turner
Flint & Shenton
Extant

The *Leicester Journal* reports the erection of this stone to commemorate King Richard's 'grave' on 2nd January 1857:

'KING RICHARD'S GRAVE. – A memorial has just been erected at Bow Bridge, whereon it is recorded that near that spot lie the remains of King Richard the Third. It is a very handsome stone, set in the gable of one of the new buildings there, and being an object likely to attract much attention can hardly fail to settle the question between the rival archaeologists as completely as the Battle of Bosworth did between Henry and Richard. The monument is in Ketton stone, designed by Messrs. Flint and Shenton, and

486 LRO 1856/800.

A fondly remembered view of Richard III's stone in its original position on Bow Bridge.

The Richard III stone today.

executed in first rate style by Mr. Broadbent[487] – the work in each case being presented as a free gift. The monument is worth a visit, and few, we think can see it without feeling that the thanks of the town are due to those gentlemen who have thus assisted in preserving the memory of one of the most interesting and best authenticated of our local traditions.'

Of course, the twenty-first century saw the discovery of Richard's actual grave and the final debunking of the myth that his bones were thrown into the River Soar during the Dissolution of the Monasteries.

The stone was built into a cottage on the estate owned by Archibald

---

487 Benjamin Broadbent (1813-1862) of Friar Lane. Monumental mason, builder and architect. His firm is still trading in Leicester.

Turner[488] and was opposite the Bow Bridge Inn, supposedly on the site of the Augustinian Friary, commemorated today by the name of the road over the Bridge, St Augustine Road.[489] The present iron bridge dates from 1861 and the area around it, including the cottage in which the plaque was built, was demolished in around 1967.[490]

In October 1856, Flint and Shenton were engaged to make alterations to a cottage on Bow Bridge in Turner's possession. Whilst the plans show that they were principally concerned with drainage, it is probable that this was the same cottage and the stone was installed at the same time.

The monument still exists on Bow Bridge but shows signs of breaks, although there are parts missing and obviously replaced. It is an inaccurate and redundant thing, but it is also part of Leicester's myth and legend and needs to be retained. It is also a small sidelight on William Flint's business activities in the 1850s.

Alteration to house
New Park Street
Richard Harris
Flint & Shenton
November 1856
Demolished

Plans to alter the entrance to Richard Harris Junior's[491] house on the right-hand corner of Braunstone Gate and New Parks Street were approved on 14th November 1856.[492] Plans A and B were presented with plan A being more ambitious with a sense of 'trying his luck' about it. The design included a bressummer (a large, horizontal, supporting beam which bears the weight of a wall starting on a first or higher floor). No more is known

---

488 Archibald Turner (1809-1876), owner of Archibald Turner and Co., elastic webbing factory at Bow Bridge. For obituary see *Leicester Chronicle* 25th November 1876.

489 Plaque on the Bridge erected by the Richard III Society, 2005.

490 *Leicestershire Architects 1700 – 1850*, (Bennett, 2001).

491 Richard Harris Junior (1812-1874). Hosiery manufacturer and town councillor of Braunstone Gate, son of Richard Harris MP.

492 LRO 1856/845.

The Harris house on New Parks Street – a rather unclear commission.

about this commission, but New Park Street still exists off Braunstone Gate and part of Harris's house is still there.

7 houses
Lancaster Terrace, Lancaster Road
John Holland
January 1857
Flint & Shenton
Extant

Approval for seven houses on Lancaster Street (now Road) for the auctioneer John Holland was given on 16th January 1857.[493] Much of the estate agent work Flint undertook was auctioned through his auction house.[494]

The row of houses appears to be simpler than its neighbours, but they still retain a good sense of proportion and space, Flint's hallmark. They are deceptively large with two floors and cellars and three rooms on each of the floors with an attached two-floor scullery. They are linked by a passageway at the back of the houses. Unusually for a Flint building of this age, there is a recessed panel showing the name of the terrace and the year of erection. They represent a rare survival of Flint's modest housing

493 Plan LRO 1857/865.
494 Later Holland, Warner and Sheppard.

Rare survivors of Flint and Shenton's domestic work in Lancaster Street.

Unusual for Flint – a name for the terrace.

work, a lot of which was built in the late 1850s when he was in partnership with Shenton. Almost all of these pleasant but unglamorous terraces have been demolished.

Office alterations
South Bond Street
Leicester Poor Law Union
January 1857
Flint & Shenton
Demolished 1975

Situated opposite the enormous complex of Bond Street Mills, the Leicester Union Poor Law office was located on South Bond Street, one of four Bond streets that formed a square around the mills. The area is quite lost under the Shires development, now the Highcross.

In early January 1857, plans were approved for alterations to the Union offices. There was evidently a lodging area of the offices as the relieving officers allowed Samuel Stinson[495] to let a room for 2s (including coal and gas) in April 1857,[496] perhaps now that the work was complete.

It looks like the building already existed and Flint and Shenton converted it to use by the Union's Guardians. As well as alterations to drainage, the plans show separate male and female waiting rooms; a pay office; two relieving offices and a boardroom.[497] A gateway allowed claimants in through a yard, in the corner of which was a urinal. Extending a water supply to the urinal was a condition of plan approval! The drain used was an existing one at Mr Manning's property.[498]

Banking house and house alterations
Horsefair Street and Market Street
Thomas Cooke
March 1857
Flint & Shenton
Partially extant

Thomas Farmer Cooke[499] was agent to the Bank of Deposit and the

---

495 Samuel Stinson (d.1858), relieving office messenger.
496 *Leicester Mercury*, 18th April 1857.
497 LRO 1857/861.
498 John Manning (1791-1869), grocer and sometime Mayor of Leicester and future client.
499 Thomas Farmer Cooke (1809-1870), banking agent formerly of Peatling Hall.

Parts of Thomas Cooke's house still stand behind Market Street.

National Assurance and Investment Association. A new entrance to the office's premises was created for this commission and there were internal alterations to the strong room, for example. A water closet was added and the plans specify Doulton pipes. A coal hole was also put in. The office stood opposite McDonald's on the corner of Market Street closest to the Town Hall. Photographic evidence of it is rare and the building seems never to have been the subject of a camera. The building next to it, now numbered 6, Market Street, has a clear Flint look and may be the same building as the banking house or is more likely connected to it.

Cooke lived on Market Street and at the same time as the work above, Flint made alterations to his substantial house altering windows and drains. It looks as though the house was reached through a passageway off Market Street somehow, as the house next to the Deposit Bank is not the same building. This house survives behind various shop buildings and, from an aerial view, the house strongly resembles Flint designs, suggesting that the original design may have been his.

Classrooms and additions
Gallowtree Gate Congregationalist Chapel

April 1857
Flint & Shenton
Demolished 1927

Gallowtree Gate Congregationalist Chapel grew out of the Bond Street Chapel and opened in October 1823. No mission hall this, the chapel was a substantial building behind the Marks and Spencer's side of the street approximately behind Boots. It was accessed through a passageway which linked to Free Lane and then to Rutland Street.

The commission doubtless came through Shenton whose stepfather, Rev Legge, was minister at the church and, given that Shenton wrote a hymn book for the chapel, it is certain that this is where he also worshipped. Longer ago, his father had been elected deacon in 1828. Indeed, Henry Shenton would be buried there in 1896 before re-interment at Welford Road when the chapel was demolished.

Built behind the chapel, the new school room extension included two yards; a vestry for the deacon and another for the minister as well as classrooms (but only for boys). It was two storeys high and followed the line of the chapel, running at a right-angle to Gallowtree Gate and Free

A very rare view of the Congregational Church on Gallowtree Gate roughly behind Boots.

Lane. The area it occupied is now a delivery and access centre to Gallowtree Gate shops and was commonly known until recently as Chapel Yard.

House
Daneshill Road
Thomas Bland
June 1857
Flint & Shenton
Extant

Thomas Bland[500] was a builder with a significant practice in Leicester. He lived at Lower Redcross Street and never seemed to live in the house he commissioned Flint and Shenton to build in 1857. In its original rural setting, it must have looked an impressive building with an entrance hall giving way to a drawing room and dining room and then scullery, staircase and kitchen. A passage led to a pantry, a closet and an increasingly common indoor water closet.

Sited immediately next to Stretton's houses on Fosse Road, at right angles on Danehsill Road, this house was for Thomas Bland.

---

500 Thomas Bland (1819-1899) of T. Bland and Sons in Harvey Lane, sometime West St Mary's town councillor and Guardian of the Poor. For obituary see *Leicester Chronicle*, 26th August 1899.

The house is connected to the building of a new street (presumably Daneshill Road) onto which the house fronted with its back to Mr Stretton's two houses and its left wing facing Fosse Road.[501] Surprisingly, it looks as if it survives on Fosse Road Central next door to William Stretton's surviving houses and fronting to Daneshill Road. The building has the same multi-coloured brick fence wall as Stretton's houses (and the wall continues across the road towards the site of the Orphan Asylum – a last remnant perhaps?).

This was Bland's second attempt at obtaining planning permission for the land as, earlier in 1856, he had asked Flint to design four houses to build. The plans show a very busy and irregular complex of four houses and look as though they were drafted in a hurry. Unsurprisingly, therefore, the Corporation refused their permission.[502]

Shop and Offices
Horsefair Street and Bowling Green Street
Thomas Cooke
June 1857 and November 1860
Flint & Shenton
Demolished 1955

The firm were back working for Thomas Farmer Cooke in June 1857 to build an office complex at the corner of Horsefair and Bowling Green Streets. This building was separated on the Horsefair Street side from Cooke's other office by just one building and it appears to back onto Cooke's house.

The design was for a shop on the corner of the streets next to a counting house with four offices behind. There was an indoor water closet and a coal chute, a lobby and a strong closet. It had a basement and sewerage was conducted into a culvert on Bowling Green Street.

The 1857 design was a single storey affair with a hipped roof.[503] In 1860 Flint and Shenton returned to add two further storeys to house the

---

501 LRO 1857/920.
502 LRO 1856/837.
503 LRO 1857/919 unindexed but with 'Flint and Shento' (sic) recorded on the plan.

Cooke offices: starting life as a single storey in1857, the firm returned in 1860 to add two more.

offices and printing works of no less than the *Leicester Journal*. The first floor had two water closets as well as three offices, coal house and urinals. The second floor housed the printing office; make up room, composition room and a two-horse boiler.[504] The decoration to the eaves and top storey are rather more elaborate than usual for a Flint building and an almost identical commission is the John Baines warehouse a few paces away on Belvoir Street.

For many years the building housed the Leicester office of Norwich Union Insurance. It was demolished along with its neighbour and Cooke's Market Street office to be replaced by a purpose-built and rather plain office block.

Warehouse and factory
Lower Brown Street

---

504 LRO 1860/1314 unindexed but with Flint and Shenton recorded on the plan.

July 1857 and April 1861
Hodges and Turner
Flint & Shenton
Demolished

Hodges[505] and Turner[506] was a firm of hosiers and their warehouse was near the present-day corner of Norton Street and Lower Brown Street. The plans show that there is an existing factory on the site, although Flint and Shenton are making significant additions. It is possible that Flint was the architect in the first place in 1856. It had four storeys each containing four water closets and a substantial basement. The portion of the plan where the architect's details are normally recorded is almost entirely missing save for a flourished 'Fl', for Flint and Shenton.[507] Hodges and Turner dissolved their partnership in 1860[508] and the firm became known as Hodges and Son.[509] Flint and Shenton were back making alterations and additions to existing premises. It contains a chimney of 110 feet and this was on the site of the 1857 privies. A new engine house looks likely to have been put in at the same time and it had an iron roof.[510] In March 1863, Shenton and Baker would come back to the site and design an impressive extension which would front onto Welford Road.

A design packaging firm called Hodges and Drake has premises in Upper Brown Street albeit in an Art Deco building.

Temporary privies
Lower Brown Street
July 1857

505 Thomas William Hodges (1807-1874), elastic webbing manufacturer and sometime town councillor and mayor. His daughter, Emma, married Thomas Cook's son, John.
506 Luke Turner (1832-1897). Son of Archibald. Elastic webbing manufacturer with premises on Deacon Street.
507 LRO 1857/938.
508 London Gazette, 3rd August 1860.
509 John Edward Hodges (1829-1892), elastic webbing manufacturer and sometime town councillor.
510 LRO 1861/1357.

Flint & Shenton
William Gimson
Demolished 1861

This was a job that nowadays would be rendered unnecessary due to the advent of Portaloos! It was concerned with erecting a two-cubicle toilet block to cater for the workmen next to William Gimson's business building a factory for Hodges and Turner. They would have been quickly built and seem to have been reasonably substantial judging by the plans.[511] They were demolished in 1861 and are mentioned on the plans of the factory for Hodges and Son above.

House
Upper Brunswick Street
Ann Pickard
September 1857
Flint & Shenton
Demolished c. 1959

That this commission is for a woman is unusual and Miss Ann Pickard[512] appears to be the only female client the firm had. She lived in the house, then numbered 129, as housekeeper to her father, Benjamin.[513]

It was a detached house with two floors and a cellar and comprised a parlour, kitchen and workroom downstairs and at least two bedrooms upstairs. There was a long garden and an outside privy and dust pit. The plans show that entrance was gained through a passage, but it is not clear why a passage was needed. [514] Upper Brunswick Street is now lost under the St Matthew's Estate, although Brunswick Street still exists as a mixture of buildings in light engineering and residential use. It is likely the house was demolished around 1959.

---

511 LRO 1857/926.
512 Ann Pickard (1822-1896), later wife of Thomas March, a warehouseman.
513 Benjamin Pickard (1794-1875). Framework knitter.
514 LRO 1857/865.

Warehouse
Yeoman Lane
John Law
February and April 1858
Flint & Shenton
Demolished

Yeoman Lane links Charles Street to Yeoman Street and Flint and Shenton built a two-storey warehouse here in 1858. Plans were approved on the 26[515]ᵗʰ February. The warehouse had a frontage to Lower Charles Street and it was an unusual building comprising separate male and female water closet; a seven feet by 20 feet six inch waiting place; yard; scullery and warehouse itself. It has not been possible to ascertain why there was a waiting place or who waited there.

There was tragedy in the warehouse's construction and this is the only recorded fatality on a Flint building:

> 'FATAL ACCIDENT TO A BRICKLAYER'S LABOURER. –
> An inquest was held on Friday on the body of William Thomas Smith,[516] aged 16, who died from the result of an accident sustained while engaged in the building of a warehouse for Mr. John Law, between Charles-street and Yeoman-lane, the previous day. It appeared from the evidence of the workman engaged at the building that the deceased, whose employment at the time of the accident was carrying bricks up to the scaffold, caught his foot against a board which was lying on the scaffold, and losing his balance, fell to the ground, a distance of 11 feet. The scaffold was constructed in the usual manner, and the deceased had passed over the piece of board in question several times without injury. A verdict of 'accidental death' was returned.'

The building contractor's name has not been traced.

On 9ᵗʰ April 1858, a second plan was approved on the same site. The plans reveal more surprises and show a gas tank over which a warehouse

---

515 LRO 1858/992.
516 William Thomas Smith (1842-1858).

was intended to be built.[517] The Council must have had some concerns as the plans show that permission is granted at the owner's risk:

"The proprietor taking on himself the risk of applying the novel arrangement of making a workplace over a gas holder".

What an extraordinary building it must have been.

John Law's firm was The Rutland Foundry, specialising in iron and brass, which seems at odds with the design of the building with its waiting place, etc., but does explain the gas holder. Flint and Shenton had used him as a contractor building the Infant Orphan Asylum in 1854. The building was auctioned off at the Stag and Pheasant Hotel in May 1890, when it passed out of the Law family's hands, and it was probably demolished when Charles Street was widened in the 1920s. This particular area of Leicester contained several foundries.

Aylestone Road
6 houses
John Holland
April 1858
Flint & Shenton
Demolished

This second commission for John Holland was for six houses of which five fronted Aylestone Road and they are clearly of higher quality than his 1857 terrace of houses in Lancaster Street.

They were large houses with three storeys and a triple seven feet six high basement for the cellar, kitchen and scullery.[518] The front five houses were at an angle facing Aylestone Road and the sixth ran behind them so that it ran at ninety degrees to the others. They all had gardens but the ones at the greatest angle had correspondingly smaller ones. The front five were surrounded by a palisade fence. They were probably situated near to the Victory Public House and the demolished Pride of Leicester on what is now an access way for the Royal Infirmary.

---

517 LRO 1858/1014.
518 LRO 1858/1003.

Entrance lodge and machine office
Sparkenhoe Street
Poor Law Union
April 1858
Flint & Shenton
Demolished 1977

Situated at the entrance of the workhouse on Sparkenhoe Street the firm built a lodge for a member of staff from the workhouse, probably the head groundsman or porter. A simple building of one storey, it comprised living room, bedroom, scullery, passage, water closet, dust pit and coal pit. There was an angular bay window into the living room and a very small garden in front of it. The (weighing) machine office was another single-storey building with a pitched roof and room nine feet and six inches high and the same angular window bay. From contemporary photographs, the buildings were in the same Jacobethan style as Flint's main workhouse building. They are almost symmetrical (the lodge is larger) and the brickwork shows a little ornamentation, for example a

An early photograph of Leicester Workhouse and the new entrance buildings, possibly on their completion in 1858?

The remains of the workhouse gates and walls in Sparkenhoe Street.

latticed side window. They were demolished around 1977 to build Moat Community College.

Warehouse
Wellington Street
April 1858
Samuel Westfahll
Flint & Shenton
Extant

Samuel Westfahll had a drapery business on Wellington Street and commissioned Flint and Shenton to add another warehouse to his premises, which was next to Ward's printing business at number 2, a business Flint put up in 1853. Given the small footprint of the site, it must have been complicated to fit in the new workshops, passageways, cellars and toilets. Westfahll died in 1893 and this building was part of the estate auction on 27th September 1893 at the Midland Auction Mart '… *at seven o'clock in the evening prompt…*' The notice in the *Chronicle* and *Mercury* trumpets the site:

'The position is unrivalled for commercial requirements in connection with the staple trades of the town'.

The main frontage has the look of a Flint building and it is possible that he was responsible for the whole site with several commissions over the years. Some of the buildings may be seen, accessed from Albion Street.

4 houses
Willow Street
May 1858
James Nicholls
Flint & Shenton
Demolished c. 1964

Willow Street still exists and runs between Taylor Street and Wanlip Street in the middle of the St Matthew's Estate. Nothing in it dates from much later than the 1970s and much has changed as the street itself used to run into Curzon Street. In 1858, Flint built four houses here in what was then a growing and fashionable new area of the town. These houses were for a slightly better off clientele. They had a front garden surrounded by iron railings on a brick base, which backed onto a bay window. Entrance was gained via a three feet wide passage and a front door that opened onto stairs to the first floor and a doorway into the kitchen on the left or into the parlour on the right. Each had a yard and a back garden; each having a separate privy. A scullery contained a large copper boiler for each house and the height of the internal rooms on both floors was 8 feet 9 inches. Plans were approved immediately before the next commission for Nicholls on Curzon Street.[519]

4 houses
Curzon Street
May 1858
James Nicholls

---

519 LRO 1858/1019.

Flint & Shenton
Demolished c. 1960

James Nicholls[520] was a solicitor's clerk (so it is rather surprising to find him building houses given the income of such a position) and plans show his next four houses were identical in every way to the Willow Street houses[521] and they were situated near to where Flint would build his large Methodist Church the following year. Although Willow Street and Curzon Street did intersect, the plans are unclear where the houses were in relation to each other, but they were probably nearby. The whole area is under the St Matthew's Estate save for one stretch of truncated remnant, separated by Dysart Way and still called Curzon Street where the Curzonia Works stands.

House additions and alterations
London Road
1858
Joseph Brookhouse

These houses in Curzon Street reflect the aspirations of 'New Leicester'.

---

520 James Nicholls (1834-1890). Solicitor's clerk later of Albion Street and law writer of Holborn, London.
521 LRO 1858/1020.

Flint & Shenton
Demolished

Joseph Brookhouse's[522] residence was situated at the corner of London Road and Prebend Street. William Flint acted as Brookhouse's agent to purchase the house at auction in 1857.[523] It cost £3675 and had been standing for at least 25 years.

Plans for alterations and additions to the house were approved by the Council on 4th June 1858.[524] It is clear that a new water closet and lavatory were put into the downstairs kitchen and the drainage was re-laid through the back of the house. After that, it is hard to see from the plans what existed and what was new. Given that this is a plan for alterations *and* additions, it is likely that the conservatory and whole back of the house were what was added. If this is the case, it involved building a new stable, stable yard and coach house and perhaps a new scullery too. It must have been a delightful villa with a decent back garden. The identity of the original architect of the house is not certain either. Could it be William Flint? The building resembles other confirmed Flint projects, so it is possible.

Flint had an association with Joseph Brookhouse's house in London Road to put him contention as the original architect.

522 Joseph Brookhouse (1805-1861), son of Benjamin Brookhouse.
523 *Leicester Mercury*, 14th November 1857.
524 LRO 1858/1029.

On New Year's Day 1859, Brookhouse advertised the Rutland Street/ Granby Street property he lived in for auction, suggesting that Flint's work in London Road did not take long. Flint had also made alterations to this property in 1851. Though the main house still exists, albeit with a modern and rather crass frontage, everything behind the main body of the building has been demolished and is now the car park for the nearby Masonic Hall. The road behind the house is named Brookhouse Street.

Warehouse
Yeoman Lane
Mr Townsend
October 1858
Flint & Shenton
Demolished

Shortly after their work for John Law, the firm went back to Yeoman Lane for Mr Townsend to remove common privies and a urinal and build water closets. The warehouse had a frontage to Yeoman Lane and it comprised two storeys; a ground floor of eleven feet six inches height and a first floor of six feet six inches. Despite considerable research, it has proved impossible to identify Mr Townsend. The plans are not indexed as theirs at the LRO, but they are obviously Flint and Shenton's.[525]

Factory extension
Bow Bridge
Archibald Turner
November 1858 and May 1859
Flint & Shenton
Demolished 1967

The factory and presumably its Strawberry Hill inspired frontage were designed for Samuel Kelly[526] by Christopher Staveley[527] before 1817 for

525 Plans LRO 1858/1074
526 Samuel Kelly (1786-1828). Hosier in partnership with William Kelly.
527 Christopher Staveley (1759-1827), architect and surveyor.

his cravats and fancy hosiery business. Archibald Turner took the site over by 1854 and regularly added to it as his elastic webbing business expanded to cope with demand in rapidly industrialising early Victorian Britain.

Flint and Shenton's plans for a three-storey extension to the factory were approved on 13th May 1859. However, a report in the *Mercury* in November 1858 shows that a large extension was opened then amid much ceremony.[528] The coverage does not include details of the architect, but it probably was Flint and Shenton who built it and then in May 1859 added a further wing of three storeys. It is possible that a new boiler house and engine house were put in at the same time. The plans reveal that there was a water closet on each storey[529] and reflect perhaps a focus on new working patterns that emphasise the 'time is money' approach that enabled such high levels of productivity.

Shenton would work on the site in July 1862 and he would again, and with Baker, in November and December 1865. The firm completed other work for the Turner family throughout their period in business. Demolition came to the whole area for the Ring Road in about 1967 and Bow Bridge

Flint and Shenton's 1858 extension is clear from the slightly different window design.

---

528 *Leicester Mercury*, 6th November 1858.
529 LRO1859/1144.

House represents a great loss to Leicester's heritage. More than fifty years later, there is still no development on the site and it lies derelict.

House alterations
London Road
Rupert Carryer
December 1858
Flint & Shenton
Demolished

This house is probably one and the same as 'The Chestnuts', which was situated opposite University Road and was set some way back off London Road in front of a large garden and driveway. It was the home of Rupert Carryer.[530] Flint and Shenton added a new roof section and possibly another storey. They also fitted an indoor water closet and extensively altered drainage. The front garden was built on in around 1888 and the house demolished after 1904.

Warehouse
Belvoir Street
John Baines
December 1858
Flint & Shenton
Extant

The *Leicester Chronicle* announced that John Baines' large warehouse was already in construction in early 1859 and it marvels at the great need for warehouses in 'New Leicester'.[531] The *Leicester Chronicle*, in its final edition for 1859, mentioned the now complete building and saw fit to commend Flint and Shenton's latest work:

'As one of the evidences of increasing prosperity, the erection of new warehouses and other buildings in this town may be adduced.

---

530 Rupert Carryer (1814-1896). Pawnbroker and salesman.
531 *Leicester Mercury*, 22nd January 1859.

The Baines warehouse in Belvoir Street has an almost identical counterpart in the now lost Bowling Green Street Cooke premises.

Of the former we may notice the warehouse in Belvoir-street, recently built for Mr. Baines, by Messrs. Flint and Shenton – a very pleasing specimen of what brick and stone may be rendered capable in architectural adornment...'[532]

John Baines[533] was a hosiery manufacturer. Situated on the corner of Stamford Street nearest Granby Street, the warehouse is three storeys high and has a basement and the plans show that the two large areas on the ground floor were for taking in and packing.[534] The warehouse has a curved frontage and other details that are strikingly similar to the Cooke building extension the firm built on Horsefair Street in 1860. The design is Italianate palazzo and, rather fittingly, the building has been occupied for much of the last two decades by the Italian restaurant chain Zizzi. The warehouse was added to the City's heritage register in 2017.

---

532 *Leicester Chronicle*, 31st December 1859.
533 John Baines (1812-1875). Hosier and sometime Leicester mayor and alderman. For obituary see *Leicester Chronicle*, 10th July 1875. Flint wanted him to stand as MP – see Chapter 20.
534 LRO 1858/1094. Unindexed as Flint but with Flint and Shenton on the plan with the date 23rd December 1858 for a 31st December 1858 approval.

Primitive Methodist chapel and school rooms
Curzon Street
April 1859
Flint & Shenton
Demolished 1999

The Primitive Methodist Chapel in Curzon Street had its origins in the George Street Chapel community who purchased the ground for a new chapel and school in around 1858 and was another contribution to 'New Leicester', much of which was planned but not yet built.[535] The Rev William Lea[536] who would become the first incumbent wrote to the *Leicester Mercury* in early April 1859 to explain what was happening:[537]

'The erection of the new chapel is to commence immediately. Mr. Flint is engaged as architect. It is intended to accommodate upwards of 600 persons, and to be so planned, as to admit of considerable enlargement without detracting from the symmetry of the whole. The outlay is expected to exceed £1,000...'

Curzon Street Methodist Church in the 1980s.

535 *Leicester Mercury*, 22nd January 1859.
536 Rev William Lea (1800-1870). Methodist minister living in Derby.
537 *Leicester Mercury*, 5th March 1859.

The *Chronicle* of the same date reveals that the Chapel *'... is designed to be respectable in appearance...'* and that the Chapel will front Curzon Street and the school rooms Charlotte Street.[538]

At the end of April, the foundation stone was laid by John Dove Harris Sr. The *Mercury* reports the occasion and notes that the weather was unfavourable and that the service began with the singing of *"Before Jehovah's awful throne"* before moving to a tea for 500 at 5pm that ended at 10pm.

The Chapel opened on 17th January 1860 and the *Mercury* was in praise of Flint's evidently modest but effective design:[539]

> 'The building is a commodious one, with some attention to architectural taste, and it is highly creditable to the body – their pecuniary capabilities being considered'.

Plans for the chapel's drainage still exist although they are not indexed as Flint and Shenton designs.[540] The Chapel, which was situated on the corner of Curzon and Arnold Streets, was added to in 1865 and external walls and railings were added in 1878 with further remodelling over the decades until the Chapel was closed in 1998, by which time (in 1967) it had been renamed All Saints and the road it was in renamed Malabar Road. Pevsner describes the style as *'Italianate'*, a style favoured by Flint throughout his career. It was demolished in 1999.

House and warehouse extension
New Walk and Wellington Street
Joseph Hames
July 1859
Flint & Shenton
Demolished

Although Joseph Hames was the client, the property was occupied by Charles Billson[541] and Josiah Fleming. Joseph Hames the elder and

---

538 *Leicester Chronicle*, 5th March 1859.
539 *Leicester Mercury*, 21st January 1860.
540 LRO 1859/1190.
541 Charles Billson (1805-1878). Hosiery manufacturer of Billson and Hames in Newark Street.

younger[542] were in partnership with Billson in the hosiery trade until 1864. The plans[543] show that the house was occupied by Billson and that it was to be extended by adding a new parlour. It was physically joined by a small part of one corner to the warehouse, which was also to be extended with a three-storey new block and its main building to be basemented. Access to the estate was through a yard fronting onto Wellington Street and past the coach house, and the house backed on to New Walk via its front garden. The 1861 census numbers the house 14, putting it at the bottom of New Walk nearest King Street. This makes the most likely location for these demolished premises near Holy Cross and on that side.

542 Joseph Hames Jr (1827-1897). Hosier of New Walk and later Rotherby Hall.
543 LRO 1859/1168.

CHAPTER 10

The Buildings of the 1860s

Hustings and polling booths
Market Place
January 1861
Flint & Shenton
Demolished 1861

The firm advertised for contractors to build hustings and polling booths on 24th January 1861.[544] Hustings were set up in the Market Place and contemporary photographs suggest it would have been a reasonably substantial wooden grandstand, large enough to accommodate the officials, candidates and their numerous supporters. It had at least four compartments; one each for the candidates and another one centrally for the civic dignitaries. The need arose due to a Westminster by-election brought about by the sudden death of Joseph William Noble.[545] It was a noticeably bad-tempered affair even for a noticeably fractious Leicester at the time. The Liberals could not agree a candidate, so two fought the election: John Dove Harris Sr attempting to return to Westminster, and Peter Alfred Taylor.[546] They split the vote and this resulted in the election of a Conservative (for the first time in nearly 25 years), William Unwin Heygate[547] in this previous Liberal seat. There was violence when the poll opened on the 6th February with several assaults and many businesses closing for safety reasons. The result was announced on 8th February,

544 *Leicester Mercury*, 26th January 1861.
545 Joseph William Noble (1797-1861) of Danett's Hall. Leicester Alderman and Liberal MP, died in the Cholera epidemic at Malaga and is commemorated by the Hospital Noble.
546 Peter Alfred Taylor (1819-1891). Social reforming MP and scion of the Courtauld family.
547 William Unwin Heygate (1825-1902). Conservative MP for various constituencies and chairman of Pares' Leicestershire Banking Company.

shortly after which the hustings would have been removed. Heygate would lose the 1865 General Election and, as a result, his erstwhile opponents Taylor and Harris would be returned for the two seats.

Drinking Fountain
Temperance Hall
Granby Street
April 1861
Flint & Shenton
Demolished 1961

The *Leicester Chronicle* reported plans for a drinking fountain in April 1861:

> 'A DRINKING FOUNTAIN is now being executed, to be erected adjoining the Temperance Hall in Granby-street. The bowl is of Scotch granite, polished, inserted in a Mansfield stone niche, with white marble plinth, and columns with carved capitals, the whole surmounted by a Ketton stone carved pediment, forming as handsome tout ensemble that will bear a favourable comparison with most of its more costly rivals in the metropolis and in the provinces. The design, by Messrs. Flint and Shenton, architects, of Leicester, is in admirable taste. The execution of the work is entrusted to Mr. Joseph Yates,[548] St. George's-street, whose long established respectability is a guarantee of it being carried out in a manner alike creditable to the projectors of the fountain, to the architects, to himself, and to the town.'[549]

The same day's *Mercury* reveals that '... *works... are now in progress*'.[550] It was built on the north side of the Hall and was adjacent to a public house and such was the popularity of the fountain that the publican tried to capitalise on it by advertising his premises more prominently. The Temperance Society was aghast and built a wall to obscure the view![551] The opening

---

548 Joseph Yates (1798-1878). Stonemason of St George's Street who also designed the base for the Robert Hall statue in de Montfort Square.
549 *Leicester Chronicle*, 20th April 1861.
550 *Leicester Mercury*, 20th April 1861.
551 *Leicester Journal*, 4th October 1861.

ceremony took place in 1861, led by the Rev Babington[552] who was President of the Temperance Society, and it was widely reported.[553]

Coach houses, stabling, granaries and warehouses
Campbell Street
Evans and Stafford
June 1861
Flint & Shenton
Demolished

This was a large commission for Evans[554] and Stafford, which Flint would not live to see beyond its early stages. The *Leicester Chronicle* published a rave review of the new additions in 1863 and quotes extensively from *The Grocer*,[555] although Flint's part in the design was overlooked. The warehouse was an imposing edifice fronting Campbell Street and Trinity Street and formed a quadrangle. The original design was by Frederick Ordish in 1858. Flint and Shenton started their additions in 1861 and they were completed by 1863 and nothing quite conjures up the Empire-wide commerce of the time as this warehouse.

Classrooms
Archdeacon Lane Chapel
June 1861
Flint & Shenton
Demolished c. 1955

Archdeacon Lane Chapel was a Baptist church whose congregation formed in 1793 and Henry Goddard[556] designed the long-lived and purpose-built

---

552 Rev John Babington (1791-1885). Clergyman. Sometime vicar of Cossington.
553 *Leicester Chronicle*, 14th September 1861.
554 Thomas Merrett Evans (1816-1892). Prominent grocer of Portland House; High Bailiff of Leicester and Liberal councillor for Middle St Margaret's ward. For obituary see *Leicester Chronicle*, 16th April 1892. The firm helped sell his previous house, Highfield House on London Road, in 1859.
555 Leicester Chronicle, 23rd May 1863.
556 Henry Goddard (1792-1868). Architect and second generation of the dynasty of Leicester architects.

Archdeacon Lane Chapel survived until 1955.

new chapel for them in 1836. It closed in 1939 as a direct result of losing its congregation to the first wave of slum clearances before the war. Flint and Shenton received planning permission for classrooms on 21st June 1861[557] and the commission is typical of the steady and utilitarian works undertaken by the firm at the time. The classrooms were built on the main school room on the right-hand side of the chapel and ran across the graveyard running parallel with Thames Street. As with the Gallowtree Gate chapel works four years earlier, the classrooms appear to be for boys only. The congregation relocated to Buckminster Road in 1939 and the chapel was demolished around 1955. Archdeacon Lane still exists, and is an almost building-less road near the flyover: nothing gives any clue to the fact it was once a densely populated community.

Warehouse additions
Church Gate
Hunt and Pickering
August 1861

---

557 LRO 1861/1391.

Flint & Shenton
Extant

The Hunt and Pickering[558] Company was concerned with agricultural machinery and operated a goulding implement works. It had premises on Gallowtree Gate and it alerted *Journal* readers to its '... *extensive additions to their workshops and machinery, extending to Church-gate.*'[559] The firm started life in about 1827 as a bar iron warehouse operated by Mary Hunt[560] and later her son, William,[561] until about 1854 when the business became Hunt and Pickering. This partnership lasted until it was dissolved in 1872 (it is likely Pickering was dying) and William Hunt then operated alone. His ploughs were evidently of good quality and won prizes at Agricultural competitions with the Paring and Light Harrow Ploughs particular hits.[562]

Hunt and Pickering's warehouse from Short Street.

558 Joseph Pickering (1828-1872). Ironmonger of Melton Road.
559 *Leicester Journal*, 11th October 1861.
560 Mary Hunt (1790-?) of London Road, businesswoman and widow of William Hunt (1785-1820), iron founder and framesmith.
561 William Hunt (1814-1874). Ironmonger and Borough Magistrate of London Road.
562 *Leicester Chronicle*, 11th October 1873.

Flint and Shenton were engaged to enlarge the premises which they did by extending the warehouse from the back of the Church Gate fronting counting house so that it backed on to Short Street. Vipan and Headly[563] took over in about 1873 and the business continued to use the Church Gate warehouse until the First World War. The firm lasted in one form or another until 1964. The building still exists.

Fence wall
Hill Street British School
August 1861
Flint & Shenton
Extant

This almost inconsequential work is included as it is the last known work with which William Flint was associated but is a rather pedestrian full stop to an illustrious career. Plans were approved on 16th August 1861[564] for a

The wall for the British School in Hill Street and possibly Flint's last work.

563 James Vipan (1827-1903) of West Walk, later Bournemouth and Edward Paget Gillam Headly (1843-1913) of Alexandra Road, ironmongers.
564 LRO 1861/1416.

wall to run from the school site on Hill Street and round the corner of the property to Eldon Street. Flint had, of course, built the school in 1834. A new entrance on the corner of the two streets was created, with a little of the remaining land given over to the Borough on condition that they lay down flagging. Hill Street still exists but it now runs into Lee Circle which has resulted in truncating Eldon Street. However, there is a wall-like structure in the right place at the bottom of the road. Could this be Flint's last stand?

CHAPTER 11

Other Work

Shop fronts
1849-1860
Leicester Town Centre
Flint & Wickes and Flint & Shenton

Shop fronts were a small but presumably steady source of income for Flint's business. There are ten surviving designs at the LRO, but it is likely there were more in the history of the firm. Given that seven of the plans are closely similar in date from late 1849 to early 1851, it is probable that what the LRO holds is only that which has survived. The 1850s was a time of such rapid growth in commerce that these commissions are probably a small representation of what must have been a good source of revenue for Flint and his partners.

1849, December: High Street for Mr Harris.[565] Flint & Wickes.
This is a frontage for Joseph Harris's legal business. The plans show that this was a small commission involving minor alterations and that the business was situated on High Street at number 63 or 65. Flint had previous involvement with the property handling the associated dwelling's letting for Harris in 1843 – one of very few pieces of work that year.[566]

1850, March: Silver Street for Mr Sharpe.[567] Flint & Wickes.
Thomas Sharpe owned a linen, woollen and silk mercers and hosiery business on the corner of Cheapside and Market Place. By 1850, a shop was opened on Silver Street and it may be that this was the new shop being fitted out. The work involved changes to plinths and pilasters.

---

565 Joseph Harris (1798-1882), attorney of Westcoats House.
566 *Leicester Journal*, 1st September 1843.
567 Thomas Sharpe (1813-1852). Silk mercer.

1850, March: Granby Street/Halford Street for Mr Robins.[568] Flint & Wickes.
This laceman's, haberdasher's and hosier's was situated on the corner
of these two streets and it was owned by Robert Robins. The shop was
replaced by Imperial Buildings around the turn of the last century.

1850, July: Market Place for Mr Jones.[569] Flint & Wickes.
At the same time as the firm was busy erecting the new Corn Exchange,
Flint and Wickes were able to complete a shop front in the Market
place for Henry Sharpe Jones and his fancy repository; an enterprise he
somehow combined with being a silversmith and toy dealer. Plans were
given approval on 26th June 1850 and involved changes to the balconies
and window projections.

1850, August: Silver Street for Mr Thompson. Flint & Wickes.
John Thompson[570] was a clothes dealer and pawnbroker at number ten
and number twelve Silver Street who also had premises at 26, Belgrave
Gate. This commission was concerned with additions to what was already
a sizeable business with its own counting house, etc.

1850, September: Gallowtree Gate for Mr Porter.[571] Flint & Wickes.
This shop front was for John Porter, who was a tobacconist at number 22
and a cabinet maker at number 24, and was another job which was about
changing the appearance of existing pilasters.

1851, March: Market Place for Mr Lockwood.[572] Flint & Wickes.
Flint and Wickes undertook another Market Place commission; this
time for William Lockwood who was about to dissolve his partnership
with Matthew Steele[573] in the drapery company Lockwood and Steele of
Cheapside. The work removed a step; altered cornices by eight inches and
moved a set of iron doors.

---

568 Robert Robins (1811-1876), whose premises were Regent House, Market
    Place, from 1869.
569 Henry Sharpe Jones (1819-1885). Fancy goods shop proprietor.
570 John Thompson (1804-1869). Pawn broker later of Nicholas Street.
571 John Porter (1803-1865). Cabinet maker and tobacconist.
572 William Salte Lockwood (1798-1862). Draper of West Street.
573 Matthew Richmond Steele (1820-1857). Draper who went bankrupt in 1855.
    For account of death see *Leicester Chronicle*, 3rd October 1857.

1856, March: High Street for Mr Manning. Flint & Shenton.

16 High Street was the premises of John Manning, tea dealer and coffee roaster and cheese and bacon factor and this new shop front was another minor job for Flint, albeit with a new partner.

1860, April: Haymarket for Mr Burton.[574] *Flint & Shenton.*

John Burton was a printer, engraver, bookseller and stationer and also acted for both the Manchester Fire and Pelican Life Insurance Companies. This job involved a long shop window and the plans also reveal that the business was in between the White Hart Hotel and Mr Hames's[575] house. The firm branched out into photography and artistry by 1870 and later achieved the Royal Warrant. The whole façade had a strong Flint look and there is a strong possibility that Flint designed it in the first place.

Streets
1851-1861
Leicester Town Centre
Flint & Wickes and Flint & Shenton

With the growth of housing, there had to be a growth in street building. Street plans are often less clear than plans for buildings as it is not always immediately clear what exists and what is proposed. Flint was heavily involved in the Leicester Freehold Land Society and it is almost certain that there are more streets that he laid out than are shown in surviving records. As with shop front plans, what follows is probably just a small sample of work that Flint undertook.

1851 Paving and tarmacking Regent Road
Flint sought tenders to pave and macadamise Regent Street in late 1851.[576] This is at a time of rapid town expansion and in turn this would lead to several commissions on the new road. He was employed by the Borough to do the work.

---

574 John Burton (1807-1881). Leicester businessman prominent in photography and printing and a prime mover in the development of the Clock Tower.

575 Francis Hames (1817-1887). Saddler of Haymarket. Father of Francis J. Hames, Town Hall architect.

576 *Leicester Mercury*, 29th November 1851.

1856 Richard Harris land

Plans to create Leamington Street, Little Holme Street, Great Holme Street and West Holme Street were given approval on 8th February 1856.[577]

Great Holme Street in 1965.

Little Holme Street in 1965.

---

577 LRO 1856/776/1 and LRO 1856/776/2.

Little Holme Street post demolition.

There are two plans which indicate some element of resubmission and they are linked to later plans – see below. Holme may be a Harris family name. They reveal that nine feet three inches below the datum line in Leamington Street, for instance, a 16 inch bore sewer was also put in. Much has changed in the area and Great Holme Street has disappeared under the ring road. Leamington Street has also gone. West Holme Street and Little Holme Street survive, but they are unrecognisable from Flint's time. Although houses were presumably well built and sought after, the area degraded into slums and was demolished in the 1970s.

1858 Leicester Freehold Land Society

Two new streets along newly built Havelock Street were laid out at the same time as a culvert of 15 inch bore was dug between Mill Lane and Gray Street.[578] The new streets were probably Deacon and Laxton Streets and the work in Havelock Street stretched as far as Raglan Street. This was part of the Leicester Freehold Land Society's Sixth Estate. In December the same year Flint and Shenton are advertising for paviours and builders to form, pave and drain two new streets for the Society, near Hinckley Road.[579]

---

578 LRO 1858/1016.
579 *Leicester Mercury*, 4th December 1858.

March 1860 Trinity Hospital Estate

Twenty years after Flint's first work for the charity in London Road, he was commissioned by them to lay out a new street. It was to have a causeway (pavement) and run into Duns Lane. The last part of the street, which had a gradient of 1 in 200, was contiguous with the Whitmore and Ellis mill.[580]

May 1860 Joseph Harris land, Lincoln Street

Flint laid out Lincoln Street in 1860 and it still exists in Highfields, linked by Andover Street to Conduit Street, with which it runs parallel. Flint had worked for Harris in 1849 when he put in a new façade to his solicitor's office in High Street. Even in the Twenty-First Century it retains a pleasant suburban Victorian feel.

1861 Richard Harris and Joseph Stretton[581] land

Richard Harris and Joseph Harris Stretton were cousins and, rather confusingly, the plans show Leamington and the Holmes Streets as new

Lincoln Street is situated behind the railway station and has a tranquil residential feel to it.

580 LRO 1860/1235.

581 Joseph Harris Stretton (1830-1889), attorney and solicitor; son of Clement Stretton of Danes Hill House.

but also include Gerrard Street and Coventry Street.[582] Both are now demolished. It is not clear if this was all laid out finally in 1861 or whether or not the 1856 plans were actually carried out.

Other business

As a surveyor (estate agent)

One of Flint's valuations still exists and is preserved at the LRO. Dated 13th January 1838 and written from Flint's office in Friar Lane, it reads:

> 'Sir,
> I have researched the Retail Shop, Dwelling House and Warehouse situate in the Gallowtree Gate, and occupied by you, and I value the premises at the sum of one thousand eight hundred and fifteen pounds.
>
> 1815£ [sic]
>
> I am Sir
> Yours faithfully
> William Flint' [583]

It is an uninteresting letter in itself, but it is remarkable in that it is the sole survivor of what must have been hundreds or possibly thousands of valuations over Flint's career. The identity of the customer was not clear due in part to Flint's handwriting, but research has proved it to be for Mark Iron, a druggist.[584] He did not appear to move until the next year and was involved in a court case centring on this property and its qualification to allow him to vote – his vote was eventually expunged![585] His premises somehow linked to Rutland Street.

---

582 LRO 1861/1370.
583 LRO DE3196/22.
584 Mark Oliver Iron (1800-1849). Druggist and sometime overseer of St Margaret's Parish.
585 *Leicester Chronicle*, 28th September 1839.

Letting

As well as surveying and work as an architect, a good portion of Flint's work was letting. Contemporary newspapers are full of his and almost every other architect's letting notices. The following is a typical example of Flint's work:

> 'TO BE LET
> and may be entered upon immediately,
> A Superior Dwelling HOUSE, situate in Church-gate, with large dining and drawing rooms, and breakfast parlour complete with five bed rooms, and six attics, large kitchen and out-offices, with one 3-stall stable, capital cellars, spacious garden and summer house, formerly the residence of Beaumont Burnaby.[586] Esq.
>
> For a view of the premises, &c apply to Mr. Flint, Architect, Leicester.' [587]

Looking down Church Gate in the Twenty-First Century, it seems impossible that this could ever have been a desirable residential location and that there could ever have been room for gardens, summer houses and stables. It must have been an attractive house if it was fit for the ubiquitous Mr Burnaby, who was a busy society solicitor and features regularly in the Leicester press of the time.

Another unusual job, and another that strains modern day credibility, was the sale of valuable building materials from the demolition of Lord Southampton's[588] kennels and stables in 1838. Situated by St George's Church, the site comprised a thatched building or coach house and all sorts of outbuildings and stables, most of which were decorated with iron spouting and piping. There was also a lead pump and cistern. The kennels were probably associated with the Quorn Hunt, where Lord Southampton had recently been master.

---

586 Beaumont Burnaby (1772-1848) of Friar Lane, solicitor and Registrar of the Prebendal Court.
587 *Leicester Journal*, 9th February 1838.
588 Charles Fitzroy, third Baron Southampton (1804-1872). Huntsman and British peer of Whittlebury Lodge.

CHAPTER 12

Flint or Not Flint?

The buildings in this chapter fall into three categories. The first group are buildings thought to be by William Flint but there is evidence to show that they are probably by someone else. The second is for buildings that are popularly thought to be by him but there is little or no evidence to prove it and the third group is buildings that look like they may be by him or whose existence is proved but it has not been possible to establish any other facts about them. Where there is an advertisement in the contemporary local press with Flint as the estate agent selling or letting newly erected or substantially improved properties (often without the involvement of another party), the property is included in section three, as it is suspected that there is a strong link between the building and selling. It may not be the case, so this is why they are in this section where attribution cannot be proved.

Group 1

For many years, the railway station at Campbell Street was assumed to be a William Flint design until research revealed William Parsons to be the architect. Attribution to Flint is given in this book to some buildings even though it is not 100% certain in some cases. These are clearly indicated in their individual entries but if they are included, it means Flint is *at least* the most likely architect. There are some surprising omissions to the tally of Flint buildings…

The Phoenix Building, Welford Place
This is universally considered to be his work and the Grade 2 listing information states that it was built by him in 1842. However, the plans no longer exist and although this is not unusual for buildings of this age, there is no building reported in the local press leading up to the year 1842. When

Phoenix House: Long thought to be Flint's work but more probably attributed to Parsons.

the original clients, The Leicestershire and Midland Counties Fire and Life Insurance Company, left their Market Street offices in 1836 to move to Belvoir Street, it coincided with a building project for their new offices in Welford Place by William Parsons.[589] Whilst it is possible that Parsons built something else for the company in the same road, it seems unlikely, which leaves Flint's former master and not Flint as the most likely architect.

2 houses, New Walk

There is a pair of houses opposite the Museum and next to Isaac Barradales's Court View. They were derelict for many years and since about 2010 have been back in use as dwellings; they are Greek Revival in style and particularly handsome. They have the anthemion and filament design that Flint (and Parsons) favoured – see Chapter 13 What Might a House have Looked Like? – and have been sometimes attributed to Parsons but more often to Flint. J. D. Bennet[590] suggests that the pair of semi-detached Greek villas featured in Loudon's *Encyclopaedia of Rural Architecture* are these houses and, with no evidence to link them to Flint, Parsons with his partner Gill is the most likely architect.

---

589 *Leicester Chronicle*, 18th June 1836.
590 Bennett op. cit.

Greek stuccoed houses, New Walk: another more likely Parsons commission.

Group 2

Waterloo House, New Walk

Built circa 1835 this large construction has all the hallmarks of a Flint commission. It has his usual simple and classical design with use of the anthemion and filament ornament. It was a large three-storey grand edifice and stood on the Hastings Street junction of New Walk and was demolished in 1973 for Tigers' Way. It is a Flint design by look and reputation. Pevsner thought it to be by him.[591]

House, New Walk

There used to stand a house at number 94 (formerly 86), New Walk. This was situated almost over the railway bridge and near the Museum on the side nearest the station. Another attractively simple Classical design with a pilastred portico and anthemion decoration; it is a strong possibility that Flint is the architect. It was demolished in the 1950s.

2 houses, New Walk

Another New Walk possibility is the pair of detached villas towards the King Street end and numbered 27 and 29. Leicester City Council's New

591 Pevsner op. cit.

Another Tiger's Way demolition: Waterloo House in the early 1970s.

94 New Walk: This house has several Flint signs. Could it be his?

Walk Character Statement[592] names Flint as do Helen Boynton in her New Walk[593] book and others. In look they have nothing against them except the bay windows which look contemporary and, if they are, would

592 *New Walk Conservation Area Character Statement* (Leicester City Council, 2004)
593 *The History of New Walk* (Boynton, 2002)

be a departure for Flint. If they are a later addition, then it makes Flint a much more likely candidate to be their architect.

House, London Road

Dr Boynton also attributes a detached house on London Road to Flint (number 172). The house was possibly stuccoed, it is similar to the New Walk pair above and is an easy possibility.[594]

Two of the earliest houses on New Walk, similarities with Flint's style are obvious.

With stucco it's easier to imagine as a Flint design.

594 Boynton op cit.

Group 3

2 shops and houses, Lutterworth
Another use of the anthemion and filament frieze is to be found on two shops in High Street. This is the only known use of the frieze outside Leicester and it is a longshot, but could this 1828 advert reveal Flint as the architect:

'VALUABLE SITUATION
TO BE LET

AN excellent Shop, with convenient Dwelling House and ample warehouses adjoining, situate in a populous and very improving Market Town, in the County of Leicester. – The Town AND Neighbourhood present a desirable opportunity for extensive business to an Ironmonger, and a part of the premises is, at present, an Ironmonger's Shop.

For particulars apply to Mr. W. Flint, Architect, King Street, Leicester.'[595]

The anthemion and palmette give this Lutterworth edifice a clear classical look.

595 *Leicester Journal*, 18th Januray 1828.

It is equally possible, however, that the architect of this building and Flint both sourced their friezes from the same dealer!

1838 five houses, Curzon Street

Flint was active in the Curzon Street area from the 1830s and another lost commission is suggested in this private contract advert for five houses '... *on the Humberstone Road, at the corner of the new street opposite Curzon-street.*'[596] It is not immediately clear where the advert means, but Kent Street is the one that matches the description best. However, the (admittedly later) Ordnance Survey map of 1913 does not show houses that match. The piece gives details of the cellars, palisaded fence in front, private yards and a backway as well as confirming that they have been '...*recently and substantially erected.*'

c. 1840 Three houses, London Road

This trio now comprising 178,180 and 182 London Road have a strong mid-Victorian look. The design with the last house at right angles is a well-known Flint device.

An obvious Flint design or copy on London Road.

---

596 *Leicester Journal*, 9th February 1838.

c. 1840 Hastings House, (three houses)
Hastings Street and Princess Road
This building has the pilasters, the frieze, the lugged architraves, string courses and overall simplicity to be a certain Flint design. It is very similar to the heavily altered London Road trio above and survived into the 1970s.

Hastings House, an almost certain
Flint construction.

C. 1840 Shops and houses, Causeway
lane and Highcross Street
More pilasters with frieze adorn this pleasing construction. These mixed retail and residential premises resemble those found in Lutterworth and the houses immediately above.

1840 two houses, New Walk
The *Journal* is the source for these two new houses on New Walk, one of Flint's most prolific patches: *'Those two handsome and newly-erected*

Another similarly dated and styled edifice, this time on the corner of
Causeway Lane and Highcross Street.

HOUSES, delightfully situate in the New Walk...'[597] the premises included a 25 feet long warehouse and fronted a newly formed back street. In the same advert he was offering for sale an *'... ornamental iron verandah...'* which stood before Mr Sarson's[598] houses on New Walk before they were taken down for the railway.

1843 Warehouse

No advert for this work has been uncovered in Leicester, but there is one in the Derby press for iron founders and smiths:

> 'PERSONS desirous of CONTRACTING to execute the CAST and WROUGHT-IRON WORK of a WAREHOUSE now building at Leicester...'[599]

It has not been possible to identify the warehouse; it could potentially be the Richard Harris premises on King Street but this is speculation only.

1844 House, West Street

Flint handled the sale of *'... the recently erected and commodious dwelling house...'* with five bedrooms in West Street in October 1844.[600] Mrs Byng[601] was already resident in this large house, which also had two kitchens and a 'spacious' garden. Could this house be the one found at the back of the three Regent Road properties (formerly the Fielding-Johnson Hospital) as it has several points of similarity? By look, it is an easily acceptable Flint building.

1848 Factory, Southgate Street

Another good candidate for a Flint building is Caleb Bedell's[602] elastic webbing factory in Southgate Street. Evidently a large affair with '...

---

597 *Leicester Journal*, 14th August 1840.
598 John Sarson (1775-1851) of New Walk, grocer and tea dealer with premises on Hotel Street.
599 *Derby Mercury*, 17th May 1843.
600 *Leicester Journal*, 18th October 1844.
601 Maria Byng née Gwyllym (1781-1851). Widow of Lt Thomas Byng of Tamworth.
602 Caleb Bedell (1807-1874). Pioneering elastic webbing manufacturer who later went bankrupt. For obituary see *Leicester Chronicle*, 28th February 1874.

Mrs. Byng's house on West Street opposite the Museum. Its later addition
to the right is obvious.

Steam Engine and Boiler thereto and the WAREHOUSES...',[603] the reason
for Flint being a candidate for architect is that the same advert has a final
line: *'The Buildings are chiefly new, and substantially erected, and contain a floor
area of 11,500 feet'*. Might Flint have built the factory in the first place?

1849 House in a parish adjoining the Borough of Leicester
An advert with the title *'A Desirable Country Residence'* appeared in the
Chronicle in 1849 looking for a let for '*... a newly erected HOUSE, situate in a
parish adjoining the Borough of Leicester...'*. This was no cottage and comprised
a pleasure garden, (normal) garden, kitchen garden and gardener's cottage,
coach house and vinery outside and a library, six bedrooms and two attics
(amongst other rooms) inside. At the time, the parish referred to may
have meant Knighton or Stoneygate.

c.1850 Terrace, Friar Lane
This row still exists and was where Flint, Wickes, Shenton and Baker
practiced. They have a pleasing clear definition and are commanding
without being ostentatious. There is no evidence to identify an architect

---

603 *Leicester Journal*, 16th June 1848.

Flint's office was here in Friar Lane. Did he design the block?

but given their look and their association with Flint, it must be an even bet that he is their architect. J. D. Bennet thought this row to be his[604].

c.1852 Houses, Asylum Street

Another set of highly likely Flint buildings which appear to continue on from his known commission for Mr. Brown in 1852, which can be seen in the background.

More houses in Asylum Street and probably for Mr Brown.

1855 Tomb, Welford Road Cemetery

Richard Harris's monument in Welford Road cemetery is also reputed to be by Flint. It is clearly a classical in design and may have been based on

---

604 Bennet, op cit.

Oft rumoured to be a Flint design for former client Richard Harris.

an entrance to the Tower of the Winds or Horologium in Athens, built c. 100 – 50 B.C. The columns have a similarity to other Flint columns and there is also use of the anthemion design at each corner. The source used by Friends of Welford Road Cemetery has not been recorded.

1857 Villa, Stoneygate
The firm were offering a let for the '... *small villa recently erected and delightfully situated at STONEYGATE, a short distance from the London-road'.*[605] It had domestic offices, two sitting rooms and six bedrooms as well as a coach house and an ornamental garden. Its location has not been identified.

1860 Warehouse, Belvoir Street
Flint and Shenton advertised a plot of land for a warehouse next to John Baines's warehouse with a frontage to Belvoir Street of 276 yards. It is not clear whether anything further was built by the firm.[606]

---

605 *Leicester Chronicle*, 11th April 1857.
606 *Leicester Mercury*, 11th February 1860.

Flint's frieze?

Several of Flint's buildings are adorned by a Greek frieze of anthemion and palmette. Anthemion is the Greek name for honeysuckle; it has been a popular adornment to buildings for millennia and can be seen on the Erechtheum at the Acropolis. The palmette is a radiating, fan-shaped motif suggestive of a palm leaf and is found in Egyptian, Assyrian, and Aegean art.

For some years the frieze has been seen as Flint's trademark; however, it is not nearly as clear as that. The following buildings have the frieze and are attributed to Flint with total certainty:

1830	*Baptist Church, Charles Street*
1836	*General Newsroom, Granby and Belvoir Streets*

This next group are almost certain to be his:

1835	*Crescent Buildings, Upper King Street*
1836	*Crescent Cottages, King Street*

This group may be his:

Anthemion and palmette frieze at Charles Street Baptist Church.

Detail on pilaster bases at Upper King Street.

1828	*Two shops, High Street, Lutterworth*
c.1835	*Waterloo House, New Walk*
c.1840	*86, New Walk*
c.1840	*Hastings House, Pribcess Road, Hastings Street*

The last group are (probably) not by him, but have the same frieze:

c.1834	*Pair of Greek style houses, New Walk (by Parsons and Gill)*
1836	*Theatre Royal, Horsefair Street (by Parsons)*

What all this probably means is that the frieze was pre-fabricated and available to buy from a building supplier or could have been cast in a mould purchased by the architect. The exact same frieze is common in Brighton, for example. Rather than being the sign of a particular architect, could it be the particular sign of a builder? Builders' identities are much harder to trace than architects, so it will probably never be known.

CHAPTER 13

What Might a House have Looked Like?

Charles Wickes's final book was published at the end of 1854 and he must have written it during his time as William Flint's partner. The following is taken from *A handy book of villa architecture* and is his description for a house which was accompanied by five plates showing internal cross sections and exterior elevations. The detail is fascinating: memel (a type of oak) used here, fir used there and the proscription about the fittings, where nothing but *The Vieille Montagne Zinc Company* (a Belgian concern) or *Maw's Encaustic Tiles* (from Worcester) will do, is eye-catching. Is Wickes an early practitioner of product placement? Flint and Wickes built similar villas and, whilst it is likely that here Wickes gives full reign to his imagination, their buildings such as the Infant Orphan Asylum and Loughborough Emmanuel Rectory that show clear debts to Wickes's work. The following gives us at least a taste of what sort of work went into the houses they built.

'OUTLINE SPECIFICATIONS AND ESTIMATES.

DESIGN No. I.

SPECIFICATION.

EXTERNALLY.— The whole of the walls to be built of good hard well-burnt and well-shaped yellowish stocks, those used for the facings to be most carefully selected and of uniform size and colour, to have neat close joints which are to be raked out and pointed with flat joint the last thing before completion.

The plinth, horizontal bands, frieze and bedmold to cornice to be formed of the very best white bricks, to correspond with the stone dressings. The splay of plinth, and also the splay to chimney shafts to be of similar bricks moulded for the purpose.

Wickes' design number 1.

The arches and keys over all windows and doors, except those of dining-room bay-window, to be formed in red and black ganged bricks, accurately worked and set in putty.

The irregular quoins at angles to be formed in good hard red bricks of approved colour.

The sill and dado, jambs, mullions, arches and keystones of dining-room bay are to be executed in Box-Ground or Portland Stone, and the mullions, sills and blocks of other windows are to be done in the same material, as also the moulded slopes or off-sets to chimneys and the shafts above necking. The Cantilevers to main cornice, also to Bay and Porch may be of Ransome's Stone, or other durable cast material.

The Roofs to be covered with best Bangor Countess slates with copper nails, and the Ridges to have Slate-saddle and Ridge-roll, fixed with brass-headed nails and properly set.

The flat on top of the roof over porch, and the covering of Bay, to be formed of 21 ounce zinc with rolls, etc., laid in the manner adopted by the "Vieille Montange Zinc Company" without solder.

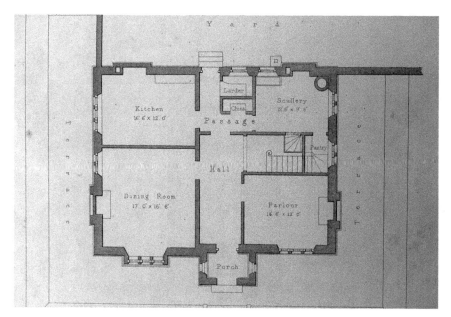

The ground floor.

The eaves gutter to be of cast-iron moulded, with all needful angles, slopt ends, and outgoings, laid to slight fall, and resting on 4 inch rough stone landing well tailed into wall and cemented on the under side. The down pipes to be 3 inch cast-iron round, with all needful bands, bends, shoes, etc. The down pipe from Bay may be 1 ½ inch lead.

The central gutter and those behind chimney stacks with step flashings to be of 6 and 5 lb. lead respectively.

The glass in all ground-floor windows to be of patent plate, and elsewhere best flattened sheet-glass all properly bedded and sprigged where needful.

INTERNALLY.— The timber to be Memel of good quality. The whole of floors, except cellars and hall, to be of battens laid straight joint, and free from all large knots and defects. The partitions forming Larder, China Closet, Bath Room, etc., to be of Fir quarters 4 x 2, lathed and plastered on both sides.

The sashes throughout are all to be double hung, and the windows to have boxing shutters hung in two heights with proper bars and fastenings.

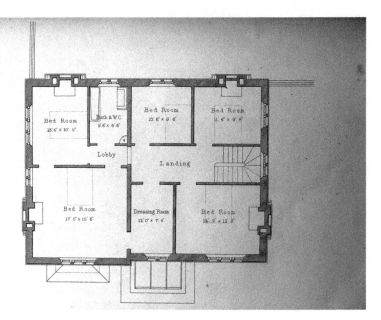

The upper floor.

The internal wood work to staircase, doors, shutters, etc., to be of the cleanest description, and be put together in the best possible manner, the panels being of pitch pine, and the whole prepared with a view to being stained and twice varnished and not covered with paint. The external work to be primed and painted in four good oils and finished an approved colour.

The Porch to be paved with Portland Stone and the Hall with Maw's Encaustic Tiles, laid to pattern on bed of concrete six inches thick.

The walls of Hall and Landing to be plastered with Cassentini's or Keene's Patent Plaster to prepare for paint. The walls of Dining-room and Parlor to be rendered, floated, set and papered with paper of the value of fourpence per yard, two front bed-rooms and dressing-room with paper value threepence per yard, other rooms of first-floor with paper value twopence per yard. Enriched cornice twelve inches girt to parlor. Plain cornice twelve inches girt to dining-room, hall and landing, and of nine inches girt to bed-rooms, to be executed in plaster, and picked out in two tints.

Provide one enrichment in centre of dining-room, thirty-six inches diameter, and one in parlour, thirty inches diameter, fixed complete.

Provide slate cistern to hold 150 gallons; Jenning's patent stool-cock, water closet apparatus with blue ware pan and trap fitted with regulator complete; zinc painted bath and urinal, with all necessary plumber's work in pipes, unions, cocks, valves, joints, solder, wall-hooks to supply same and carry off water; also to connect bath with oven and boiler-range in kitchen, for the supply of hot and cold water, together with all necessary joiner's work in seat, riser, casing, etc.

Lay on water to supply sink in scullery, and also tap in small lobby first-floor landing.

    Provide for one bell, hung complete from each room, and one to front door.

    Also for finger-plates, and Pitt's Patent Porcelain Furniture to all doors on ground-floor.

    Provide stoves and chimney-pieces to all chimney openings, those in dining-room, parlour and front bed-room to be of marble.

All fittings or finishings, not before enumerated, to be finished in a style to correspond and be consistent with the foregoing, and with the size and character of the building.

ESTIMATE.

This Villa can be erected in a good and substantial manner, according to Plates Nos. 1, 2, 3, 4 and 5, including two cellars, etc., in Basement, earth-work, steps, and gravelling to form Terraces, Drainage, Stoves, Chimney-pieces, Dresser, Copper, Bath, Bell-hanging and other Fittings and Decorations as described in the foregoing Specification, for the sum of Eleven hundred and twenty-five pounds

£1,125 0s 0d

If dressings are executed in Portland Stone instead of Box-Ground add £25 0s 0d.'

CHAPTER 14

The Pupils: William Millican

William Henry Millican was born on 22nd August 1830 and christened on 8th December 1830 at St George's. He was the son of Thomas,[607] a tailor of Gallowtree Gate and his wife Marianna.[608]

The Directory of British Architects and his RIBA nomination papers[609] record that William Millican was a pupil of William Flint between March 1847 and March 1851, however, his obituary in the *Leicester Mercury*[610] records an apprenticeship with Smith[611] and Dain, which is not recorded anywhere else!

He is in business by mid-1851 in partnership with John Kellam and in October of that year they moved from Millstone Lane to offices lately occupied by Palmer[612] and Billson in Friar Lane, thus becoming neighbours of Flint.[613] Surviving plans for the firm show that shop frontages and warehouses, e.g. for William Hardy's business in Hotel Street in 1856 or James Plant's[614] Norton Street fancy box and stationery warehouse in 1853, are a staple part of the business. Much of their work was building houses on streets such as Painter Street, Sparkenhoe Street or Aylestone Road. They were responsible for laying out Brudenell, Cardigan, Gloucester and Alma Streets in 1855 – long since demolished they were situated off Mill Lane near the canal. Of note to antiquarians is the firm's hand in the (partial) demolition of the historic Angel Inn on Cheapside to make way

---

607 Thomas Millican (1799-1872), tailor.

608 Marianna Freeman (1805-1878).

609 RIBA nomination papers F v5 p.123.

610 *Leicester Mercury*, 9th November 1889.

611 William Beaumont Smith (1828-1899), architect.

612 William Palmer (1809-?) and William Billson were a firm of solicitors, later of New Street.

613 *Leicester Journal*, 17th October 1851.

614 James Plant (1818-1892). Fancy box maker, printer and stationer; consulting engineer; amateur scientist; museum creator and pillar of the Philosophical Society of West Street. For obituary see *Leicester Chronicle*, 12th November 1892.

for Richard Morley's[615] drapery business expansion. The partnership with Kellam was dissolved on 14th August 1856 and coincidentally Millican moved to chambers on William Hardy's '*more eligible*' premises opposite the Assembly Rooms on Hotel Street.[616] The move has the feel of an acrimonious separation.

Millican did not practise alone for long as he was already working with his new partner Thomas William Smith[617] by March 1857 and the firm's trade was similar to commissions Millican had undertaken with Kellam. A late project was the Gothic National School at Enderby liked by Pevsner, but their alterations to St Egelwin the Martyr in Scalford he rates as '*dismal*'.[618] This partnership came to an end on 5th July 1860 probably due to Smith's financial problems as he was declared bankrupt on 29th March 1862. Just days later, on 5th May he died of '*effusion of blood to the brain*'.[619]

In practice on his own, in 1861 he competed to design the new Town Hall at Northampton and came third behind another Flint pupil, Charles Baker,[620] but trade seems to have carried on as before with similar work such as warehouse additions and alterations; although not very many plans from this period in practice seem to survive. In 1860, he designed another National School in Gothic, this time in Birstall. In 1862, he extensively restored Allexton's St Peter's Church and restored St Thomas a Becket in Skeffington. In 1864, and waiving his fee, he restored Parsons's St George's tower roof and south gallery. A further commission around this time was for Thomas Ingram[621] to build his new house at Wigston. Known as Hawthorn Field it stands in the grounds of Wigston Academy near the site of the Conduit which Ingram relocated there before it was finally lost under the school's development.[622]

---

615 Richard Morley (1805-1884). Draper and sometime conservative councillor of Victoria House, London Road.
616 *Leicester Mercury*, 30th August 1856.
617 Thomas William Smith (1835-1862), architect of Millstone Lane.
618 *Leicestershire and Rutland* op. cit.
619 *Leicester Chronicle*, 5th May 1862.
620 *Leicester Chronicle*, 4th May 1861.
621 Thomas Ingram (1810-1909), prominent Leicester solicitor and legal registrar.
622 The author is Executive Headteacher of Wigston Academy and the neighbouring Wigston College. The ground floor currently houses the Trust's nursery!

Now a nursery for Wigston College, Abington House was built for Thomas Ingram.

Millican married Susannah Tuffney[623] in 1852 and their only child, Kenneth William[624] was born in 1854. In 1861, he was living at 47 Regent Road a few steps away from his master at number 76.

By 1866, he is in partnership again and this time, rather confusingly, with Thomas Smith.[625] It looks like the surname is purely coincidental as there is no connection to the first Thomas Smith. This business saw lots of work and, once again, houses were a large part of their activity with work on St Leonard's Street, Crown Street, Norfolk Street, Bradgate Street, Walnut Street and London Road amongst others. In 1867 the firm were involved in a row over a design for a competition to improve traffic around the Haymarket; a real traffic hazard in the city at the time. The East Gates Improvement Committee sprang up and launched a competition to sweep away obstructions and replace them with a clock tower. 105 designs were submitted, including the one by Shenton and Baker, and eventually the choice fell between Millican and Smith's Perpendicular and Joseph Goddard's Gothic. Subscribers voted for Millican and Smith with 24 votes over Goddard; however, when the Town Council's Clock Tower

---

623 Susannah Loseby Millican (1828-1875).

624 Kenneth William Millican (1854-1915). Physician and champion of homeopathic medicine.

625 Thomas Smith (1833-1886), architect of Aylestone.

Committee met, they voted by 30 votes to 14 in favour of Goddard. Controversy ensued, as it transpired that Goddard had altered his original design in light of criticism from the committee. It was announced to cries of *'No, no'* and *'Order'* and as a *'Robbery of the brains'*[626] and councillors were passionate in their sympathy for Millican. Nevertheless, Goddard's design is what they chose.

Millican and Smith were responsible for the vicarages for St George's on Saxe Coburg (now Saxby Street) and also St John's on Ashwell Street. An early commission was the extensive restoration of St Peter's church in Arnesby in 1866 and in 1872 they built Holy Rood Church in Bagworth (demolished 1968 due to subsidence). They also designed the Board school on Belgrave Road as well as another for St George's Church in Colton Street. In May 1876, they undertook work on the cellar in Flint's General Newsroom with their last known commission being ten houses on King Richard's Road for Messrs Carr and Elvey[627] in July 1876. On 24th January 1877 the partnership was dissolved with Millican taking responsibility for all debts. (This is unusual and may hint at another

Holy Rood Church fell victim to subsidence, common in the Leicestershire coal field area.

---

626 *Leicester Chronicle*, 4th January 1868.
627 Mr Carr fl. 1870s and William Elvey (1848-1919). Master bricklayer of Beaconsfield Villa, Aylestone. Later bankrupt.

unhappy ending.)[628] It looks like the official dissolution took place after Millican started operating on his own as he is listed as the sole architect for the striking Greek-inspired Midland Auction Mart on Market Street complete with its bust of Mercury![629]

The Midland Auction Mart of 1876: a temple of commerce.

Their greatest work is the National Provincial Bank on the site of the Three Crowns Hotel, an old and well-known coaching inn. Started in 1868 and completed in 1872, the bank occupies the corner of Granby Street and Horsefair Street. The design is Italianate in white brick which Pevsner describes as

Subsequently extended, Millican owes a clear debt to Flint with his National Provincial bank of 1868.

628 Leicester Journal, 26th January 1877.
629 LRO 1876/10930

'modest'.[630] In this building can be seen William Flint's influence on his pupil as this is a building in his style and in his taste. It still exists and still impresses: quietly but commandingly.

Back in practice on his own, business seems to have been booming. At this stage in his career his work is much more commercial rather than domestic in character. There are houses, as might be expected, for example, two villas on Knighton Drive in 1879 for W. Wilkinson or houses and villas on Victoria Road, Great Holme Street, Stoneygate Road and Mowbray Street, but they are not nearly as numerous as before. He carried out work on several, now lost, public houses: the Anchor Hotel on Halford Street and the Eclipse on East Gates both in 1888 and the Fountain on Humberstone Gate and the Pelican in Gallowtree Gate both in 1881. A prestigious job was the free library given to Leicester by local businessman and benefactor Israel Hart[631] in 1881 which opened, much delayed, in 1883. Situated on the corner of Garendon Street and Upper Kent Street (now Maidstone Road), the building is in rather flamboyant Italian Gothic and shows Millican as an architect in his own right with

Garendon Street Library not long after opening.

630 *Leicestershire and Rutland* op. cit.
631 Sir Israel Hart (1835-1911), prominent Liberal town councillor and mayor, philanthropist and wholesale merchant.

Garendon Street Library today, now a mosque.

little or none of Flint's influence on display. The building is no longer a library and has changed into the Tajdaar-e-Madina Mosque.

Millican had at least two pupils who would set up practices as architects in their own right. The most notable was F. J. Hames, the designer of the Leicester's Queen Anne style Town Hall (and almost nothing else!). J. C. Traylen[632] was another pupil from 1855-1863, staying as his assistant until 1867 and he would practice in Leicester and Stamford during the latter half of the Nineteenth Century. One of Barradale's pupils, Thomas Fosbrooke,[633] would also become Millican's assistant towards the end of his life.

Millican was a fellow of the Royal Institute of British Architects and was proposed by Traylen's sometime partner F. W. Ordish and Joseph Goddard in 1878. In turn he was an active proposer of others including Henry Shenton in 1879 and Albert Sawday (with Shenton) in 1891.

His architectural career was just one aspect of his life and from a Twenty-First Century perspective he is the epitome of the self-made

---

632 John Charles Traylen (1844-1907). Architect and partner of F. W. Ordish, later of Stamford.

633 Thomas Henry Fosbrooke (1862-1925). Architect, later of Keites and Fosbrooke and then Keites, Fosbrooke and Bedingfield. Respected restorer of the Guild Hall and expert on Rothley Temple. Designed the art deco Belvoir Street extension to Johnson's later Fenwick's. For account of his life by Christine Taggart, see *The Leicestershire Historian* number 45, 2009.

civically minded Victorian. Volunteer reservist, JP and town councillor, he managed to combine all of these things with his business, married life and fatherhood. He was first elected to Leicester Council in a fiercely contested election for St Mary's East in 1872. He sat in the Conservative interest and would later be the leader of their group on the seemingly perennially Liberal dominated council. He resigned in February 1876, his obituary records that it was never explained why but it was maybe due to a public row about the Town Hall chimney, and he was not an assiduous attender either, it seems. In 1880 he was appointed magistrate and was known for his independent minded views and he contested the 1885 General Election increasing his party's vote. In 1859, he joined the Leicester Rifle Volunteers and by the time he died he had been made their honorary Lieutenant-Colonel. He was '*... a strict, if not a stern disciplinarian.*' but also '*... he was ever the jovial companion*'.[634]

Millican was also an artist. He painted several buildings in Leicester and a good example is the Exchange in the Market Place which he painted in 1850, whilst he was Flint's apprentice. Shortly after he painted it, the building was demolished to make way for the present (albeit with major additions) Corn Exchange by William Flint and Charles Wickes.

Susannah Millican died in 1875 and Millican married again the same year to Ellen Howell[635]

William Millican's grave at Welford Road Cemetery.

---

634 *Leicester Mercury*, 9th November 1889.
635 Ellen Millican (1836-1887).

with whom he had three children and whom he also survived. He and his family lived at Upton House (number 42) on de Montfort Street and this is where he died on 5th November 1889 after a long illness. Tributes were heartfelt and lengthy and it was publically noted that the children he had with Ellen were now orphaned at a young age. His funeral was a large public event and Isaac Barradale and J. C. Traylen were among the mourners. There was a wreath from the indisposed F. J. Hames and another from the Millican's Masonic Lodge with the rather neat inscription from Hebrews Chapter 10 verse 11: '*Looking for a city whose builder and maker is God.*' His will was proved on the 2nd January 1890 and his friend Francis James Hames was one of the executors.

His descendants were also interesting. His son, Kenneth, was a leading proponent of homeopathy and was persecuted by the British medical establishment because of it to the extent that he had to find work in America. Kenneth's daughter Dorothy, known as Jane Millican, was an actress and appeared in 'The life and death of Colonel Blimp' and 'A Canterbury Tale' amongst other films.[636]

---

636 Dorothy Bertha Millican (1902-1997). Actress.

CHAPTER 15

The Pupils: Charles Baker

The son of Robert Baker [637] (a draper) and Elizabeth Parker,[638] Charles Baker was born in Leicester in 1834. He never married and lived at 12, The Crescent, on King Street for over 30 years after 1870 before which he lived at Flint's 5, Museum Square.

He was articled to William Flint at the age of 16 in 1849 and stayed as his pupil until 1854. He is still with William Flint in April 1857 and is mentioned in the *Leicester Journal* account of a bad tempered and complicated litigation between Mr Holland (et al) and Mr Hutchinson[639] involving wood at the lunatic asylum. Charles Baker gave evidence about a store of gravel and is described as *'Charles Baker, assistant to Mr. Flint, architect...'*[640] William Millican was also engaged to measure gravel. At some point he went to Maidstone to work for Martin Bulmer,[641] then to John Bland[642] in Birmingham in about 1858 and finally to John

Charles Baker's house at 12, The Crescent, whilst he lived in it.

---

637 Robert Baker (1793-1874), lived at Flint and Wickes's Museum Square.
638 Elizabeth Baker (1802-1877).
639 John Hutchinson (1803-1869). Builder and paviour of Humberstone Gate.
640 *Leicester Journal* 24th April 1857
641 Martin Bulmer (1809-1879). Architect and County Surveyor for Kent.
642 John George Bland (1818-1898). Architect in practice at Market Harborough and then Birmingham where he designed several churches.

Johnson[643] in Adelphi, London. However, he is in Leicester on census night in 1861, living with his parents in Market Place and describing himself as 'an architect's assistant.' He went into partnership with Henry Shenton in 1863, the year after Flint died.

After Shenton retired in 1883, Baker carried on in business and retained offices at 18, Friar Lane and the practice remained busy. He was assisted for some of this time by Albert Gimson,[644] who later became an architect and surveyor in his own right. Gimson was a mourner at Shenton's funeral so his association with the firm may have stretched back to his time. In 1883, he extended Wyggeston Boys' School and also built the vicarage for St. Mary's Knighton and the next year built new factory buildings for William Yeomanson[645] in York Street. Sheds, extensions and warehouses feature heavily during these years including yet more work at the Whitmore Ellis mill at West Bridge in 1883, 1886, 1891, 1893, 1895, 1896 and 1900. He built several houses for several clients, for

THE BOYS' SCHOOL

Albeit without railings and much extended, the Wyggeston Hospital School still exists.

643 John Johnson (1807-1878). Hackney Borough Surveyor and co-designer of Alexandra Palace.

644 Albert Starkey Gimson (1863-1945) of Ashleigh House, Danes Hill. He kept offices at 18, Friar Lane well into the 1920s.

645 William Yeomanson (1820-1894). Fancy hosiery manufacturer of Lorne House, Regent Road.

The quiet and secluded vicarage for St. Mary's Knighton.

Baker followed in Flint then Shenton's footsteps to extend the Museum in 1891.

example two for William Gimson (father of his assistant Albert) at Dane Hills in 1883 and a pair of cottages for Samuel Partridge[646] in Friar Lane in 1887. In 1891, he extended the Museum in New Walk and the following year was involved with the Clarendon Park Estate once again laying out

---

646 Samuel Steads Partridge (1839-1919), solicitor, living two doors down from Baker at 10, The Crescent.

streets. The same year he built a business premises for Partridge on High Street, which still stands.

No plans designed by Baker exist at the LRO after 1904 at which time he must have more or less retired, although his work restoring the tower, clerestory and north isle of St Nicholas Church in 1904-1905 is commemorated by a plaque at the church along with a small display of the plans. It did not meet with universal acclaim. J. D. Bennett[647] suggests that the practice went to Albert Herbert, but there is no formal partnership. Herbert joined with James Tait[648] (whose pupil he had been) to form

A Dutch inspired elegant premises for Samuel Partridge on High Street.

Tait and Herbert in about 1900. Herbert's obituary by a member of the Leicestershire Archaeological and Historical Society in 1964[649] indicates that he 'absorbed' Baker's practice with Herbert transferring from 28 to 18 Friar Lane when he did so.

Charles Baker died on 11th February 1911 and his funeral took place on 16th February at Holy Trinity, a 30 metre walk from his house and a church he would have helped Flint remodel in 1853. That day's *Leicester Mercury* describes the event:[650]

'The funeral took place yesterday, at Welford-road Cemetery, of Mr. Charles Baker, who had practiced as an architect in Leicester for nearly forty years and who died at his residence, 12, The Crescent,

---

647 *Leicestershire Architects* op cit.
648 James Tait (1834-1915). Leicester architect of 28, Friar Lane. Shenton proposed his FRIBA nomination in 1882.
649 *Journal of the Leicestershire Archaeological and Historical Society*, 1964.
650 *Leicester Mercury*, 16th February 1911.

The commemorative plaque to Baker's work at St. Nicholas.

on Saturday at the age of 77 years. The funeral service took place at Holy Trinity Church, the clergymen officiating there and at the graveside being the Rev. F. Pepprill, vicar of Holy Trinity and the Rev. E. Atkins, master at Trinity Hospital. The latter gentleman was for many years associated with Mr. Baker at St. Martin's Church, when he was curate, and Mr. Baker was churchwarden. The mourners were Mrs. J. J. Bond (sister), Mr. and Mrs. Sydney Bond, Miss. Mabel Bond, Mr. R. M. Baker, Mr. T. Y. Baker, Mr. W. Baker, Misses. Ruth, Alice and May Baker, and Mr. A. S. Gimson (who was professionally associated with the deceased gentleman), Mr. W. M. Baker, Mr. Charles Baker's only brother was prevented from attending through illness.

In addition to the wreaths from the family, one was sent from the churchwardens and past churchwardens at St. Martin's with the following inscription: "In affectionate remembrance of an old and valued colleague whose earnest work for our church will long be remembered." Other wreaths were sent by the Misses. Abrahams, Mr. and Mrs. Berridge, Mr. and Mrs. Haviland, Mr. and Mrs. Hancock, Mr. and Mrs. A. Cowling, Mrs. Alfred Cook and sons, Mrs Mallam (Oxford), Mr. and Mrs. Edward Bayley and family, Mrs. Salusbury, Mrs. Lockwood, Mrs. Jacques, Messrs. Tait and Herbert, Dr. Cecil Marriott and Mrs. Garratt.

Mr. Hancock, organist at St. Martin's was at the organ and played "I know that my Redeemer liveth.'

The Baker family gravestones at
Welford Road Cemetery.

He is buried at Welford Road Cemetery and he left an estate valuing £1065 5s 6d. His younger brother, William Baker,[651] a draper like their father, died three months later and his estate was three times higher at £3722 15s. Whether this demonstrates that Charles Baker was a lesser businessman is a matter of conjecture.

The Warner, Sheppard and Wade catalogue for the auction of his effects survives at the LRO[652] and perhaps reveals a quiet and unostentatious man: there is nothing showy or

glittering in the auction. The lots range from Lot 323, a Japanised hip bath to lot 375, a 14 volume history of European morals and a more sentimental Lot 180, an engraving in an oak frame of 'The Strawberry Girl' by Samuel Cousins.[653]

An interesting survivor: the auction
catalogue for Charles Baker's estate.

---

651 William Mason Baker (1836-1911). Draper of Market Place whose second wife was William Gimsons's daughter, Elizabeth.
652 LRO DE61531/1.
653 Samuel Cousins (1801-1887). Highly regarded British mezzotint engraver.

CHAPTER 16

The Pupils: James Frank Smith

James Frank Smith was baptised on 5th April 1837 at St George's. His parents were Francis Smith[654] and Elizabeth Hames.[655] Francis Smith is one of the most celebrated and enigmatic figures of Victorian Leicester and is rumoured by some to be one of Conan-Doyle's inspirations for Sherlock Holmes. He is none other than 'Tanky' Smith, one-time police inspector and later private detective and renowned as a master of disguise, many of which are depicted in stone at Victoria Terrace on London Road, now known as 'Top Hat Terrace'. It was built by his son.

James Frank Smith's relationship with Flint is not clear. Both in 1862 and in Smith's obituary in 1895, Flint is described as his 'uncle'.

Victoria, later Top Hat, Terrace, showcasing Tanky Smith's disguises.

---

654 Francis Smith (1815-1888). Legendary Police Officer and later private investigator.
655 Elizabeth Hames (1814-1904).

A contemporary view showing the Top Hat Terrace's front gardens.

One of Tanky Smith's disguises.

He does not appear to be a blood relative as, of William Flint's two siblings who survived into adulthood, John Flint did not appear to marry or have children and Elizabeth Flint was a spinster who married Arthur

Whitewood, had no children and did not remarry after his death. This points to Ann Flint's family, but no connection has yet emerged. There is an Elizabeth Hull to Francis Smith marriage in 1833 which fits Ann Flint's maiden name of Hull but little else and most sources name Tanky Smith's wife as Elizabeth Hames whom he married in 1836.

He evidently went into tutelage with Flint in around 1851, after his formal education at the Green Coat School, later Alderman Newton's. Shortly after announcing his entrance to the profession in 1862, he is advertising for an assistant: *An intelligent youth wanted as pupil. Small premium only required.*[656] from his new address at 24, Market Place. A year later there are notices to *'Builders and small capitalists'* as well as *'Paviers and others'* to build *'New Leicester'*,[657] in other words the rapidly expanding edges of the town. In the same edition, he puts himself forward as a candidate for Surveyor to the Leicester District under the new Highway Act and boasts of his twelve years of experience. On 17th July 1868 he is on the front page of the *Leicester Journal* offering 25-year terms and excise and parochial assessments; ecclesiastical and other dilapidations; the building of labourers' cottages and draining.

He seems to have cornered the market in parish surveying posts. As his obituary records, he was parish surveyor at St Mary's for 35 years and eventually occupied that post for all of the other Borough parishes except St Margaret's. He rated St Mary's three times and saw its value rise from £34,125 in 1860 to £136,508 in 1895.[658]

As an architect he had a busy career with some prominent commissions. Pevsner highly rates his 1863 building for the Midland Brewery Company on Humberstone Gate. Known as Green's Electrical for some time he describes it as '… *a jolly little Italian palazzo.*'[659] Although the stucco has been removed, it remains an unusual and impressive construction and the late Flint Italianate influence is obvious. In 1864 he built the distinctive and great fun Top Hat Terrace for his father with its 18 differently hatted heads to represent his father's disguises as a detective.

After an abortive attempt to create an estate in Stoneygate with no terraced houses in the 1870s, similar to Alexandra Road which he laid out

656 *Leicester Mercury*, 1st March 1862.
657 *Leicester Mercury*, 14th March 1863.
658 *Leicester Chronicle* and Mercury, 15th June 1895.
659 *Leicestershire and Rutland* op. cit.

Well known in Leicester as Green's Electrical, the building actually started as a brewery.

A contemporary engraving of the Midland Distillery.

in 1876, he created and built Francis Street and Allendale Road and he possibly owned some of the houses there, as his widowed mother had a house in Francis Street in 1901.

A real sense of space in Allendale Road

Like Flint and almost every other contemporary architect, Smith was active as a surveyor and estate agent; for example, valuing the Nottingham Arms Public House in New Bond Street at £40 as part of a criminal case in 1872[660] or handling the renting of an 18-bedroom house four minutes from London Road Station in 1889.[661]

Looking at surviving plans at the LRO, Smith had a similar, although perhaps not quite as busy, practice to Flint. In 1863, he built nine houses for ex-Flint client Thomas Bland in Sycamore Lane (off Friars' Causeway) and in 1867, twelve cottages for Samuel Hodgkinson[662] in Framland Street (near Sparkenhoe Street). Houses in Saxe-Coburg Street in 1874 and the laying out of Stoneygate Road followed in 1877. In 1878 he was advertising for tenders for the New Bath Hotel in Bath Lane[663] and the 1880s saw much work in Francis Street and Stoneygate Road. In 1880, Smith also handled the sale of nearly 2,000 square yards of land in Abington Road, Evington Foot Road and Evington Lane (Road) and

660 *Leicester Chronicle*, 28th September 1872.
661 *Leicester Mercury*, 7th March 1889.
662 Samuel Hodgkinson (1823-1889). Currier and leather dealer of London Road.
663 *Leicester Journal*, 18th October 1878.

In his master's footsteps: Smith's version of the Fish Market.

probably laid the roads out.[664] He was responsible for the Fish and Poultry Market which was rebuilt in 1881 and still stands today, albeit encased in modern day shops. His tender was for £2,000.[665] His last major work was in 1892 with a factory for Stretton and Sons[666] on Castle Street and Southgate Street.

He had at least one pupil, Renfrew Spencer[667] who lodged with Smith and his family in Oadby in 1891. He was articled to him from 1889-1893 and later practised mainly in Nottingham.

He seems to have inherited some colourful characteristics from his father and it also looks like he had a sense of humour. He was involved in a trespass case and fishing without permission in 1873. He seemed to like fishing and attended meetings of the Leicester Angling Preservation Society at the Blue Boar Inn (*'Toasts interspersed with songs'*). Did he get this from his 'uncle'? Flint was a fisherman, as revealed by the auction of his estate. He had a further brush with the law over building irregularities at

---

664 *Leicester Journal*, 20th August 1880.

665 *Leicester Chronicle*, 4th June 1881.

666 Samuel Stretton (1789-1859) and his sons Stephen Dudgeon Stretton (1820-1910) of Aylestone Hall and Simeon Stretton of Kirby Muxloe (1822-1891), hosiery manufacturers.

667 Renfrew Spencer (1872-1961). Gedling based architect.

Victoria Terrace with the law catching up with him in 1874, seven years after his alterations. He was fined 40 shillings.[668] He was also something of an inventor and had a series of patents on self-acting gates and sluices cancelled in 1876.[669] As a pamphleteer, he published in 1877:

'Observations on the object and effect of some of the regulations of the Leicester Sanitation Authorities, and of the schedule attached to the Leicester Improvement and Drainage and Market Act, 1868'

which was a complaint about stringent building regulations and how this damages '*the advancement of mercantile prosperity.*' In 1875 he wrote to the *Chronicle* and *Mercury* to poke fun at the Local Board of Works and their flood scheme in the Great Holme Street area (following in Flint's footsteps again as he had laid the street out in 1856 and reported on drainage in it in 1845):

'My idea is that the streets should be channelled out, and make a sort of Venice of our ancient city. It would be very jolly to have boats sailing up and down the streets and the noise of the traffic would be less than the wood pavement.'

His greatest flight of fancy was in 1861 and got as far as the French Emperor before its manifest weaknesses were examined more closely:

'ENGLISH AND FRENCH SUBMARINE RAILWAY

AMONG the numerous schemes for effecting a land communication between England and the Continent, our attention has been directed to one by Mr. F. Smith, architect and engineer, Leicester, who proposes to carry a railway through a wrought-iron tube of vesical form in section, and laid on its side, at a level of about six fathoms beneath the surface of the sea. It is computed that the space of water displaced by the tube, supposing its length 23 miles, would be about 2,347,840 cubic yards, or 1,821,600 tons weight; consequently, deducting the weight of the tube and the ballast, about 800,000 tons, there remains 1,021,600 tons required to make the tube of

668 *Leicester Journal*, 24th July 1874.
669 *Leicester Chronicle*, 15th January 1876.

the specific gravity of sea water, or upwards of 25 tons per lineal yard for the entire length of the tube, and it is proposed to distribute this weight along the bottom of the sea, to which chains are to be attached, and secured to the tube by adjusting rods, so that it may be kept level throughout. And, further, in cases where practicable, and the rock hard enough, "Lewises" may be made in the rocky bed of the sea, and so connect the tube with the immovable bottom. Besides these, chain-weights every 50 feet apart, diagonal strain and tie chains are to be employed, as indicated on the plan, to connect the tube weights, or by Lewises as the case may be, to prevent any disturbance of the tube by tidal waves or under-current, if any.

It is thought that with the sectional form proposed there would be little or no vertical surface for the pressure of water, or to resist the gentle action of tidal waves or under-current, and the tube being submerged to the depth of six fathoms, no surface waves could ever reach it, it being an authentic fact that in our narrow seas they seldom extend to a depth of more than 15 to 20 feet; if so much; consequently the tube may be supposed to lie in quiescent water; but, further, and for the removal of all doubt, it is proposed to build each side of the tube, every mile apart, immense piers of masonry, connected together with wrought-iron rods above and below the tube.

It is proposed to carry out the works simultaneously on either shore, the tube to be built in lengths of 100 feet, and after being proved, to be floated to their position, made of the specific gravity of sea-water by weights, so as to be moved about with pleasure and with the slightest power, and attached by screw bolts through flanches projecting all round the tube, externally and internally, and the weights to be removed when the tube has been attached by chains to the bottom. The water would be prevented entering the ends of the tube by iron plates, so constructed that they may be removed afterwards internally, as length by length is attached.

The drawings show that there are two cases or shells inclosing the "railroad", the inner one consisting of inch-thick wrought-iron plates, riveted to T and angle iron, and the outer one of two similar plates, or two inches in thickness of wrought metal enveloping the whole, so, that in case a train got off the line of rails and tore away the inside shell, the tube would still be sound and comparatively uninjured.

It is proposed to inclose the end of the tube at either shore with immense blocks of masonry, which are to support tower lights 100 feet high, so as to give mariners an idea as to the locality of the "railway" and appendages.

It is proposed to descend from the level of the respective countries to the tube by a corkscrew tunnel, with an easy gradient, and to keep the tube itself level throughout.

The ventilation of the tube would be accomplished wither by passing currents of air through it, or by floating ventilators attached to the tube below.

In respect to the cost of the tube it is considered that it would not exceed ten and a half millions sterling, and that it would cost very little to keep in repair after completion.

"As to the advantages of the 'roadway' when completed," says Mr. Smith, "their extent is beyond conception, and the most ignorant must allow that the greatest boon to a commercial country is its easy communication with its neighbours, and the whole of Europe; and we cannot close our eyes to the fact that a waggon load of goods may then travel from London to Paris without unloading, and Englishmen visit the Continent of Europe without the sickening sea voyage and consequent trouble and risk."[670]

The article reappears in the *Leicester Journal* in December 1861 and is augmented by a disclosure from Smith that the plans were laid before the French Emperor in April that year and that the idea can go no further as the Prime Minister, Lord Palmerstone has vetoed the topic![671] There are several plans for submarine railways in the early 1860s and the idea would run on for another few decades. Smith's plan looks far from original and others look like they had the idea first. Nevertheless, it must have been good publicity for an architect about to start private practice...

He married Hephzibah Hickling[672] in July 1861 and they had four children: Kate Isabella[673] in 1862; Frank Anthony[674] in 1863; William

---

670 *Building News*, 6th December 1861.
671 *Leicester Journal*, 13th December 1861.
672 Hephzibah Smith (1840-1921).
673 Kate Isabella Smith (1862-1947).
674 Frank Anthony Smith (1863-?).

Montague[675] in 1864 and Edith Maud[676] in 1870 He died on 6th June 1895 at his house in Hoby and is buried alone in the small cemetery in Hoby village. Hephzibah Smith died in 1921 at Carlton House in Countersthorpe.

The people who worked with Flint fall into two categories: respectable and applied to their profession and public life like Shenton, Millican, Baker and Barradale or colourful and faintly sulphurous like Wickes. James Frank Smith fits this last category better. Nothing more aptly illustrates this than his third brush with the law in October 1881 at Six Hills, near Burton-on-the-Wolds on land belonging to Lord St Maur.[677] He was convicted of poaching a hare and fined £2 with costs. The *Journal* reports that he was found by Lord St Maur's gamekeepers and told them all '… *to go to hell…*' although the decorous *Journal* substituted '_____' for the word 'hell'. He was with a friend, Etienne Gonty,[678] who was also found guilty and fined. James Frank Smith seems rather fun.

James Frank Smith's grave at Hoby.

675 William Montague Smith (1864-1933). Rate collector of The Elms, Countersthorpe.

676 Edith Maud Smith later Hobson (1870-1944).

677 Lord St Maur (1813-1894), later 14th Duke of Somerset.

678 Etienne Gonty (1831-1910), silk and cotton dyer and sometime Guardian of St Nicholas and town councillor for All Saints ward. Smith would add a conservatory to his Talbot Lane home in 1884.

CHAPTER 17

The Pupils: Isaac Barradale

Isaac Barradale does not have the prominent reputation that he perhaps deserves. He is important in that he introduced the 'Domestic Revival' style to Leicester and it characterises much of Knighton and Stoneygate. The high status homes he built then are still high status homes today. His death at the age of only 47 is partly to blame and it may also be that he is eclipsed by the reputation of his pupil, Ernest Gimson,[679] an exponent of the Arts and Crafts movement with a national if not international reputation. However, he was a pupil of William Flint and reached greater heights than William Millican, Charles Baker or James Frank Smith. He was also more daring and somehow smarter: his work looks different to the others'.

He was born in 1845, the son of Isaac Barradale[680] and his wife Ann Standley née Allen[681] at 22, Wellington Street. He was named after his father and an older brother who had been born in 1840 and died in 1841. He married Elizabeth Collins[682] on 3rd November 1876 at Derby and they had three children: Charles Geoffrey,[683] Hubert Collins[684] and Margaret Elizabeth.[685] In the 1870s and 1880s they lived In Castle View and this may well have been where Flint lived as a child seventy years before.

In the 1861 census his profession states 'architect office'. Barradale must have started his apprenticeship in approximately 1857 aged about 12 and it is probable he is the pupil Flint and Shenton were seeking in their advert in January of that year in the *Leicester Journal*:

---

679 Ernest Gimson (1864-1919), architect and designer prominent in the Arts and Crafts movement.
680 Isaac Barradale (1803-1883). Scottish born tailor of Market Street.
681 Ann Barradale (1802-1885).
682 Elizabeth Barradale (1846-1919).
683 Charles Geoffrey Barradale (1875-1938) of Stratford House, London Road, perhaps one of his father's designs.
684 Hubert Collins Barradale (1878-1896).
685 Margaret Elizabeth Barradale (1880-1880).

Barradale's first home as a married man in Castle View.

'TO PARENTS AND GUARDIANS MESSRS. FLINT & SHENTON, of Leicester, Architects and Surveyors, have a Vacancy in their Office for an Articled Pupil.' [686]

As an architect, he was in business by 1870, although plans in the LRO only appear from 1875. He operated from Stanley House Chambers in Gallowtree Gate and clearly started to prosper as in 1877, he designed and built St George's Chambers at 3, Gray Friars. He moved in by 1880 and was advertising tenancies of suites of offices there to solicitors and others the same year.[687] A graceful and elegant high-gabled four floor expression of English Domestic Revival, it is virtually untouched, except for the paintwork under the window bays and the entrance which were dull terracotta when the building was new. Pevsner calls it *'his best building'.*[688]

Much admired then as now, Barradale's business premises at St. George's Chambers.

---

686 *Leicester Journal,* 16th January 1857.
687 *Leicester Journal,* 24th September 1880.
688 Pevsner op. cit.

Elmhurst in Stanley Road.

And Carisbrooke, Elmhurst's twin.

Much celebrated in Leicester are an almost matching pair of substantial villas called Carisbrooke and Elmhurst (now the Croft Hotel) on the corner of London Road and Stanley Road. Reputedly built for a pair of sisters in 1878 by their father, and former Flint customer, John Whitmore (who died at Elmhurst in 1881). They still impress today as they impressed the *Leicester Journal* at the time:

> 'Red Whitwick bricks have been used for facing on all fronts of the buildings, and red Dumfries stone for the window dressings. The roofs are covered with strawberry-coloured Broseley tiles, with red Maidenhead ridges, and the cove to the waves (sic) is formed with plaster. The timber framing is red deal, carefully selected and coloured with Stockholm tar. Including granite walling and gates, the cost will be about £5,400' [689]

A few steps away down the road is a housing development appropriately named Barradale Court.

He made a foray into Stoneygate, in an almost art nouveau Queen Anne style, for Charles Robinson[690] in 1879 with four houses (now de Montfort Court) in Stoneygate Road, before he began to settle into his preferred domestic revival style. Barradale himself lived in the third house from London Road and his widow remained there after his death. The same year he was elected to the fellowship of the Royal Institute of British Architects and had been proposed by Joseph Goddard, William Millican and Frederick Ordish.

The already much missed Fenwick's occupied another of his works which was originally put up as a department store for Joseph Johnson[691] starting in 1880. The building faces onto Market Street and is in Barradale's domestic revival style with obvious similarities to St George's Chambers. The Fenwick's complex is made of several buildings and the Market Street/Belvoir Street corner building is also by Barradale. It was erected in 1883 for Richard Allen, whose initials are inscribed in a cartouche along with another showing the construction date.[692] Pevsner does not like it and describes its later upper storeys as '*overblown*'.[693] Few people

---

689 *Leicester Journal*, 14th November 1879.
690 Charles Stephen Robinson (1839-1933). Gas Works Manager and husband of John Whitmore's daughter, Priscilla.
691 Joseph Johnson (1844-1906). Fancy draper later of Kirby Muxloe.
692 Richard Allen (?-?). Barradale may have been a cousin through his mother, whose maiden name was Allen.
693 Pevsner op cit.

Built for Richard Allen, the building became Joseph Johnson' and then Fenwick's for many years.

know that the building is named Gresham House and it is not entirely clear what business Richard Allen transacted there, although he appears to be a mineral water producer and also perhaps brewer. This seems at odds with the scale and ambition of the building. There is a niche for a statue on the corner which has led some to believe there may have been a religious aspect to the business, but this has not been substantiated. The building directly opposite on Market Street, with its turreted corner, is another Barradale work and was built as a hotel for John Lorrimer in 1885. It replaced the Dog and Gun Hotel with a grander hotel, eight shops and a three-storey warehouse.

Out of the county, he was responsible for the splendid Hambleton Hall, built for Walter Marshall[694] as a hunting box and now a Michelin starred hotel and restaurant. It has strong gables, tiles and half timbering in domestic revival style. More in this vein followed in 1882 with The Hawthorns on Knighton Park Road. It is still well regarded and is a very attractive Victorian villa, once the home of Wilmot Pilsbury[695] whose tiles adorn the outside. This essay in domestic revival with an early arts and crafts influence contains a triple aspect studio on the first floor.

In 1881, he built an unusual-looking and now demolished mission hall in Abbey Gate. Two years later he designed the Cottage Homes at Countersthorpe for the Leicester Board of Guardians; a series of twelve

---

694 Walter Gore Marshall (1845-1899), wealthy shipping magnate and businessman.
695 Wilmot Pilsbury (1840-1908). Artist and headteacher of the Leicester School of Art.

A quirky foray into religious architecture for Abbey Gate Mission Hall.

(now ten) slightly different children's homes or cottages opened in 1884. In Station Road, Hinckley there is the free library with its Franco-Flemish gables, which he put up in 1887-1888; he had used this crowstepped design in St Margaret's Street (now French Street) for some striking workers' cottages and in Campbell Street on a warehouse for William Vincent's[696] hat business in 1885. More work in Stoneygate followed the same year with more hearty domestic revival houses at 43-53 Stoneygate Road.

An unusual but very stylish set of homes in Countersthorpe, now much sought after residences.

696 William Wilkins Vincent (1843-1916). Bristol born hatter, later of Knighton Hall.

Barradale employed crow-stepped gables on several designs including in this row on St. Margaret's now French Street.

He built a photographic studio in 1887 on New Walk for the Rev John Hopps[697] of the Great Meeting. Now known as Court View, it still stands opposite the Museum and is an interesting design in its simplicity and boldness. A late work was the Flemish style 10-20 Alexandra Road in 1891.

Much of his work survives into the Twenty-First Century and, as parts of the city see people moving back in to live there again, it is being adapted. A good example is the building popularly known as 'Leif's Pawn Shop' at 27a and 27b Wharf Street built on land for the former cricket ground in 1880 for an unidentified Mr Smith. This spikey and unusual building with its angular gables was converted to studio flats in 2017 after some years lying empty as well as usage as a haulage company office, pawn broker's and brothel!

Isaac Barradale sometimes followed in Flint's footsteps, but to a lesser degree than his other pupils. He did work at Rust's worsted spinning mill in 1878, built more additions in 1881 and 1886 and he designed the two houses for Flint's former customer, John Whitmore, but his style and

697 Rev John Page Hopps (1836-1911). Celebrated author and preacher. For obituary see *Melton Mowbray Mercury* and *Oakham and Uppingham News,* 13th April 1911

A most unusual pair of shops now dwellings in Wharf Street.

business owe very little to his master and there is no trace of any of Flint's classical influence in any of his work.

In addition to Ernest Gimson, Barradale had three other pupils: Thomas Fosbrooke who later worked for Millican, Amos Hall,[698] articled in 1873 and George Bankart.[699] Bankart came from Leicester and was articled to him in the early 1880s before going to London, first to Grays's Inn Road and then Richmond in Surrey (where Messing Dain retired). He specialised in decorative plasterwork and worked with Gimson. The roots of his pupils' arts and crafts futures are clear to see in Barradale's work. De Montfort Court has obvious arts and crafts traces as does his work in English Domestic Revival in the wider sense. Barradale *had* to come before Gimson. Barradale was also assisted for a time by Samuel Pick,[700] who came to him after six years with Frank James Smith and

698 Amos Hall (1858-1930). Leicester architect responsible for the Silver Arcade.
699 George Percy Bankart (1866-1929), architect who completed the ceiling at the Royal Naval College, London in 1904 and was author of several books on decorative plasterwork and occasional collaborator with Ernest Gimson, e.g. the White House, Leicester.
700 Samuel Perkins Pick (1858-1919), architect and later partner of J. B Everard (the company is still trading in Leicester). Together they built the sumptuous Parr's Bank in St Martin's and alone he created the striking façade to the Marquis Wellington on London Road.

Obvious Arts and Crafts roots: de Montfort Court.

who also included strong Arts and Crafts influences in his work.[701]

Isaac Barradale died on 19th February 1892. He is buried at Welford Road Cemetery with his wife and two youngest children. His will was proved the same year and his friend and perhaps early partner in business, Stockdale Harrison, was one of his executors. His assistant in business and another former pupil was also remembered:

> 'To Amos Hall £10 and all the instruments and books in my possession as an architect and surveyor.'

Barradale's grave at Welford Road Cemetery.

Hall would succeed Barradale to the practice.

His gravestone is as modest as he was in life and bears the inscription:

'In affectionate remembrance of Isaac Barradale FRIBA of this town who died on the 19th February 1892 aged 47 years.'

He had become a RIBA fellow in 1879 on the same day as Shenton and Baker. He was proposed by Joseph Goddard, William Millican and Frederick Ordish. His nomination papers survive and record his works up till that point:

'Pupil of the late William Flint Esq, architect to the Corporation of Leicester. Additions and alterations municipal buildings Dudley. Mansion for the Mayor of Dudley and buildings. House for the headmaster of Leicester School of Art. Residences in Stoneygate for John Whitmore Esq and Charles Smith Esq[702] and other buildings and warehouses. Offices in Leicester.'[703]

Like Flint, he is commemorated by a panel at Welford Road Cemetery and also like Flint he had a road named after him. William Millican had a granddaughter who pursued the arts and Barradales's great-grandson is the manager of the rock band The Arctic Monkeys. The loss of Barradale so young and at the height of his powers is tragic. What else could this rather modest and very talented man have imagined and brought into being?

Memorial plaque at
Welford Road Cemetery.

---

702 Charles Smith (1828-1905). Hosier and tobacco manufacturer. The house was on London Road and called Lyndwood.
703 RIBA nomination papers.

CHAPTER 18

Flint Trivia

Plans and buildings are only a part of William Flint's life. The paucity of details as to the man has been charted elsewhere in this book, but this section at least gives some idea as to where his personal sympathies might lie. There is Victorian conformism in the charities he supports, but by no means did he subscribe to everything. He seems to stand out as an independent. It is the same thing with his politics: he votes Liberal or Whig for both candidates in elections *mostly* but not always. Flint was clearly a thinking man.

Events

16th August 1840, a seven year old boy was badly bitten by a donkey belonging to a potter called Wainwright on land in Morledge Street owned by Flint.[704]

19th October 1840, Flint was a jurist at the General Borough Quarter Sessions.[705]

18th May 1843, he was a Grand Jurist at Borough Sessions which included several housebreaking cases and the theft of a horse and gig.[706]

23rd August 1844, he tendered for the valuation position for St Margaret's vestry at £2 2s per day.[707] (He lost to Daniel Mansfield[708] at £1 10s per day.)

14th October 1844, he was a Grand Jurist at Borough Sessions which included several breaking and entering cases and thefts, some of which resulted in transportation.[709]

---

704 *Leicester Herald* 22nd August 1840.
705 *Leicester Journal*, 23rd October 1840.
706 *Leicester Chronicle*, 20th May 1843.
707 *Leicester Mercury*, 28th August 1844.
708 Daniel Mansfield (1801-1867). Architect and surveyor of Halford Street.
709 *Leicester Mercury*, 18th October 1844.

31st December 1845, he was elected to the General Newsroom Committee.[710]

17th March 1849, he was a jurist at the Easter Sessions concerning a large number of *'ordinary and uninteresting'* cases.[711]

1849 October, he was a committee member of The Leicestershire Fine Arts Society and Arts Union.[712]

On Thursday 25th January 1849, Flint was one of a number of local dignitaries who accompanied W. Ranger Esq,[713] General Board of Health Inspector on a 'perambulation' of the town, including visits to Great Holme Street, Porkshop-yard and Grange Lane ditch as part of the latter's inquiry into Leicester's sanitation.[714]

1850 May, his voting papers for the election of St Margaret's Guardians were lost.[715]

9th October 1856, William Flint was foreman of the Grand Jury at the Borough Michaelmas Quarter Sessions. A fellow jurist was William Millican's father, Thomas.[716]

10th November 1856, he was one of 51 burgesses of the East St Mary's ward to write to John Baines asking him to stand for election to the Town Council following Richard Harris's appointment as alderman. Henry Shenton and Isaac Barradale Sr were fellow signatories. John Baines replied in the affirmative the next day.[717]

11th September 1857, Flint's dark Oxford mixture great coat was stolen from his house in Southfields-place.[718]

15th July 1858, he was foreman of the Grand Jury again at the Borough Assizes involved in a case of forgery and another of perjury.[719]

9th November 1859, Ann Flint was the victim of attempted fraud when a labourer, George King, tried to use her name to defraud Isaac

710 *Leicester Chronicle*, 10th January 1845.

711 *Leicester Mercury*, 17th March 1849.

712 *Leicester Mercury*, 27th October 1849.

713 William Ranger C. E. (1800-1863). Public Health inspector and civil engineer.

714 *Leicester Mercury*, 27th January 1849.

715 *Leicester Mercury*, 11th May 1850.

716 *Leicester Chronicle*, 11th October 1856.

717 *Leicester Mercury*, 15th November 1856. Election day was 20th November and he stood against John Mortin (Conservative) who beat him 213 votes to 102.

718 *Leicester Mercury*, 18th September 1857.

719 *Leicester Mercury*, 17th July 1858.

Horton[720] of eight yards of black silk. He didn't get away with it and was sentenced to six months' imprisonment.[721]

Charitable works

He was a regular and public subscriber to charity and contributed to the following good causes:

1833 April, subscriber to the Leicester General Dispensary, 10s 6d.[722]

1835 November, Flint purchased one share in the Leicester and Leicestershire Collegiate School proposal.[723]

1837 April, subscriber to the Leicester General Provident Society, £1 1s.[724]

1837 June, subscriber to the Leicester General Provident Society, £5.[725]

1840 January, subscriber to fund for Unemployed Operatives, £10.[726]

1844 July, subscriber to the restoration of St Mary's Church, £5.[727]

1846 March, subscriber to the further restoration of St Mary's Church, £5.[728]

1846 April, subscriber to the proposed monument for the late Rev John Brown, £3 3s.[729]

1847 January, subscriber to the Coal Charity, £2.

1847 January, contribution to the Irish and Scotch destitution fund for clothing, 10s.

1847 February, another £3 subscription to the Rev Brown Monument.[730]

1847 February, contribution to an appeal for William Gimson after a fire at his business, £5.[731]

1847 June, subscription to the Fund for the Relief of the Unemployed Poor, £5.[732]

---

720 Isaac Horton (1828-1863). Draper and mercer of Silver Street.
721 *Leicester Guardian*, 7th January 1860.
722 *Leicester Journal*, 26th April 1833.
723 *Leicester Journal*, 20th November 1835.
724 *Leicester Mercury*, 29th April 1837.
725 *Leicester Mercury*, 24th June 1837,
726 *Leicester Chronicle*, 4th January 1840.
727 *Leicester Journal*, 26th July 1844.
728 *Leicester Journal*, 6th March 1846.
729 *Leicester Journal*, 3rd April 1846.
730 *Leicester Journal*, 26th February 1847.
731 *Leicester Journal*, 5th March 1847.
732 *Leicester Journal*, 11th June 1847.

1849 January, subscriber to the newly formed Leicester School of Design.[733]

1856 January, for the Relief of the Poor of Leicester, £5.[734]

1857 August, to continue the Race Course concerts, £1 1s.[735]

1857 September, for the Relief of the Sufferers of the Mutiny in India,[736] £5 (with Henry Shenton).

---

733 *Leicester Mercury*, 13th January 1849.
734 *Leicester Mercury*, 12th January 1856.
735 *Leicester Mercury*, 1st August 1857.
736 *Leicester Journal*, 2nd October 1857.

APPENDIX 1:

The Buildings of William Flint

The following table shows the complete list of all of Flint's *known* architectural work. Dating has not been straightforward. Where plans exist at the Leicestershire and Rutland Record Office, this is the date that has been taken for the work and they are identified by 'ROP' (Record Office Plan) in the table. If the source of identification has been through minutes or newspaper reports, the earliest date with a link to Flint has been taken, thus the West Bridge is listed as '1836 12' as his first report for the project was written in December 1836. Wherever possible a month has been given after the year in order to create a timeline of Flint's activity. Newspapers are iterated as 'LC', 'LJ' and LM' for the *Leicester Chronicle, Journal* and *Mercury* respectively and 'Pevsner' denotes his *Leicestershire and Rutland* volume. The table also shows if Flint was working alone or in partnership; gives the road or street name of the property worked on and also gives a source for each job. 148 commissions have been identified of which 39 are thought to exist in one form or another.

Building	Year	Where	Client	Architect	Notes	Source	Status in 2018
Church	1830	Charles Street	Baptist sub-scribers	William Flint		LJ 01/04/1830	Extant and in use as Leicester Central Baptist Church
Library and meeting hall	1831	Wellington and Belvoir Streets	Subscribers	William Flint		LC 28/05/1831	Extant and in use as The Leicester People's Photographic Gallery
Church tower	1832	Kibworth Beauchamp, St Wilfrid's Church	Church of England	William Flint		Arch-bishop Bonney's accounts, LRO	Extant and in use as a church

Church and presbytery	1832 11	Loughbor-ough, Ashby Road	Loughborough Catholic com-munity	William Flint		LJ 16/11/1832	Extant, remodelled and in use as a church
Factory	1833	Braunstone Gate	Richard Harris	William Flint		LC 20/07/1833	Converted into Flats and Natterjacks bar / restaurant
Lime shed	1834 4	Soar Lane Wharf	Leicester Swan-nington Railway	William Flint		LC 03/05/1834	Demolished
School	1834 5	Hill Street	British Schools	William Flint		LJ 23/05/1834	Demolished
Houses	1835	Upper King Street	N/K	William Flint		Pevsner	Extant and in use as houses, flats and businesses
Chapel	1835	Northamp-ton Street	N/K	William Flint		LC 10/02/1844	Demolished
Houses	1836	Alfred Street	N/K	William Flint		LM 28/11/1837	Demolished
Houses	1836	Crescent Cottages	N/K	William Flint		Pevsner	Extant and in use as houses, flats and businesses
Library and news room	1836 11	Granby and Belvoir Streets	Subscribers	William Flint		LM 5/11/1836	Demolished
Bridge	1836 12	West Bridge	Leicester Town Council	William Flint		LJ 16/12/1836	Demolished
Workhouse	1837 9	Sparkenhoe Street	Leicester Poor Law Union	William Flint		Poor Law Guardian minutes 27/09/1836	Demolished
Workhouse	1837 12	Lindfield Road, Barrow-up-on-Soar	Barrow-up-on-Soar Poor Law Union	William Flint		Poor Law Guardian minutes 28/12/1837	Partially extant and in use as houses
Banking house	1838 12	Granby Street	Leicestershire Banking Com-pany	William Flint		LJ 28/12/1838	Demolished
Houses	1839 9	Lancaster Place, Lon-don Road	Trinity Hospital	William Flint	3 houses	LJ 20/09/1839	Demolished
Fish market	1839 12	Market Place	Leicester Town Council	William Flint		Council Estates Com-mittee minutes 06/12/1839	Demolished

Chapel	1840 5	York Street	Baptist Church	William Flint		LM 27/05/1840	Unknown
Houses	1840	Regent Road	N/K	William Flint	3 houses	LJ 26/04/1844	Partially extant and used as business premises
Houses	1841 12	Princess Street	N/K	William Flint	2 houses	LJ 03/12/1841	Extant and used as business premises
Church	1842 11	Leicester Road, Market Harborough	Congregationalist subscribers	William Flint		Receipt LRO	Extant and in use as a church
Shops and Houses	1844 8	N/K	Harborough Charity	William Flint		LJ 16/08/1844	Unknown
Church	1844 10	St Mary de Castro	Leicester Town Council	William Flint	Chancel repairs	LJ 18/10/1844	Extant and in use as a church
Factory	1845	King Street Marlborough Street	Richard Harris and Sons	William Flint	Approximate date	ROP	Extant and in use as flats
Warehouse	1845	Granby Street	John Corah	William Flint		Company History, 1965	Demolished
Post Office	1846 7	Granby Street	Postmaster General	William Flint		LM 11/07/1846	Demolished
Museum	1846 10	New Walk	Leicester Town Council	William Flint	Conversion from school to museum	Council Estates Committee minutes 27/10/1846	Extant and in use as a museum
Fever House	1847 7	Union Workhouse Melton Mowbray	Melton Mowbray Poor Law Union	William Flint		LJ 16/07/1847	Demolished
Cattle market	1847 12	Horsefair Street	Leicester Town Council	William Flint		LJ 31/12/1847	Demolished
Mill	1848 7	West Bridge	Whitmore and Ellis	William Flint		Company History,1948	Extant and used as the Land Registry and other business premises
Gaol	1848 11	High Cross Street	Leicester Town Council	Flint and Wickes	Alterations Borough Gaol	Council Estates Committee minutes 09/11/1848	Demolished

Cottage	1849 9	Knighton Hill		Flint and Wickes		LJ 14/09/1849	Unknown
Houses	1849 11	Princess Street	Mr Shuttle-worth	Flint and Wickes	2 houses	LM 17/11/1849	Unknown
Shop front	1849 12	High Street	Joseph Harris	Flint and Wickes		ROP	Demolished
Shop front	1850 3	Granby Street, Hal-ford Street	Mr Robin	Flint and Wickes		ROP	Demolished
Shop front	1850 3	Silver Street	Mr Sharpe	Flint and Wickes		ROP	Demolished
Houses	1850 3	Hotel Street	William Stretton	Flint and Wickes	2 houses	ROP un-indexed	Demolished
Houses	1850 3	Emmanuel Church vicarage Loughbor-ough	Church of England	Flint and Wickes		ROP	Extant
Warehouse	1850 4	Welford Place	Messrs Henrys	Flint and Wickes		ROP	Demolished
Fence	1850 4	Trinity Hos-pital, The Newarke	Trinity Hospital	Flint and Wickes		ROP un-indexed	Demolished
Warehouse	1850 5	Albion Street	John Biggs	Flint and Wickes	Additions	ROP	Unknown
Warehouse	1850 6	St Nicholas Square	Thomas Rust	Flint and Wickes		ROP	Demolished
Market House	1850 7	Market Place	Leicester Town Council	Flint and Wickes		LC 06/07/1850	Partially extant and in use as the Corn Ex-change Public House
Shop front	1850 7	Market Place	Mr Jones	Flint and Wickes		ROP	Demolished
Shop front	1850 8	Silver Street	Mr Thompson	Flint and Wickes	Addition to Shop	ROP	Demolished
Shop front	1850 9	Gallowtree Gate	Mr Porter	Flint and Wickes		ROP	Demolished
Warehouse	1850 10	Free Lane	Thomas John-son	Flint and Wickes		ROP	Demolished
Houses	1850 11	Museum Square	Thomas Swain	Flint and Wickes	5 Houses	ROP	Extant and in use as business premises
Toilets	1851 1	Marlbor-ough Street, King Street	Richard Harris and Sons	Flint and Wickes	Soil cess pool	ROP un-indexed	Demolished
Warehouse	1851 2	Rutland Street	John Corah	Flint and Wickes		ROP un-indexed	Demolished
Shop front	1851 3	Market Place	Mr Lockwood	Flint and Wickes	Shop front	ROP	Demolished

Warehouse	1851	Newarke Street	Robert Warner	Flint and Wickes	No approval date on plan	ROP	Demolished
Spire	1851 5	King's Norton church	Church of England	Flint and Wickes		LJ 23/05/1851	Demolished
Houses	1851 6	Hastings Street	Mr Blackwell (Midland Railway)	Flint and Wickes	4 houses	ROP un-indexed	Demolished
Toilets	1851 6	Hastings Street	Mr Blackwell (Midland Railway)	Flint and Wickes	Drainage	ROP un-indexed	Demolished
Outbuildings	1851 7	Rutland and Granby Streets	Benjamin Brookhouse	Flint and Wickes	Change to out buildings and drainage to ware-house	ROP	Demolished
Warehouse	1851 7	King Street	Richard Harris and Sons	Flint and Wickes	Additions and drainage	ROP	Extant and in use as flats
Houses	1851 7	St Nicholas Square	Rev Clarke	Flint and Wickes	2 cottages	ROP	Demolished
Warehouse	1851 9	King Street	Robert Overton	Flint and Wickes	Additions	ROP	Demolished
Factory Ware-house	1852 5	Marble Street, Newarke Street	Charles Billson	Flint and Wickes	Factory and Ware-house Exten-sion	ROP un-indexed	Demolished
Houses	1852 6	New Walk	Joseph Hames	Flint and Wickes	6 Houses	ROP un-indexed	Extant and in use as flats and houses
Houses	1852 9	Asylum Street	Mr Brown	Flint and Wickes	3 houses	ROP	Demolished
Houses	1852 9	Midland Street	John Carrington	Flint and Wickes	4 houses	ROP	Demolished
Factory Ware-house	1852 10	Marble Street	Charles Billson	Flint and Wickes	Alter-ations (exten-sion) to factory	ROP un-indexed	Partially extant and in use by 'johnewright' printers
Public house	1852 12	Marquis of Granby Inn	Leicester Town Council	Flint and Wickes	Altera-tions and additions	LM 25/12/1852	Demolished
Church	1853 2	Holy Trinity Church, Re-gent Road	Church of England	Flint and Wickes		LC 12/02/1853	Partially extant and in use as a church
Warehouse	1853 3	Newarke Street	Frisby and Chawner	Flint and Wicks	Addition to ware-house	ROP	Demolished

Warehouse	1853 8	Pocklingtons Walk	Joseph Whit-more	William Flint		ROP	Demolished
Houses	1853 8	Regent Street	Nathan Wester-mans	William Flint	2 houses	ROP	Demolished
Fence	1853 9	de Montfort Square	Leicester Town Council	William Flint	fence	LC 10/09/1853	Demolished
Warehouse	1853 9	Wellington Street	Ward and Sons	William Flint		ROP	Extant and in use by the Adult Educa-tion Service and a printers
Warehouse	1854	Gas Street	Leicester Gas Light Company	Flint and Shenton	Gas holders and sheds	LC 25/02/1854	Demolished
Houses	1854 8	Regent and Lower Hast-ings Streets	Thomas Swain	Flint and Shenton	5 houses	ROP un-indexed	Demolished
Houses	1854 9	Mowbray and Infirma-ry Square	Henry Mowbray	Flint and Shenton	16 Houses	ROP	Demolished
Asylum	1854 9	Fosse Road	Leicester Female Infant Asylum	Flint and Shenton		ROP	Demolished
Houses	1854 10	Deacon Street	James Wootton	Flint and Shenton	5 Houses	ROP	Demolished
Warehouse	1854 12	Lower Brown Street	William Gimson	Flint and Shenton		ROP	Demolished
Houses	1854 12	Infirmary Square	Henry Mowbray	Flint and Shenton	8 Houses	ROP	Demolished
Houses	1855 2	New Bridge Street	Henry Mowbray	Flint and Shenton	2 houses	ROP	Demolished
Houses	1855 2	London Road	William Rushin	Flint and Shenton	2 houses	ROP	Demolished
Houses	1855 2	Upper Prin-cess Street	Cornelius Herbert	Flint and Shenton	5 Houses	ROP	Demolished
Drainage	1855 2	Upper Prin-cess Street	Cornelius Herbert	Flint and Shenton	Drainage	ROP	Demolished
Warehouse	1855 2	Newarke Street	Charles Billson	Flint and Shenton	Additions to ware-house	ROP	Partially extant
Houses	1855 3	Hastings Street	Jonathon Collins	Flint and Shenton	4 houses	ROP	Demolished
Road	1855 8	New Bridge Street	James Wootton	Flint and Shenton	New Street	ROP	Demolished
Houses and Public House	1855 8	New Bridge and Raglan Streets	James Wootton	Flint and Shenton	4 houses and a public house	ROP	Demolished
Toilet	1855 9	Wellington Street	Josiah Fleming	Flint and Shenton	Privies changed to water closets	ROP	Demolished

Houses	1855 10	Nicholls Street	Thomas Colt-man	Flint and Shenton	4 houses	ROP	Demolished
Houses	1855 10	Rutland Street	George Ander-son	Flint and Shenton	2 houses	ROP	Demolished
Factory	1855 10	Pocklingtons Walk	Mr Warner	Flint and Shenton	Additions	ROP	Demolished
Houses	1855 12	Deacon Street, At-kins Street	Thomas Nor-man	Flint and Shenton	4 Houses	ROP	Demolished
Land	1855 12	Rutland Street	George Ander-son	Flint and Shenton	Exchange of land	ROP	Demolished
Streets and Drainage	1856 2	Great Holme Street, Little Holme Street, Leamington Street, Duns Lane	Richard Harris	Flint and Shenton	Streets & Culverts to be Built num-bered 766 & half	ROP un-indexed	Partially extant
Warehouse	1856 2	King Street, Marlbor-ough Street	Richard Harris and Sons	Flint and Shenton	Additions and base-ment	ROP	Extant and in use as flats
Shop front	1856 3	High Street	John Manning	Flint and Shenton		ROP	Demolished
House	1856 3	London Road	Henry Kemp	Flint and Shenton	Altera-tions to House	ROP	Demolished
Factory	1856 4	St Nicholas Square	Thomas Rusts	Flint and Shenton		ROP	Demolished
Houses	1856 5	Fosse Road	William Stretton	Flint and Shenton	2 Houses	ROP un-indexed	Extant and in residential use
Drainage and sewerage	1856 7	Gas Street	Leicester Gas Light Company	Flint and Shenton	Sewerage	ROP	Demolished
Stone	1856 10	Bow Bridge	Archibald Turner	Flint and Shenton	Stone inset in cottage	LC 02/01/1857	Demolished
House	1856 10	Bow Bridge	Archibald Turner	Flint and Shenton	Altera-tion to cottage	ROP	Demolished
Street	1856 11	New Park Street	Richard Harris and Sons	Flint and Shenton	Change to street opening	ROP	Demolished
Houses	1857 1	Lancaster Street	Mr Holland	Flint and Shenton	7 Houses	ROP	Extant and in residential use
Office	1857 1	South Bond Street	Leicester Poor Law Union	Flint and Shenton	Altera-tion of premises	ROP	Demolished
House	1857 3	Market Street	Thomas Farmer Cooke	Flint and Shenton	Altera-tions	ROP	Partially extant and in use as business premises

Chapel	1857 4	Gallowtree Gate	Congregational-ist Church	Flint and Shenton	New school-rooms	ROP	Demolished
Water Closets	1857 4	Gallowtree Gate	Gallowtree Gate Chapel	Flint and Shenton	Water closets and drainage	ROP	Demolished
House	1857 6	Daneshill Road	Thomas Bland	Flint and Shenton	1 house	ROP	Extant and in residential use
Office	1857 6	Bowling Green Street	Thomas Farmer Cooke	Flint and Shenton		ROP un-indexed	Demolished
Factory	1857 7	Lower Brown Street	Hodges and Turner	Flint and Shenton		ROP un-indexed	Demolished
Toilets	1857 7	Lower Brown Street	William Gimson	Flint and Shenton	Privies	ROP	Demolished
Office	1857 8	Horsefair Street	Thomas Farmer Cooke	Flint and Shenton	Additions	ROP	Demolished
House	1857 9	Upper Brunswick Street	Ann Pickard	Flint and Shenton	1 house	ROP	Demolished
Warehouse	1858 2	Yeoman Lane	John Law	Flint and Shenton		ROP	Demolished
Street	1858 4	Havelock Street	Leicester Freehold Land Society 6th Estate	Flint and Shenton	New Streets and culverts	ROP	Partially extant
Houses	1858 4	Aylestone Road	John Holland	Flint and Shenton	6 houses	ROP	Demolished
Lodge and ma-chine office	1858 4	Sparkenhoe Street	Leicester Poor Law Union	Flint and Shenton	Entrance lodge and machine office	ROP	Demolished
Warehouse	1858 4	Wellington Street	Samuel West-fahll	Flint and Shenton	Additions	ROP	Demolished
Houses	1858 5	Willow Street	James Nicholls	Flint and Shenton	4 houses	ROP	Demolished
Houses	1858 5	Curzon Street	James Nicholls	Flint and Shenton	4 Houses	ROP	Demolished
House	1858 6	London Road	Joseph Brook-house	Flint and Shenton	Additions	ROP	Demolished
Drainage	1858 6	Newarke Street	Chawner and Co	Flint and Shenton	Drain-age and toilets	ROP	Demolished
Warehouse	1858 7	Charles Street	John Law	Flint and Shenton	Ware-house	ROP	Demolished
Warehouse	1858 10	Yeoman Lane	Mr Townshend	Flint and Shenton	Addition to ware-house over foundry	ROP un-indexed	Demolished
Factory	1858 11	Bow Bridge	Archibald Turner	Flint and Shenton		ROP	Demolished

Roof	1858 12	Gas Street	Leicester Gas Light Company	Flint and Shenton	Roof and additions	LJ 03/12/1858	Demolished
House	1858 12	London Road	Rupert Carryer	Flint and Shenton	Additions	ROP un-indexed	Demolished
Warehouse	1858 12	Belvoir and Stamford Streets	John Baines	Flint and Shenton		ROP un-indexed	Extant and in use as a restaurant called Zizzi
Warehouse	1859 2	Welford Road	William Gimson	Flint and Shenton		ROP	Demolished
Warehouse	1859 3	Marble Street	Charles Billson	Flint and Shenton	Additions	ROP un-indexed	Partially extant and in use by 'johnewright' printers
Church	1859 4	Curzon Street	Primitive Methodist Church subscribers	Flint and Shenton	Primitive Methodist Church	ROP un-indexed	Demolished
House and warehouse	1859 7	Wellington Street and New Walk	Joseph Hames	Flint and Shenton	Additions and alterations	ROP	Demolished
Warehouse	1859 9	Marlborough Street	Richard Harris and Sons	Flint and Shenton	Additions and alterations	ROP	Extant and in use as flats
Gas tanks	1860 3	Gas Street	Leicester Gas Light Company	Flint and Shenton	Additions and alterations	LM 03/03/1860	Demolished
Street	1860 3	Trinity Hospital Estate	Trinity Hospital	Flint and Shenton		ROP	Demolished
Shop front	1860 4	Haymarket	John Burton	Flint and Shenton		ROP	Demolished
Street	1860 5	Lincoln Street	Joseph Harris	Flint and Shenton		ROP un-indexed	Extant
Office	1860 11	Bowling Green Street	Thomas Farmer Cooke	Flint and Shenton		ROP un-indexed	Demolished
Hustings	1861 1	Market Place	Leicester Town Council	Flint and Shenton		LM 26/01/1861	Demolished
Drinking Fountain	1861 4	Granby Street	Leicester Temperance Hall	Flint and Shenton		LC 20/04/1861	Demolished
Factory	1861 4	Lower Brown Street	Hodges and Sons	Flint and Shenton		ROP	Demolished
Warehouse	1861 6	Campbell Street	Evans and Stafford	Flint and Shenton		LM 15/06/1861	Demolished
Chapel	1861 6	Archdeacon Lane Chapel	Baptist subscribers	Flint and Shenton	Class Rooms	ROP	Demolished
Warehouse	1861 8	Church Gate	Hunt and Pickering	Flint and Shenton		ROP	Extant and semi-derelict use as business premises
School	1861 8	Hill Street	Trinity Hospital	Flint and Shenton	New Fence Wall	ROP	Demolished

Streets	1861	Fosse Road	Richard Harris and Joseph Stretton	Flint and Shenton	2 plans	ROP	Demolished
Factory	1870	St Nicholas Street	Thomas Rust	Flint and Wickes		ROP	Demolished
Houses	Un-dated	Fosse Road, Dane Hills	Thomas Bland	Flint and Shenton	4 houses, not ap-proved	ROP	Unbuilt

Extracts from Borough Accounts

It is difficult to know how much William Flint earnt a year or indeed per project. Whilst a good rule of thumb is that payment on a project is a percentage (often 5%) of the total building cost, this isn't always the case. What makes it even more difficult to work out Flint's profit is that he will have had to have paid craftsmen and labourers from monies he received. The following are abstracted from the Borough Accounts and they shed some light on his earnings from the Town Council. They make odd reading and it certainly seems to be the case that he was only paid for work from 1848, 1849 and 1850 in 1851. This must have represented quite a wait and perhaps confirms that he was only paid on completion of work, with no advances or part payments:

Date	Account	Description	Payment
Mar 1837 – Sep 1837	Sale	Cash to Mr Flint for laying out Streets and Building Land	£45 19s 0d
Sep 1838 – Sep 1839	Sale	Mr Flint bill as surveyor	£61 5s 0d
Sep 1840 – Sep 1841	General Sale Gaol	Surveyor [W. Flint] Feb 15th 1841 Surveyor's bill [W. Flint] Apr 16th 1841 Surveyor's bill [W. Flint]	£43 8s 0d £15 1s 0d £69 6s 2d
Sep 1841 – Sep 1842	General Sale	Surveyor (Wm. Flint) Flint as architect and clerk to works	£67 10s 0d £250 0s 0d
Sep 1842 – Sep 1843	Sale	Mr Flint, Architect	£112 5s 0d
Sep 1843 – Sep 1844	Creditor account	Architect's Bill, per W. Flint	£10 13s 6d
Sep 1847 – Sep 1848	Estate, rent and Tithe Town Improvement	Mr Flint 4 years' bills Surveyor, Mr Flint	£122 7s 0d £76 16s 0d
Sep 1848 – Sep 1849	Town improvement Museum	Mr Flint – Commissions on Cattle Market contracts Ditto on Dun's Lane ditto Mr Flint – Commissions on contracts	£141 17s 6d £4 15s 6d £34 10s 6d

Sep 1850 – Sep 1851	Payments	Town Survey per Mr Flint (balance)	£66 7s 4d
Sep 1851 – Sep 1852	Payments	Surveyor and Architect (Mr Flint) on account of general bill for 1848, 1849 and 1850	£200 0s 0d
	Payments	Plans, surveys &c &c per Mr Flint in 1848, 1849 and 1850 (balance)	£19 5s 6d
	Payments	Sanitary Inquiry 1848: – Mr Flint, for attendance upon Mr Ranger, plans &c	£46 17s 0d
Sep 1852 – Sep 1853	Estate	Sale Fund in re-payment of part of the sum of £200, paid out of the General Account, on account of Mr Flint's bill for 1848, 1849 and 1850, chargeable to sale Fund.	£79 6s 6d
	Payments	Surveyor – Mr Flint's bill for 1851 and 1852.	£34 18s 1d
Sep 1854 – Sep 1855	Payments	Architect and Surveyor (Mr Flint) for surveys &c	£10 12s 0d

Afterword

We still know so little about William Flint and his work. There is a sense that whilst his classical style is timeless and eminently tasteful, it is cursed by being unremarkable. It doesn't always please in the same way Barradale's Greyfriars office somehow cheers the soul. It doesn't startle in the same way perhaps Teulon's Holy Cross does, and it doesn't impress in quite the same way as Goddard's bank on Granby Street. Had his General Newsroom on Granby and Belvoir Streets survived I suspect a biography and a body of research would have been undertaken many years ago. Without this key building to dominate that part of the city and command attention, he has drifted a little into anonymity. Flint was working in Leicester at its most strongly non-conformist and working with non-conformist clients to whom the plain and simple classical style was modest and more acceptably 'Godly'. It is no surprise that he was unable to break free into new designs as all of his pupils did.

Many of his surviving buildings have been rediscovered in this book or identified in print for the first time. I hope that this will spur on others to look for more of Flint's work and find concrete sources to definitively attribute work to him. Some of the houses on New Walk, the Harris factory on King Street and the former Fielding Johnson Hospital all need more certainty attached to the identity of their creator. Some of the buildings mentioned in Chapter 12 also need to be tracked down. Finally can any more light be shed on what William Flint was doing in 1843 and what the reason was behind his contracting a marriage so far from home in Herne Bay?

In conclusion, Flint led a useful life and contributed to the growth and prosperity of late Georgian, William IV and Victorian Leicester. Through his work and through his surviving buildings and through his pupils' pupils and their pupils, he still does.

Bibliography

Bennett, J. D. (2001) *Leicestershire Architects 1700 – 1850.* Friends of Leicestershire Museums; Leicester

Boynton, Dr Helen E. and Seaton, Derek (1999) *From Tollgate to Tramshed,* Helen Boynton; Leicester.

Boynton, Dr Helen E. (2000) *The History of Victoria Park.* Helen Boynton; Leicester.

Boynton, Dr Helen E. (2001) *The Changing Face of London Road.* Helen Boynton; Leicester.

Boynton, Dr Helen E. (2002) *The History of New Walk.* Helen Boynton; Leicester.

Brandwood, Geoffrey K. (2002) *Bringing them to their knees: church building in Leicestershire and Rutland 1800 – 1914.* Leicestershire Archaeological and Historical Society; Leicester.

Brodie, Antonia (ed.) (2001) *Directory of British Architects 1834-1914.* Two volumes Continuum; New York.

Clinker, C. R. (1977) *The Leicester and Swannington Railway.* Avon-Anglia Publications; Weston-super-Mare.

Dhaliwal, Balwinder (2002) *The Central Lending Library Belvoir Street.* Leicestershire Historian, Volume 38; Leicester.

Leicester City Council (2004) *Supplementary planning guidance: New Walk Conservation Area Character Statement.* Urban Design Group; Leicester.

Lott, F. B. (1935) *The Centenary book of the Leicester Literary and Philosophical Society,* Thornley and Son; Leicester.

Mackness, A. M. (1948) *Patons and Baldwins Ltd. Story of West Bridge Mills Leicester 1839 – 1948.* Manuscript at LRO DE2043.

Mitchell, Sheila (1984) *Not disobedient ... a history of the United Baptist Church, Leicester, 1760 – 1983,* private printing for local Baptist churches; Leicester.

Moore, Andrew (2003) *Ellis of Leicester: A Quaker family's vocation,* Laurel House Publishing; Leicester.

Moore, Andrew (2008) *Where Leicester has worshipped*, Laurel House Publishing; Leicester.

Newitt, Ned (ed.) (2009) *The slums of Leicester*, DB Publishing; Nottingham.

Pevsner, Nikolaus revised by Williamson, Elizabeth (2003) *The buildings of Leicestershire and Rutland*, Yale University Press; New Haven and London.

Soer, John (1997) *The Royal Mail in Leicestershire and Rutland*, The Midland (GB) Postal History Society; Newark.

Wilshere, J. E. O. (1974) *Leicester Clock Tower,* Leicester Research Services; Leicester.

Webb, C. W. (1959) *Corah's of Leicester,* private printing for Corah's; Leicester.

Anon (1966) *Holy Trinity and its surroundings 1838 – 1966*, A. T. Shelley & Co; Leicseter.

Index

Street Index

Tertiary Index